CAMBRIDGE LIBF

Books of enduri

MW00790251

Maritime Exploration

This series includes accounts, by eye-witnesses and contemporaries, of voyages by Europeans to the Americas, Asia, Australasia and the Pacific during the colonial period. Driven by the military and commercial interests of powers including Britain, France and the Netherlands, particularly the East India Companies, these expeditions brought back a wealth of information on climate, natural resources, topography, and distant civilisations. Their detailed observations provide fascinating historical data for climatologists, ecologists and anthropologists, and the accounts of the mariners' experiences on their long and dangerous voyages are full of human interest.

A Voyage to Madagascar and the East Indies

Published in English translation in 1793, this was the first study of Madagascar by a European. A member of the Académie des Sciences, Alexis-Marie de Rochon (1741–1817) was a distinguished French physicist, astronomer and traveller. He was involved in scientific voyages of discovery in the 1770s, conducting a hydrographic survey of the Indian Ocean. The present account was intended to show the advantages of French settlement in Madagascar and includes details of geography, anthropology and agriculture. In discussing cocoa and sugar, Rochon outlines the potential advantages of steam engines in sugar factories. He also provides an exploration history of the region and an interesting account of colonial leaders, notably Maurice Benyovszky (1746–86), the explorer-adventurer who was appointed governor of Madagascar by Louis XV. The work also includes a 'Memoir of the Chinese Trade', which details the many products traded between Europe and China in the late eighteenth century.

A Voyage to Madagascar and the East Indies

To Which is Added M. Brunel's Memoir on the Chinese Trade

ALEXIS-MARIE DE ROCHON
TRANSLATED BY JOSEPH TRAPP

CAMBRIDGE UNIVERSITY PRESS

Cambridge, New York, Melbourne, Madrid, Cape Town,
Singapore, São Paolo, Delhi, Mexico City

Published in the United States of America by Cambridge University Press, New York

www.cambridge.org
Information on this title: www.cambridge.org/9781108060905

© in this compilation Cambridge University Press 2013

This edition first published 1793
This digitally printed version 2013

ISBN 978-1-108-06090-5 Paperback

The material originally positioned here is too large for reproduction in this reissue. A PDF can be downloaded from the web address given on page iv of this book, by clicking on 'Resources Available'.

A

V O Y A G E

TO

MADAGASCAR

AND THE

EAST INDIES.

BY THE ABBE ROCHON,

Member of the Academies of Sciences of Paris and Peterſburgh, Aſtronomer
of the French Navy, Keeper of the Royal Cabinet of Natural
Philoſophy, Inſpeƈtor of the Machines of the Mint, &c.

TO WHICH IS ADDED,

M. BRUNEL's MEMOIR ON THE CHINESE TRADE.

ILLUSTRATED WITH

AN ORIGINAL MAP OF MADAGASCAR,
DRAWN BY M. ROBERT.

TRANSLATED FROM THE FRENCH,

By JOSEPH TRAPP, A. M.

L O N D O N:

PRINTED FOR EDWARD JEFFERY, PALL-MALL; R. FAUL-
DER, NEW BOND-STREET; T. AND J. EGERTON,
WHITEHALL; J. CUTHELL AND J. DEIGHTON,
HOLBORN; J. BANNISTER, BELL-YARD;
J. WALKER, PATER-NOSTER-ROW, AND
W. MILLER, OLD BOND-STREET.

M,DCC,XCIII.

TO

SIR JOSEPH BANKS, Bart.

P. R. S. & S. A.

SIR,

IT has been at all times the privilege of men of letters, to exprefs their admiration, refpect, or gratitude, by dedicating their labours to fome perfon of

a 3   diftinguifhed

diftinguifhed merit; yet a cuftom
fo laudable, has as frequently been
proftituted to various purpofes of
felfifhnefs and contemptible vanity.
But fince I have the honor to do you
homage of this tranflation, I find
it incumbent on me, to affure you
and the public at large, that I have
availed myfelf of this privilege, free
from all bafe adulation or fordid views.

Deign therefore to receive it as the
genuine tribute due to a protector
of fcience, to a man whofe invaluable
and

and fuccefsful exertions in the field
of ufeful knowledge, have gained
him, not only the particular efteem
of his own country, but the veneration and gratitude of all mankind.
I am not the leaft of your admirers,
and feel a peculiar happinefs, in this
opportunity to exprefs, unbiaffed by
prejudice, impartial and fpontaneous,
how much I value and prize your
excellent qualifications and high deferts, and how much happier I would
deem myfelf, to have it in my power
to give you a better, and worthier

proof

proof of the unfullied refpect and
unfeigned gratitude, in which I fhall
ever pride to remain,

S I R,

Your moft obedient,

humbly devoted fervant,

JOSEPH TRAPP.

T O

TO THE PUBLIC.

THE Translator finds it necessary to premise, that he has been obliged to omit in his version many tedious passages and uninteresting digressions which crowded the original, and must consequently appear disgustful and unpleasant to every judicious English reader. He has had an opportunity to peruse the German and Dutch translations of this work, which, in this respect, entirely correspond with his own.

With regard to the map of Madagascar, it was drawn by M. ROBERT, in the beginning of the present century, who presented and dedicated it, in 1725, to the Duc de Chaulnes, together with a plan for forming a colony in the North of that Island. It has never been published, and the author obtained it of the French Minifter, and now prefents it to the world at the head of this work. The learned and celebrated FORSTER *has found it both inaccurate and deficient, and publifhed another of his own de-lineation at* Hamburgh, *a few weeks ago.*

PRELIMINARY

PRELIMINARY DISCOURSE.

As foon as Vafco de Gama had opened to the European nations the route to the Eaftern Seas, the Portuguefe ftrove to arrogate to themfelves the rich commerce of that vaft continent, excluding all other nations.

Previous to that epoch, fo memorable in the annals of navigation, the Moorifh flag was the only one floating in the Gulphs of Perfia and Bengal.

When the Moorifh fhips failed from the ports of the Red Sea, they fteered their

courfe

courſe, moſt frequently, through the Perſian Gulph, but it was not extraordinary to ſee them follow the coaſts of Abyſſinia, and enter the Channel of Mozambique, without loſing ſight of the land. Here they traded alternatively with the inhabitants of the coaſt of Africa, and the natives of Mada-gaſcar.

The harbours which they chiefly fre-quented were Querimbo and Mozambique, on the coaſt of Africa, and Vingara and Bombetoque at Madagaſcar.

The people of Aſia, regardleſs of the imperfection of their charts, and the utter ignorance of their pilots, would oftentimes embark in more hazardous enterprizes.— They not only reſorted to the Malabar coaſt, but even ventured themſelves to loſe ſight of land. They ſailed on the main ſea, and having traverſed the Gulph of Bengal, pur-ſued their route to the Moluccas and Philip-pines, through the ſtreights of Sunda and Malacca.

The

The dangers infeparable from a voyage, both long and difficult to failors hardly initiated in the elements of navigation, did not difhearten them : the pilots were tempted to vifit the ftreights and the Moluccas, for the fake of a lucrative commerce; they were fure of finding in that archipelago, fhips from China and Japan, that failed thither to get nutmegs and cloves; moreover the bartering of Perfian and Indian merchandize for Chinefe and Japanefe commodities, conftituted a commerce equally fubfervient to the intereft of the Indian and the Chinefe,

Thus, at a period when the Portuguefe doubled the Cape of Good Hope, the voyages of the Moors were not confined to cruifing along the coaft; and certain it is, that thefe cruifes, undertaken without any other compafs than what depends on the imperfect knowledge of the apparent movement of the fun and ftars, may be an object that deferves to be known to the lovers of
hydrography

hydrography and its promoters. That kind of inſtrument which the Indian pilots make uſe of to take the latitude, has the form of a chaplet, the beads of which point out the altitude of the ſtars for different places where they wiſh to land. The poſition of the beads, in reference to the eye and the horizon of the ſea, ſupplies the place of an index.

A great deal of dexterity and practice are required for the proper uſe of this inſtrument, the imperfections of which will be felt by all thoſe who have the leaſt notion of ſteering a ſhip. Several times have I tried to make uſe of this inſtrument at Pondicherry, and could never find out the altitude of a ſtar to the preciſe truth of a degree. I muſt however own, that my being very ſhort-ſighted, renders obſervation more difficult and inconvenient to me than to others.

Although the Mooriſh commerce in the Indian ſeas fall ſhort, in every point of
compariſon

comparifon of that which has been fince carried on by the Europeans; it was not altogether beneath notice. It would be in vain for me to fay any thing here refpecting the profperity and gradual decline of the European fettlements in India, this fubject having been fully exhaufted by the pen of too many celebrated writers. A full account of the ifland of Madagafcar, and a clear demonftration of the benefits which might be reaped by eftablifhing colonies there, having for their foundation the happinefs and inftruction of the good-natured inhabitants, conftitutes the fole defign of the prefent work.

But notwithftanding every poffible care and precaution, the firft fettlements will always be in a great ftate of dependance on the Ifle of France and Bourbon, on account of their being fo adjacent to Madagafcar. It is therefore a matter of moment to make the reader acquainted with them.

If

If the isles of France and Bourbon are at present the chief settlements of the French in the Indian seas, they owe this pre-eminence to no other cause than their locality.

The harbour of Isle de France is the arsenal of the French forces, and the staple of their commerce.

The Portuguese were the first who discovered the isles of France and Bourbon. They gave the name of *Mascarenhas* to *Isle of France*, and that of *Cernea* to *Isle de Bourbon*. The Isle of Bourbon has no harbour spacious enough to receive large ships; it has fifty leagues in circumference; its form is pretty near circular, and its mountains very lofty. The summit of the mountain called the *Three Salasses*, is reckoned to be 1600 fathoms above the level of the sea: this summit reaches almost the centre of the island.

St. Denis is the chief town at *Isle de Bourbon*, and the residence of the governors

of

of the colony. The *Abbe de la Caille*
has fhewn by aftronomical demonftration
the fituation of the town, which is in 20
deg. 51 min. lat. and 53 deg. 10 min. long.
Eaft from the meridian of Paris.

The difficulty of effecting a landing at
St. Denis, gave rife to the invention of a
kind of bridge, the head of which is ftretch-
ed far into the fea, and rifes above its level,
but it is fo contrived, as to be out of the reach
of the higheft furges. To the end of this
bridge a rope-ladder is tied. The boats place
themfelves in fuch a fituation, as enables
thofe who wifh to land, to lay hold of the
ladder, at the moment when the fea, through
the violence of the furf, has attained to its
higheft degree of elevation. This mode of
landing, however ingenious, is attended with
great inconvenience, on account of the ofcil-
lation of the ladder, and the fhock it receives from the agitation of the fea; but the
furf is here fo ftrong, and breaks with fuch
impetuofity againft the fhore, that the com-

munication

munication between the town and the road would be frequently interrupted without this contrivance.

Though the eruptions of the vulcano of Bourbon be very common, yet no damage has been done by them, ever fince this ifland has been inhabited. The fettlers took care to keep at a proper diftance from this gulph; the accefs to which is formidable, if we judge of it by the defcription given of it by that learned naturalift, M. de Commerfon.

M. de Cremont, then Intendant of the Ifle of Bourbon, fpared neither efforts nor money, to enable M. de Commerfon to approach as near as poffible to the mouth of the Vulcano, and to examine its produ&ions. He even went further, he attended him, and this enlightened zeal in a governor, is, doubtlefs, well deferving the gratitude of thofe men who cultivate the fciences, and intereft themfelves in their progrefs.

The

The avenues leading to this vulcano are
difficult, the country is burnt and defolate
to a circumference of more than fix miles.
Heaps of afhes, lava, and fcoriæ, together
with fiffures and precipices, render its afcent
hard and perilous. It requires a ferene and
cloudlefs day to vifit the mouth of this
gulph; for a few drops of rain are fufficient
to excite an eruption; it would coft him his
life, who would be fo imprudent as to approach it in unfettled weather. The view
of a vulcano in eruption is a very awful
and majeftic fpectacle. The ftudy of thefe
fubterraneous fires, and ftill more that of
their productions, cannot be too ftrongly
recommended to thofe who, as travellers,
wifh to render themfelves ufeful in advancing the fciences.

The productions of a vulcano are infinitely
variegated. There has been gathered, at a
confiderable diftance from the vulcano, filaments of glafs, extremely fine and perfectly
b 2

crinigerous.

crinigerous. This species of lava is not very common.

The origin of the colonies of Ifle de France and Bourbon is connected with the firft French fettlements at Madagafcar. There is no other reafon but the great proximity of Madagafcar to this ifland, that can make us conceive how they were chofen to form a confiderable colony. Thefe two little'iflands are fcarcely perceptible on the chart of the vaft Indian Ocean.

It is matter of fact, that feveral Frenchmen, injured by the unhealthinefs of Madagafcar, took the refolution of relinquifhing that great ifland, to form a fettlement in the fmall ifle of Bourbon, the air of which is exceedingly propitious to health.

It was towards the year 1664 they put their project in execution. They wifely took care to carry with them fheep, cows, and a young bail.

The

The ifland was, at that period, uninhabit-
ed and uncultivated ; but the coaft abounded
with fifh, and was covered with turtles of
an immenfe fize. The colonifts ublifted
in the beginning on fifh, turtles, rice,
potatoes and yams. They abftained from
living on butchers meat, fince the prefervation of their lives was a matter of the greateft
importance.

When the feafon became favourable, they
planted fugar-canes, and fowed wheat.—
Their firft crops exceeded their expectation,
and foon the fuccefs of the little fettlement
ceafed to be doubtful. The lives of the
ancient patriarchs does not exhibit a truer
picture of the happinefs ever infeparable
from the man that keeps to the ftate of nature, and lives under a ferene fky in innocence and labour.

The inhabitants of Bourbon took to making a kind of fermented liquor of their fugar-
canes. The natives of Madagafcar had

b 3   taught

taught them the method of making this liquor, which, in my opinion, is preferable to the genuine good cider of Normandy. It is a pity that fo ufeful a liquor cannot be preferved any longer than twenty-four hours after its fermentation.

The fmall droves of oxen and fheep carried from Madagafcar to Bourbon, far from falling away, multiplied gradually every day on that ftrange foil. They found in the woods, with which this ifland is covered, a fhelter from the fcorching heat of the torrid zone; they fed on fucculent herbage, and appeared, above all, extremely fond of thofe vaft favannahs, the productions of which are analogous to thofe of Madagafcar.

When the inhabitants of Bourbon had duly provided for their fubfiftence by a good agriculture, the principal and moft fecure fource of all wealth, they began thinking that coffee might, in courfe of time, make a material branch of commerce between their

their ifland and Europe; they procured in the year 1718 fome young coffee plants from Mocca and Oude. The inhabitants of Bourbon found their fpeculation anfwer their purpofe; thefe young fhrubs being carefully planted, yielded a good quantity of coffee in a few years, and afforded the late French Eaft India Company an impoitant article of commerce.

While the little French colony of Ifle de Bourbon continued to be profperous, that of the Dutch at Ifle de France was in a ftate of languor and diftrefs. I do not know what induced the Dutch to fettle in this ifland, which they called Mauritius. All I know is, that they complained much of the havock made by the locufts and rats.

In 1712, they took the refolution to abandon completely, the fettlement they had formed at Ifle de France, to remove to the Cape of Good Hope. It m y be eafily con-

b 4   ceived

ceived why they preferred a vaft continent to a fmall ifland loft by its fituation.

The inhabitants of Ifle de Bourbon did not in the leaft regret the departure of the Dutch, and were eager to take poffeffion of their fettlements   The Ifle of France has two good harbours, and lies only at a diftance of thirty-four leagues from Bourbon. The air is falubrious; it is lefs fertile, and lefs extenfive than that of Bourbon. But thefe difadvantages are amply compenfated by the commodioufnefs of its harbours, and its being one of the windward iflands.

In 1734, the Company refolved to make fome important fettlements here, which pro-ject was left to the execution of the cele-brated Mahe de la Bourdonnais. That noble-man, born to govern men, whom he had both a perfect knowledge of, and knew how to make obey, fhewed, in thefe remote regions, that he was as good a governor as able a feaman; and the French are indebted

to

to him, and to him alone, for the aqueducts, bridges, hofpitals, and principal ftore houfes of the ifland; in fhort, every thing ufeful it contains, is the work of that juftly cele- brated man. La Bourdonnais had a tolerable knowledge of thofe mechanical arts which are the moft common, and moft neceffary for our fubfiftence. Oftentimes was he feen at dawn of day driving the wheel-barrow, or working with the trowel and compafs, at the head of the workmen, merely to excite and keep up a fpirit of emulation among them.

After the example thus fet by himfelf, it was a hard matter for any one to dare refufe his concurrence as far as poffible to promote the fuccefs of the public enterprife. Hence whatever he planned, or undertook for the benefit of the colony, during the twelve years his adminiftration lafted, was always crowned with complete and fpeedy fuccefs.

It

It is likewife to this governor, the French owe the choice of the harbour to the North-weft of the ifland. A man of a leffer fhare of good underftanding might, perhaps, have preferred the harbour fituate to the South-eaft, becaufe it is more fpacious and more commodious. But this experienced navi-gator knew, as much as any body, the in-numerable advantages of a harbour to the leeward. In thofe latitudes where the ge-neral winds prevail, leeward ports are alone fufceptible of an eafy defence, in cafe of an attack on the part of the enemy, becaufe the latter are always obliged to tow their fhips to bring them into harbour; for the fame reafon the wind is always favourable in fail-ing from fuch a port; another advantage which, though lefs than the former, de-ferves confideration.

The cultivation of corn is the moft pro-fperous of all the branches of agriculture, practifed at the Ifle de France; there the fields yield in regular fucceffion every year a crop a crop of wheat, and another of maize, commonly called Indian wheat; the manioc, which has been brought from Brafil by M. la Bourdonnais, ferves at prefent as common food to the blacks.

The continual fupplies received by fhips and fquadrons has checked the increafe of cattle. The ifland produces neverthelefs, excellent pafture, which fprings up in the beginning of the rainy feafon. It completes the whole courfe of its vegetation in the courfe of three months. The inhabitants profit by this interval to feed their herds; but no fooner the epoch of its growth is elapfed than nothing remains but a kind of ftraw, too hard for thefe animals to digeft. This ftraw is fo very dry, that the leaft fpark will fet it on fire, and this fire fpreads with fuch rapidity in the leeward parts of the ifland, as to leave no phyfical remedy to prevent its progrefs. Sometimes thefe ftraw fires will confume the adjacent woods.

When

When such an accident happens, the herds leave the favannahs, and retire to browſe in the woods.

When the Portugueſe firſt diſcovered Iſle de France, the ground was covered with woods up to the ſummits of the mountains. The whole iſland was, properly ſpeaking, but one immenſe foreſt full of beautiful trees. We remarked in it different kinds of the palm-tree, bamboos, ebony, mat-wood, tacamacca, ſtinking-wood, and ever ſo many other valuable trees.

This iſland, during the firſt epoch of its population, had its ground cleared with fire. More prudent however, had it been, to have left ſmall ſkirts of trees to and fro in the country. The rains, ſo neceſſary in hot climates to fertilize the ground, hardly fell on the cleared ſoil ſince the foreſts attract the clouds and ſuck their moiſture: more-over, the cultivated lands are no longer ſcreened from the violence of the wind.

The

The clearing of grounds without meafure or referve, has been productive of more hurt than good.

Thofe eminences of ground in vicinity of the harbour, which fcreen it from the impetuous blafts of wind, have been cleared to their very fummits. The brows of the mountains became arid; and the fruitfulnefs of vegetation funk from thofe tops into the vallies. They cut down or burnt thofe large trees which fecured the ground againft all danger of finking or giving way when the ifland was firft inhabited. From this epoch, torrents formed themfelves, and the beft part of the mud which they carried down with them, choaked up the harbour. The anchorage of fhips is now no more fafe againft the eruptions of the high fea and of hurricanes. Thus, by an abfolute want of forefight, and for the fake of the temporary benefits of the firft fettlers, the French have been at the eve of feeing themfelves deprived of a fea-port, which they confider as the

bulwark

bulwark of their naval forces, and the moſt convenient ſtaple of their commerce in the Indian Ocean.

M. Tromelin, late a captain in the French navy, an officer equally fertile in reſources, and able and experienced in every part of his profeſſional ſcience, found that the evil was not paſt remedy ; but it became urgent to have recourſe to the latter. The celebrated M. Poivre, then Intendant of the Iſles of France and Bourbon, convinced of all the advantages of Tromelin's projeƈt, ſolicited, in concert with M. Steinauer, a general officer, truly valuable by his virtues and merits, and then aƈting as governor per interim, of the Duke of Praſlin, Miniſter of the French Marine, in the name of the whole colony, the ſpeedy execution of a plan, which would give the iſland a ſafe har-bour, where the ſhips could ride without any danger of being damaged or deſtroyed by hurricanes.

As

As foon as thefe works were ordered, the firft object of M. Tromelin's care was, to turn off the courfe of the torrents by dykes and canals, which ferved to gather the main body of the waters, and to carry them into the fea, behind Ifle du Tonnelier (Cooper's ifland) where the obftructions could do no hurt to the navigation.

This was doubtlefs the moft urgent operation. The clearing of the harbour, or rather of the channel, could afterwards be brought about without obftacles in a period of time, proportionate to the number of machines required to take out the flime and mud; for it is well known, that each machine clears very near to the depth of twenty feet per day, ten cubical fathoms of ordure, when the wheels, which put the ladles in motion, are worked by thirty-fix men.

M. Tromelin's plan was not only confined to the works requifite for clearing the channel, and preventing its being choaked up in future.
This

This officer had more modern and more extensive views. He had remarked, a communication with a vaſt baſon, perfectly ſafe againſt the moſt violent winds. This baſon, known by the name of *Trou Fanfaron* or Braggard's Hole, takes up three hundred fathoms in length. Its breadth meaſures ſixty fathoms, and the main depth of the water does not exceed ten feet; it was neceſſary therefore, to make it twenty-five feet deep, to render it fit to receive ſhips of the largeſt burthen. Nothing was required therefore, than to take up the mud and ſlime, and two machines could clear out forty thouſand cubical fathoms of mud, which encumbered the baſon. But the clearing of the mud and ſlime was not the moſt difficult part of the operation; the mouth of the baſon was cloſed by a coral bank, the removal of which appeared to be an enterprize attended with great difficulty and expence. This obſtacle could not diſmay M. Tromelin. After a ſcrutinous ſearch of its extent, and many cloſe ſoundings, he
found

found himfelf able to hit on a proper expedient. And by means of gunpowder, and digging of holes at a certain diftance from the centre where the explofion was to take place, he fucceeded in blowing up, and removing beneath the water, that part of the bank which obftructed the paffage of the fhips.

There is no rock that can refift the expanfive force of an elaftic fluid, when the engineer who makes ufe of that expedient, knows, by cavities contrived at proper diftances, to cut off the communications of the movement, fo as to render the force proportionate to the mafs; it is really an aftonifhing fact, that gunpowder is too little made ufe of to blow up rocks under water, yet there is no force greater, and more economical, when directed by perfons of fkill.

Had it been poffible for M. Tromelin to be acquainted with the ingenious method invented by M. Coulomb, a celebrated academician

c

demician, for the purpofe of removing fuba-
queous obftructions, that experienced foldier
would doubtlefs have had recourfe to it, and
this famous experiment would have enlarged
the knowledge of engineers charged with
fimilar operations in the French harbours.
When great hydraulic works are undertaken
in countries expofed at certain periods to the
rage of winds and hurricanes, the execution
of thefe enterprizes fhould be entered on
with all poffible celerity and perfeverance, to
oppofe a great refiftance to the combined
efforts of wind and water.

Nothing but perfonal experience can
enable us to form a proper idea of that
formidable meteor, a hurricane. It is almoft
conftantly accompanied by rain, thunder and
earthquake; the atmofphere is, as it were,
on fire, and the wind blows with equal fury
from all parts of the horizon. A hurricane
is a kind of fpout which feems to menace
that part of the earth which it lights on,
with total fubverfion. It is at leaft under
this

this form navigators defcry it from at a diftance, and their fhips frequently remain becalmed, at a fmall diftance from the places where thofe dreadful ftorms break out with the moft violent explofion. If the rapidity of the wind exceed an hundred and fifty feet a fecond, its force then becomes irrefiftible, the loftieft trees are torn up by their roots, and the beft-built dwellings hurled into heaps of ruins. Neither the ponderofity of anchors, the ftrength of cables, nor the ftoutnefs of bottoms, are capable of fecuring the moorings of fhips, the wind drives them afhore, and dafhes them to pieces, unlefs they drive on a bank of fand or mud.

In the hurricane of March, 1671, I faw the ftruck main-topmaft of the Mars, of fixty-four guns, broke in the cap; and yet that hurricane was far from being fo violent as that which raged in February the fame year. Able mariners muft be well acquainted with the force neceffary to break a main-

topmaft

topmaſt when ſtruck; they will not therefore tax me with exaggeration, when I
compute the velocity of the gale in its moſt
impetuous guſts, at an hundred and fifty feet
a ſecond. The extraordinary variation of
the barometer, in latitudes ſituate between
the two tropics, is the only index hitherto
known, by which a hurricane may be fore-
ſeen ſome hours previous to its beginning.

At the epoch of the hurricane in February 1771, the ſubitaneous fall of the
mercury cauſed ſome anxiety to me and
Mr. Poivre; it was four o'clock in the
afternoon, Mr. Poivre invited the Captain
commanding in harbour to his houſe; that
officer, who had been an ocular witneſs
to the hurricane of 1761, was not ſtruck
like us with the variation of the barometer;
he ſaid there were more certain omens;
twenty-four hours, added he, before the
hurricane, you will ſee the blacks come
down the mountains and announce it.
Moreover, ſun-ſet will make me reſolve on
the

the meafures which I ought to take to prevent, as much as in my power lies, the
accidents infeparable from thofe dreadful
ftorms. The urgent intreaties of M. Poivre
and my conjoint obfervations would not
avail to convince the officer; we were forced
to wait fun-fet: the fky was thin, pure, and
ferene; but the mercury ftill continued
finking lower in the tube of the barometer.
The fetting of the fun was truly beautiful.
The Captain, who had long ferved on board
the Indiaman, left us quite pleafed and eafy
about the fcourges which threatened to
overwhelm the ifland. He feemed to pity
us for fo much ado about the barometer
Seldom does it happen that we overcome
the obftinacy of a man, who having no
other experience than the practical part of his
bufinefs, is alfo infected with the abfurd
prejudice, that theory is good for nothing.
This clafs of people unfortunately is but
too common, and he that would make it his
bufinefs to expofe the evil which refulted,
and ftill do refult from the conduct of

ignorant

ignorant and prefumptuous commanders, would furely trace no ufeful picture to humanity.

The hurricane manifefted itfelf about feven o'clock in the evening, that is to fay, one hour after fun-fet. Before nine o'clock all the veffels were driven afhore, except the fhip Ambulante, armed *en flute*, and a fmall cutter called *Le Verd Galand*; in a fudden whirlwind, the Ambulante was forced out to fea, and the cutter faftened to her with a cable, was fwallowed up by the waves.

The Ambulante, ftripped of her fails and rudder, and deprived of provifions for her crew, confifting of failors and a detachment of the Irifh regiment of Clare, who did duty on board as marines, was buffetted about for upwards of twelve hours in the ftorm. The winds fhifting frequently, fhe was toffed all round the ifland, and at laft caft, as it were, in a miraculous manner, upon the only part of the coaft where men
could

could find fafety in fuch a violent ftorm.
What renders fimilar difafters the more
afflictive, if the impoffibility of affording
mutual affiftance to one another, men muft
not ftir from amidft the ruins which encompafs them; they muft patiently await
their fate, without being able either to forefee, or to prevent it; the violence of the
wind, the rapidity of the torrents forbid
them to quit the fheltering place they have
chofen.

The hurricane raged for eighteen hours
with inceffant and unabating fury; thick
fhowers, thunder and lightning could not
calm the violence of the wind; but at three
o'clock, the mercury, which had fallen
twenty-five lines, ftood ftill for fome
minutes; a little while after it rofe; when
the fudden gufts ceafed, the wind became
more fteady, and finally rendered it poffible,
at fix o clock in the evening, to give affiftance to the unhappy fhipwrecked wretches.
In fuch dreadful fiuations, man over-

whelmed

whelmed by the power of imperious neceſſity, ſeems to have loſt all ſenſibility, he
waits with a kind of ſtupefaction the blows
which are ready to fall on him; he bears
in ſilence and without a murmur, the ills
that afflict him. During this hurricane,
the communications eſtabliſhed in the different parts of the iſland were cut off by
inundation, and the fall of trees; three
whole weeks elapſed before any tidings could
be received reſpecting the Ambulante, which
had been wrecked only ſix leagues diſtant
from Port Louis, at Iſle de France. All
the crops were deſtroyed.; it required the
utmoſt efforts to repair even thoſe ſhips which
had ſuſtained the leaſt damage.

It was, however, M. Tromelin who rendered this important ſervice to the colony
and its trade. Neceſſity required to ſend moſt
of thoſe ſhips in great haſte to Madagaſcar
for proviſions, and ſupplies of all kinds. It
is in ſuch unhappy predicaments the talents
of a governor ſhine forth with the greateſt
luſtre.

luftre. M. Poivre, who, in the courfe of his government, had difplayed an equal fhare of knowledge and wifdom, had taken the falutary precaution to let feveral fhips winter at the Cape of Good Hope. Thefe fhips, informed of the calamitous fituation of Ifle de France, brought likewife abundant fupplies which faved the colony ; for they arrived a fhort time after the fecond hurricane, whofe frefh devaftations had entirely depreffed both the fpirits and hopes of the diftreffed inhabitants of Ifle de France.

The damage which the fhips in the harbour fuftained by the impetuofity of the waves, and the violence of the wind in this fecond hurricane, was much lefs confiderable than that which they had fuffered by the firft. The variation of the barometer forewarned them of their danger, and every one was eager to provide for his fafety.

Had M. Poivre's merit been not fo well known, I would eagerly have fnatched this
opportunity

opportunity to render to his memory the tribute of praife referved to that rare number of men, whofe ftation made them benefactors of the human race; my heart felt the greater impulfe to perform this piece of duty, as he honoured me with the tendereft friendfhip. But the life of this illuftrious man has been publifhed by M. Dupont; that celebrated writer is profeffionally more capable than me, to appreciate the talents of a governor. Moreover, I do not boaft of literary merit, and this affertion of mine will fufficiently fpeak for itfelf in retrofpect of the prefent work, the want of fyftematic order is every where confpicuous. In publifhing this book I had therefore no other end in view than that of public utility.

Addicted from my tendereft age to folid fciences, I am an utter ftranger to the art of government; the numerous and long voyages which I have made to different parts of the globe have, perhaps, given me
some

fome knowledge of mankind; but the greater the knowledge, the ftronger is the averfion one feels to the honourable function of guiding and directing them.

The zeal which animated M. Poivre for the improvement of agriculture, induced him to advance confiderable fums to the fettlers for the purpofe of cultivating corn. The Magazines were always well ftocked with provifions, becaufe he always laid it down as the firft condition to repay him with the natural produce of the country. For this reafon the price of bread had feldom a great variation of rife or fall.

M. Poivre, who wifhed to enrich the colony entrufted to his care, with all the ufeful productions fcattered with profufion over the four quarters of the globe, purchafed of the late French Eaft-India Company, the great garden of Montplaifir, which he wanted to cultivate himfelf, and to naturalize the exotic plants. He fet the firft example of

grubbing

grubbing up the foil, eradicating all noxious weeds, and fecuring by this operation the fuccefs of his nurferies.

It is univerfally known, that the French colonies ftand folely indebted to M. Poivre for the nutmeg and cloves ; and this benefit, which is on the eve of opening a new branch of trade to France, will certainly not be buried in oblivion. To him they likewife owe the rima or bread-tree, and the dry rice of Cochinchina. In fhort, his garden of Montplaifir contains a vaft quantity of rare plants, of which M. Cere, our mutual friend, has given an excellent defcription. To the care of M. Cere the keeping of that treafure is now entrufted, and the colonial minifters could furely not have fixed their choice on an abler, and more expert agri-culturift.

I have here almoft exhaufted all that is worth notice, refpecting the Ifles de France and Bourbon. The mountains of the former

do

do not exceed four hundred and twenty-
fix fathoms in height; the foil is ferruginous
and productive. No venomous animals but
fcorpions and millepedes are known here.
For finenefs of climate, and falubrity of air,
thefe ifles may be compared with the Fortunate Iflands ; but they are feparated from the
Indian Ocean by an archipelago, abounding
with fhoals and fand-banks. I made it one of
the principal objects of my voyage, to defcribe
their fituation; and it is likewife to M.
Poivre, navigators ftand indebted for this
important difcovery.

The fhips which fet fail for India from
Ifle de France, were obliged to take, during
the two monfoons, long and indirect routes,
in order to keep off that archipelago of ifles
and fhoals, fituate to the North of Ifle de
France. While the dangerous pofition of
thefe obftacles remained latent and unknown,
it was but little fafe for a fquadron to fteer
a direct courfe. In the South of the line,
from the eighteenth degree of latitude to the
twenty-eighth,

twenty-eighth, fouth-eaftern gales blow all
the year round. From the eighteenth degree to equinoctial line, the fouth-eaft
monfoon begins in April, and continues till
October, at which epoch it is fucceeded by
the weftern monfoon. In the north of the
line, the cafe is entirely the reverfe.

If they fail from Ifle de France to India,
in the fine feafon, they proceed in fight of
the northernmoft point of Madagafcar, and
fteering afterwards between the flats of
Patrom and the Amirantes, crofs the line in
the fiftieth degree of longitude ; and finding
the weftern monfoon in the North, they
pafs along the Maldives, between Keloe and
Shewlipar, and approach Cochin. The reft
of the voyage is but mere coafting.

Ships that fet fail from Ifle de France to
Pondicherry, during the bad feafon, are
obliged to fteer a far longer, and more
indirect route. They go without variable
winds as far as the thirty-fixth degree of
south

ſouth latitude; they afterwards direct their
courſe in ſuch a manner, as to be able to
croſs the equinoctial line in the eighty-
fifth degree.

If the moſt perfect knowledge of that
archipelago permits ſhips to venture on ſteering a more direct courſe in both the ſeaſons,
I may flatter myſelf with having borne ſome
ſhare in the merit of this eſſential ſervice
rendered to navigation, having been the firſt
that aſcertained by aſtronomical obſervations,
the local poſitions of the moſt dangerous
parts. A perſon, however little verſed in
the nautical ſcience, muſt be ſenſible that
enquiries of this nature are attended with
continual dangers. The principal parts
which I have found out are Secheyla Iſland,
the flats of Cargados, and Salha Maha, together with the iſlands of Diego Garcia
and Ado.

The iſland of Secheyla has a good harbour, and is ſituate in the latitude of 4 deg.
38 min.

38 min. fouth, and in the longitude of 53
deg. 15 min. eaft from Paris. This ifland is
wooded up to the fummit of the mountains.
It has plenty of turtles and tortoifes, fome of
which weigh three hundred pounds. In
1769, when I refided there a whole month,
to determine its local fituation, it was inhabited, befides all the iflands adjacent, by
monftrous crocodiles; but fince that time,
a little colony has been eftablifhed on it,
and the fettlers cultivate nutmeg and clove-
trees. In one of thefe iflands, called Palm
Ifland, we find the tree which bears the famous fruit known by the appellation of
Cocoa of the Maldives, or fea-cocca, the
defcription of which is given after that of
the plants of Madagafcar.

I made it my province to dwell in this
preliminary difcourfe on thofe objects only,
which moft excited my attention. Among
the number of thefe I reckon, for inftance,
the harbour of Diego Garcia, and the
profpect of the ifland itfelf is pleafant. We
judged

judged to have twelve leagues in circumference. Its form refembles a horfe-fhoe.
Its greateft breadth is not above a quarter of
a league ; the ground is however fufficiently
elevated to ferve as a fence and fhelter to a
vaft refervoir or canal, which affords fpacious
room to the moft numerous fleets. This
canal is four leagues long, and its main
breadth is about one league. Its excellent
harbour has two entrances to the north.
The roads are extremely fine. Its fituation
I afcertain it to be in the 7 deg. 14 min.
fouth latitude, and in the 68 degree eaft longitude from the meridian of Paris.

Hitherto the fhoals with which this archipelago abounds, are not all known. They are
not to be feen on the ancient charts by M.
d'Apres. This hydrographer was fomewhat
deftitute of that fpirit of enquiry, fo neceffary for the perfection of charts, for which
reafon he has not quite made the beft of the
materials he had in his hands, which a truly
able aftronomer might have made of them,

for the safety of the navigator. I here do speak from a knowledge of causes. The collection of the charts of Isle de France is replete with notes of my own hand-writing, where I clearly show that he confounds Artova with Agalega, and Cargados with St. Brandon, though he had among his papers the different plans of those islands and their shoals, he farther made a multitude of other mistakes, all of great importance. I have certainly corrected them with all possible energy. In objects that regard so nearly the safety of the seamen, no private considerations ought to check or leave in suspence, any thing tending to promote the perfection of hydrography. But if I treat M. d'Apres with some severity, I do not mean to deprive him of the praises to which his zeal and desire of rendering his labours useful, do really entitle him on my part. More he could not require of a man who only states facts, leaving individuals out of question. Moreover, having been on the point of being shipwrecked off Cargados, only because this

hydrographer

hydrographer took it in his head to miftake
Cargados for St. Brandon, while the plan of
the former had been taken by the boats,
Charles and Elizabeth, while that of the
latter is printed in the Englifh pilot, fhould
not I have made it a duty to demonftrate,
that thofe two dangerous fhoals differ vaftly,
both in point of form and longitude ? for
they are remote fifty leagues from each
other. Cargados bears the form of a crefcent,
and St. Brandon reprefents an equilateral
triangle. M. d'Apres confounding thefe two
places, gave them in his chart a main pofition, without any other motive, than becaufe
he found them in the ancient charts, both
placed in one latitude. A falfe pofition and fo
very fallacious, that the moft wary pilot
miffes the courfe he ought to fteer to get
clear of them.

On the memorable day of the tranfit of
Venus over the difk of the fun, in June of
1769, I could not make the important obfervation of the paffage of that planet, though

the

the weather was cloudlefs and ferene, becaufe the cutter, on board of which I had
embarked, was within an inch of being
fhipwrecked off Cargados. To avoid deftruction, we were obliged to double to the
leeward, the moft eaftern lands-point of that
formidable fhoal; thus I leave the reader to
judge if, after fuch an accident, I had not
the greateft right to diftruft that opinion,
unfortunately become too popular, refpecting
the precifion of the charts drawn by M.
d'Apres

I cannot enter here into farther particulars, refpecting the archipelago which parts
India from Ifle de France, but I dare affirm,
that it is highly neceffary to be acquainted
with it, before one undertakes to fteer more
direct courfes during the two monfoons.
Thefe direct routs are by no means new, the
ancient navigators ufed to fteer them, as
may be feen by their knowledge of the
winds, and by an infpection of their charts.
Hence

Hence to expatiate by a longer diſſertation, would be foreign to my ſubject*.

I ſhall now give an account of ſome ſhip-wrecks, which prove that men, caſt by accident on an arid coaſt or barren iſland, find a ſafe ſubſiſtence on fiſh and the animals which are to be found abundantly on the ſea ſhores.

The ſhip L'Heureux, having ſailed on the 30th of Auguſt 1769, from Iſle de France to Bengal, fell in, at a moment when leaſt expected, with the iſlands of Juan de Nova. The Captain wanted to bear away from them to the leeward, and eſcape by this manœuvre, from the dangers which ſurrounded theſe iſlands. The moment he had doubled them, he ſteered his courſe

---

* This paragraph concludes with an apology on the part of the Author for a long digreſſion he makes in the original on the utility of tranſportation, which being a ſubject quite foreign to this work, has been omitted in the tranſlation.

North

North Eaſt, ¼ North, with a view of rendering his paſſage ſhorter by ſome days.
He was ſenſible that he ought to have
neglected no means which could accelerate
his arrival in Bengal, ſince the ſeaſon
was then too far advanced. But in this
route, the ſhip bore in the middle of the
night on ſome flats, ſurrounded by a row
of breakers, which encreaſed his alarm;
all manœuvres became uſeleſs, and the ſhip
was on the point of going down, when the
Captain caſt an anchor in ſuch a manner as
gave him hopes ſhe would bear on ſome high
flats. This manœuvre proved ſuccefsful,
and the crew could at leaſt wait the approach
of morning on the top of the maſts. Day-
break however, did not extricate them from
their dangerous ſituation; but at half paſt
ſix the ſame morning, they had ſome ſmall
glimpſe of hope to get off. They perceived
at a diſtance a little iſland covered with ſand.
The whole crew tranſported themſelves
thither by degrees, in the boat which the
Captain had wiſely ordered to be launched,
previous

previous to the fatal moment when the ſhip ſtruck. But the ſuppoſed little ſand-iſland was nothing but a ſhoal, which was left dry at low water. In this cruel ſituation, the Captain ſaw no other reſource than to ſend his boat to ſeek aſſiſtance on the coaſt of Africa. The wretched crew fell in, eight hours after they had ſet ſail, with a rock, which they called *Providence Iſland*. This rock was not entirely barren, and they found on it freſh water, turtles and cocoas. Nine men of the boat's crew remained there, whilſt two of the moſt vigorous rowers uſed their utmoſt endeavours to reach the ſhoal where they had left the reſt of their com-panions, until ſuch time as aſſiſtance could be obtained for them. Their expectation was the more anxious, ſince they ſaw them-ſelves bordering on the fatal moment of being ſwallowed up by the high tides, the ſeaſon of which was on the point of ſetting in. The boat was three whole days on its paſſage thither, and was not large enough

to

to take in all thofe that had been fhipwrecked. This defect they had, however,
the ingenuity to fupply by a raft conftructed
of the wreck of the fhip. They made it
large enough to contain all the provifions
and utenfils required for the building and
victualling of a large floop. This floating
raft was towed by the canoe as far as Providence Ifland. The crew of the fhipwrecked
remained two months on this rock, which
time they employed in building a floop of
twenty-five feet, on which they finally had
the good fortune to reach the ifland of Madagafcar, without any accident furvening.
The latitude of Providence Ifland was taken
8 by 9 deg. 5 min. its longitude 49 min.
and its fituation from Ifle de France north
north-weft, and fome odd degrees weft.

M. Moreau, captain of a fmall fhip, called
Le Favori, being bound on the 9th of February 1757, from Ifle de France to Nafa-
pore, fell in on the 26th of March of the
fame year with Adu Iflands. He found
their

their latitude to be 5 deg. 6 min. fouth, and
calculated this longitude in the 76th degree
eaft from the Meridian of Paris. He
launched a boat to attempt a landing, but
faw himfelf forced to abandon the party
embarked in it, becaufe he could find no
mooring, and the current drove his fhip
with great violence to the leeward. M.
Moreau informed me, that he found at the
diftance of fix leagues to the fouth of thefe
iflands a fand bank, of a good and folid bottom; and crowded all the fail he could to
overtake his boat. I am fure that the reader
will perufe with intereft the extract of the
account which M. Riviere, the officer commanding the boat's crew, gives of thofe
iflands, and of the fufferings he endured
there with his companions.

The boat's crew confifted of three whites
and five lafcars. M. Riviere failed round
the iflands without finding a fafe landing-
place. Meanwhile, having loft fight of the
fhip

ſhip for two days, he reſolved to hazard a
landing on a ſmall iſland, which had not
quite a league in circumference, and which
purpoſe he accompliſhed with the greateſt
difficulty.

Theſe iſlands are twelve in number, joined by a reef of rocks which, at low water,
afford paſſage from one iſland to the other.

M. Riviere farther told me, that they form
a bay of about ſix leagues in circumference.
The road or entrance is in the weſtern part;
he ſounded it, and found it to be thirty fathoms deep. This bay, the form of which
is circular, has in its middle a bank, which
is almoſt ſquare, and meaſures about a quarter of a league in circumference. The bank
furniſhes plenty of ſhell-fiſh and fiſh.

The iſlands lie low and are covered with
cocoa-trees. The largeſt has not quite one
league in circumference. The company
ſubſiſted

fubfifted there on birds, fifh, fhell-fifh, and
cocoas, during three months. They could
neither find frefh water nor turtles.

As foon as the axes, which ferved
them to cut down cocoa-trees, were grown
blunt and worn out, M. Riviere formed a
refolution to proceed to the coaft of
Malabar, though he had neither charts
nor compafs. That officer ordered his boat
to be laden with cocoa-nuts. He embarked
with two whites; the lafcars made a raft,
which the Indians call *catimaroo*. The boat
was to tow this catimaroo, which carried
the reft of the provifions. In fteering their
courfe north north-weft, they difcovered a
high fand-bank, four or five hours after they
had loft fight of land. A few days after
their departure, the fea running very high
overfet the raft. The whites propofed to
M. Riviere to abandon the lafcars, the boat
being too fmall to hold them. This generous officer rejected their propofal with
indignation. He took the lafcars into his
boat,

boat, though it contained provifions only for thirteen days, and landed fafely at Cranganore, near Calcutta, twenty-eight days after he had failed from Adu Iflands. It would be a hard matter to defcribe the dangers and fatigues he went through in this paffage ; but the manly and humane conduct of that officer, in fo trying and cruel a condition, merits the higheft eulogiums.

Sand Ifland was difcovered in 1722, by the fhip *Diana*, commanded by Captain La Feuille. It is flat, and has not much more than a quarter of a league in circumference. There was however, at its northward and fouthward points, drinkable water at the depth of fifteen feet. The fhip L'Utile, M. La Fargue, was wrecked there in the year 1761. The officers and company of that fhip, who were for the moft part blacks, fought refuge on that little ifland. Here they built of the wreck a floop, in which the whites embarked fix months after, and made good their landing at St. Mary's, in the

the ifland of Madagafcar, after a fhort paffage. The blacks remained on the fhoal, always expecting to receive fome affiftance from the whites, in which they were however difappointed. Every man that is endowed with the leaft fentiment of humanity, muft fhrink with horror, when we tell him, that thefe poor blacks were fuffered to perifh undefervedly, without the leaft effort being ufed to fave them.

The corvette *La Dauphine*, commanded by M. Tromelin, a lieutenant in the French navy, brother to the gentleman before mentioned, came in fight of Sand Ifland, on the 29th of November 1776. He triumphed over all the obftacles which threw themfelves in the way of thofe who wifh to land on that dangerous fhoal: he went on fhore, and had the good fortune to bring back to Ifle de France, the fad remains of the crew of the *L'Utile*. Eighty black men and women had perifhed, fome for want, others

in

in endeavouring to save themselves on rafts. Seven negresses suffered, during fifteen years, all the rigours of the most cruel and trying situation. The most elevated spot of this shoal is only fifteen feet above the level of the sea. It is six hundred fathoms long, and three hundred broad. The blacks had built themselves a hut of the wreck of the ship, which they covered with turtle-shells. Birds feathers most ingeniously tied together by these negresses, served them as covering and cloaths. This isle is absolutely barren, and does afford no shelter from the violence of the waves during storms. The seven negro-women who out-lived all the horrors resulting from famine, and the absolute want of every necessary, brought with them a little infant, which bore the same marks of misery and suffering as its unhappy mother. These women related, that they had seen five ships, of which several attempted to land on the place of their captivity, but saw all their efforts frustrated.

The

The fmalleft of thefe veffels, called *La Sauterelle*, had given them fome momentary hopes of deliverance; but the boat belonging to it, no doubt from fear of being wrecked, bore off fo rapidly as to leave one of the failors behind on the ifland. This man, a victim of his courage and humanity, feeing himfelf thus abandoned by his companions, took the defperate refolution of making his way to Madagafcar on a raft. He embarked with three black men and three black women, ten weeks before the arrival of the *Dauphine*.

If I have taken the liberty in this introductory addrefs to infert a differtation on the Ifles de France and Bourbon, and on the archipelago full of fhoals and flats, fituate to the north of thofe iflands, it is, as I have already obferved, from a conviction that it is highly neceffary to reprefent to the navigator, the obftacles which he has to conquer, in fteering a direct courfe to the coaft

of

of Coromandel during the bad feafon. I had propofed to myfelf a vaft fcope of particulars on this head, in the firft plan I projected of this work, agreeable to which, it was to have been divided in two diftinct parts; but for fome unforefeen circumftances, that part of my work which relates to navigation, will not appear at prefent, though it has been printed upwards of five years, as well as that which I now lay before the public.

NARRATIVE

NARRATIVE

OF

A VOYAGE to the EAST INDIES.

Defcription of the Ifland of Madagafcar.

NO fooner had the Europeans acquired
fome fmall knowledge of Madagafcar,
than that ifland unfortunately became the
object of their avarice.   Its extent, richnefs
of foil, and variety of productions, feemed
to offer to the people that fhould conquer it,
commercial advantages which they could
never have configned to neglect.   Till now
the unhealthinefs of the air has luckily faved
it from the yoke of thofe civilized nations,
who unjuftly and barbaroufly pretend to bend
forcibly to their fway, focieties of men

whom

whom they have denominated *savages*, for
no other reafon but becaufe they have not
the fame manners and cuftoms as thofe of
the Europeans.

There is not one of thofe civilized nations
that can boaft of having facrificed fome
flender commercial intereft to the facred principles of the law of nature.   They have all
fhewn themfelves unjuft and cruel ; almoft
every one of them have ravaged with fire,
fword and peftilence all the places whither
the love of gain has attracted them.   Ought
they to have forgot that the foil which thofe
favages inhabit is theirs, the fame as the foil
which we inhabit is our own ?

More folid   and   permanent   advantages
would have been acquired by the Europeans,
had they taken pains to difleminate their arts
and induftry in thofe climes where they are
wanting.   Prefents of that nature would not
have been fterile, and commerce would foon
have felt how much more preferable muft
have

have been a meafure fo gentle, fo humane, to the lawlefs and cruel expedients which they tried in fubduing all the ill-fated natives of the countries which prefented fome new objects of wealth.

The ifland of Madagafcar was difcovered in the year 1506, by *Lawrence Almeyda*. It was however known to the Perfians and Arabs, from times immemorial, under the name of *Sarandib*.

Alphonfo Albukerque ordered *Ruy Pereira da Conthintho* to vifit its interior parts. This General difpatched *Triftan d'Acunha* to make the tour round the ifland, and to take the foundings of the principal capes.

It is divided in twenty-eight provinces, viz.

Anoffy,	*Ycondra,*
Manapani,	*Etomampo,*
The valley of Am-	*Adchimouffi,*
boul,	*Erengdranes,*
Vohitzban,	*Vohitz-Anghombes,*
Watte Manahou,	*Manacarongha,*

B 2   *Mantatana,*

Mantatana,	*Mandrarey,*
Antaveres,	*Ampatra,*
Ghalemboul,	*Caremboul,*
Tamatava,	*Mahafalley,*
Sahaveh,	*Houlouveh,*
Voolou-Voolou,	*Sivah,*
Andafoutchy,	*Yvandrhou,*
Manghabey,	*Mafhicores.*
Adcimoutchy,	

When 'the Portuguefe firft difcovered Madagafcar, they would give it the name of *St. Lawrence.* The French in the reign of the fourth Henry, called it *Ifle Dauphine.* Tho' its real name be *Madecaffa,* it is more generally known by that of *Madagafcar.*

This great ifland is, according to feveral learned geographers, the ancient *Cernea* of Pliny, and the *Menuthiafde* of Ptolomy.

Its fituation is pretty near north-north-eaft and fouth-fouth-weft. Its limits of latitude are the 12th and 26th degrees.

The

The furface of this ifle may be valued at 200 millions of acres of good and arable ground, celebrated for the fertility and variety of its productions. All the different parts of Madagafcar are watered by torrents and large rivers, and above all by a great number of little rivulets, which take their fource at the foot of that vaft ridge of mountains, which feparates the eaftern from the weftern coaft. *Vigagora* is the higheft mountain in the north, and *Botiflmena* in the fouth.

Thefe mountains contain in their bowels precious minerals, and curious foffils. The traveller who perambulates for the firft time and for the purpofe of inftruction, the mountainous wilds, interfected by valleys and declivities where nature, abandoned to genial fertility, difplays the moft fingular, and moft variegated productions, frequently cannot refift the furprife and terror that ftrike him at the fight of thefe precipices, whofe fummits are crowned with lofty trees as ancient as the

B 3   world.

world. His aftonifhment increafes at the noife of thofe great cafcades, whofe borders are inacceffible. But thofe views truly picturefque vanifh alternately before rural profpects, pleafant hills, plains, the vegetation of which is never troubled by the intemperatenefs, or viciffitude of the feafons. The eye contemplates with pleafure the fpacious commons, which afford pafture to numerous droves of oxen and flocks of fheep. The rice and potatoe fields, exhibit likewife a new and moft interefting fpectacle. One beholds a flourifhing agriculture raifed almoft at the fole expence of nature. The happy natives of Madagafcar do not moiften the earth with their fweat, they hardly turn it with the fpade, and this labour is alone fufficient. They dig little holes in the ground, at a fmall diftance from each other, in which they drop a few grains of rice, and fill up thefe holes with earth, by a gentle motion of the foot; but what furnifhes the moft convincing proof of the extreme fertility of the

foil

foil is, that a field thus fown, yields an hundred for one.

The woods prefent a prodigious variety of trees, palm-trees of all kinds, woods ufed in dying, ebony, bamboos of an enormous thicknefs, orange and lemon trees.

Timber for building fhips or houfes is not lefs common here than other forts of wood of a lefs ferviceable nature. Flacourt fays, that in the year 1650, he fent to France fifty-two thoufand aloe-trees of the firft quality. Phyficians call this wood *agallochum*, and the Portuguefe give it the name of *eagle-wood*.

A maze of plants of the parafitic kind crowd this multitude of trees and bufhes. The forefts abound with agarics and mufhrooms, of a pleafant and lively colour and an exquifite flavor. The natives call them *holas*, and very judicioufly deftroy thofe which are prejudicial to health.

B 4   Gums,

Gums and ufeful refins are likewife gathered here.   The lacteous juice which the
iflanders draw from the trees they call *finguiera*, yields by coagulation that fingular fubftance known to naturalifts by the name of
gum elaftic.

The elafticity of this refinous gum, has
of late been tried fuccefsfully for the benefit
of the arts.   Surgery has even derived fome
advantages from it, relative to the improvement of probing inftruments and bandages.
But it is alfo evident that this precious fubftance may be applied to many other ufes.

The whole furface of the woods is covered
with herbs unknown to the botanift, fome
are aromatic and medicinal, others of great
fervice to dyers.

Flax, a kind of hemp which both in
length and ftrength exceeds that of Europe,
fugar-canes, wax, different forts of honey,
tobacco, indigo, white-pepper, gum-lack,
amber,

amber, ambergris, feveral filky fubftances and cotton, would long fince have become articles of trade which Madagafcar might have furnifhed with profufion, had the Europeans, fince they refort to this ifland, taken pains to fpread among the iflanders, thofe points of knowledge which are requifite to prepare and render valuable the divers articles I have juft enumerated. The moft indefatigable botanift could fcarcely, in the courfe of a long life, glance on the natural hiftory of the vegetation of the different parts of this ifland, whofe extent in latitude, comprifes feveral climates.

All thofe enquiries that fhall tend to procure us the knowledge of the productions of Madagafcar, will not be lefs ufeful to commerce than to the progrefs of our arts and manufactures.

There are, I am certain few countries on earth which afford refrefhments of all kinds more abundantly and at a cheaper rate to the navigator.

It

It was in the innermoft recefs of the great bay of Antongil, where Monfieur *Mahe de la Bourdonnais* found means, with equal fkill and activity, to compenfate the misfortunes and diforders which had feized on his fquadron. But for the refources this able feaman found here, he muft perhaps have been unable to put to fea, and to reap thofe great fucceffes in India, which have illuftrated his memory.

The long refidence which Bourdonnais made in the bay of *Antongil* to careen his fhips, made him regret it all his lifetime, to have not had a better knowledge of the productions of Madagafcar whilft he was governor of the ifles of France and Bourbon. This celebrated man was fenfible how ufeful that great ifland could be to the colonies over which he once commanded.

Timber, pitch, tar, fpermaceti, faline fubftances of all kinds, indigo, tobacco, the dreffing of flax and hemp, cotton and various

forts

forts of filk, appeared to him commercial articles of no fmall importance. The dexterity with which the women of Madagafcar weave and twift thofe beautiful *pagnas* which ferve to cover them, attracted his admiration. Some are made of the filaments of the leaf of a plant called *raven*. Others, moft efteemed by the iflanders, but lefs fought after by the Europeans, are manufactured of filk and cotton.

The induftrious mode in which thefe people forge and caft their iron and other metals, ftruck next the attention of *Bourdonnais;* but what he fet the greateft value on, was their manner of twifting the little cables deftined to catch whales and to moor their veffels.

He conceived hopes that the natural fkillfulnefs of thofe iflanders, joined to their fondnefs of the mechanical arts, might pave the way of introducing into this ifland, feveral branches of commerce ufeful to Europe, and

to

to the colonies of the ifles of France and
Bourbon. He propofed to himfelf to perfuade the governors of the late Eaft-India
company, to eftablifh manufactures of canvafs
forges, foundries, and rope-yards. The
population of Madagafcar is confiderable
enough to leave hopes that eftablifhments of
that nature will be attended with fuccefs.
Befides manual labor and materials are extremely cheap here.

There was no fear of Bourdonnais's having
had an intention of making the governors of
the Eaft-India company run high in expences
for ftorehoufes and buildings: he, on the
contrary, wifhed them prudently to imitate
the fimplicity and parfimony adopted by the
natives in building their dwellings. There
could indeed be nothing more ruinous, than
to erect in thofe favage regions, edifices fimilar to thofe we have in Europe for conve-
niences of that nature. It is a thing but too
common among us, to fee ufeful eftablifhments linger, and even fometimes hurry on
the

the ruin of the proprietors, for no other reafon than becaufe thefe have been filly enough
to give way to a luxurious ftile of building,
feldom or never conducive to the principal
end of their enterprize.

It would be folly to attempt drawing any
degree of comparifon of the induftry of thefe
iflanders with that of the Europeans ; we
cannot even precifely calculate the enormous
lofs of time the former fuftain through the
roughnefs of their tools, and the imperfect
ftate of their handicrafts.

The favage knows not, like us, the advantages arifing from the divifion of work, which
gives to each individual the higheft degree of
fkill he is fufceptible of, and faves the time
which is ever loft in leaving one fort of work
to take up another.   But if we had once
witneffed the fatiguing drudgery of the favages, and their patience to fucceed in the moft
common crafts, we could not help feeling the
grateful fenfation due to thofe among us,
who

who devote themfelves entirely to the improvement of arts and manufactures.   It
wants but a few new inventions to change
the induftry of a great nation.

The invention of weaving ftockings, the
difcovery, ftill more recent, of fpinning
cotton by the machines of Manchefter, have
produced a great revolution in thofe two
branches of induftry.   Neither knitting nor
manual fpinning can forthwith come in
competition with the works performed by
machines.

Europeans, who travel in thofe diftant
climates, communicate to the people, whom
you call favages, your learning and your
knowledge.   Make it your duty and law
to teach them that juftice, that equality,
that attachment which ought to rivet beings
of the fame kind; the enlightened era of
your age will never more permit you to dif-
own that facred duty.   Forget not how im-
menfely you are yourfelves indebted to fome
truths

truths unknown to your anceſtors.   It is to thoſe you owe the rapid progreſs you have made in the exact ſciences, and in the uſeful arts.

The improvement of reaſon has on the happineſs of man an influence which the art of the moſt ſubtle ſophiſter cannot invalidate. From that only period knowledge is ſuſceptible of increaſe, and the amelioration and happineſs of a man has no other ſcale of proportion than that very knowledge ; for can there be a ſyſtem more dangerous, more falſe, than that which would be founded on an oppoſite principle ?   Can it be doubted that a careful education given to ſome natives of Madagaſcar, who would be ſent back to their native land after having acquired a perfect knowledge of the induſtry of our manufactures, would not be a ſignal ſervice rendered to that iſland ?   But that nothing might be wanting to give all poſſible energy to ſuch an act of beneficence, it would be proper to keep thoſe young iſlanders free

from

from that fpirit of frivoloufnefs which defolates Europe, and France in particular.
Take care above all things that they do not
bring into their ifland the feed of that deftructive fcourge, which ftifles every fort of
ufeful induftry, and fcatters over whole nations evils paft calculation. In the great ca-
pitals this fcourge is chiefly felt. Millions of
men perifh in the fields by mifery and fatigue,
while the rich and opulent value nothing but
the pleafing talents and the arts of luxury.
The unbounded paffion which indolent men
fhew for the moft ufelefs, and frequently
the moft pernicious of things, is become fo
general, as to ceafe to make impreffion on
us. Pray what has Europe fo commendable as
makes her defpife all the reft of the world ?
Let her confider her manners and her laws,
fcarce will fhe find herfelf extricated from
barbarifm, and men of the moft enlightened
caft cannot thus far forefee the epoch and
moment, when the wifeft nation will rid
herfelf of thofe ridiculous prejudices, which
deftroy

deftroy ufeful induftry, and give importance only to objects pernicious, or at beft ufelefs.

The inhabitants of Madagafcar call them-felves indiftinctly *Malegafhes*, or *Madecaffes*. They are in general well-fhaped, and above the middling fize. The colour of their fkin is various, fome tribes are of a deep black, others tawny; fome have a coppery com-plexion, but the greateft number are of an olive color.

All thofe that are black have woolly hair like the negroes of the coaft of Africa. The hair of thofe who have the complexions of Indians or mulattoes, does not frizzle more than that of the Europeans, their nofe is not flat; their forehead is broad and open, their lips not pouting, and every feature of their face is pleafant and regular. Their phyfiog-nomy bears in general the marks of a cha-racter replete with franknefs and amenity. They never fhew any eagernefs of learning things, except fuch ones as relate to wants

C

of

of the firſt neceſſity; and this deſire is always tempered by moderation. They manifeſt even leſs than indifference to objects that require reflection. A natural ſupineneſs and general apathy renders inſupportable to them every thing that rouſes intellectual attention. Sober, nimble, agile, they waſte the beſt part of their life in ſleeping and diverting themſelves.

The native of Madagaſcar is, like the ſavage, without vice and without virtue; he only minds the preſent; he is void of all forecaſt, and does not even think that there are men on earth who trouble themſelves about the future. Theſe iſlanders are free beings, with an eaſy mind and a ſound body. Such is the organization of man, whether in his moral or phyſical ſtate, that he whoſe misfortune it is to turn his thoughts upon himſelf, is almoſt in a perpetual ſtate of malady. Indeed, if a man has a good conſtitution, he little values the advantage he has in this reſpect, over moſt of his fellow-creatures.

creatures. Our ills, if I am permitted to exprefs myfelf thus, are our own, and our pleafures belong to the external objects that procure them. Man is a good, fenfible, fympathizing being, and it is our conftitution that leads us invincibly to fuccour thofe whom we fee in pain. It is this falutary organization which by ftifling, as it were, felf-love in every individual, replaces at once laws and virtues, among thofe who live in a ftate of nature. It is nature who prevents the favage from depriving the child, the helplefs old man of his fubfiftence, however much neceffitated to procure himfelf that very fubfiftence by expofing himfelf to dangers and fatigues. In fhort, it is to that precious organization the favage owes that natural averfion to hurt his equal; and this natural, involuntary fentiment is fortunately independent of the principles of education.

The native of Madagafcar, like the favage, is abfolute mafter to do as he pleafes; no obftacle, no conftraint difturbs his freedom;

he

he goes, exerts himſelf, does what he likes, except what may hurt his neighbour. No Malegaſh ever took it into his head to predominate over the thought or action of any perſon. Every individual has a characteriſtic mode of being of his own, without his neighbour's troubling or caring about him. The people of Madagaſcar are, in this reſpect, more prudent than the Europeans, who have the cruel method of deſiring all nations on earth to be conformable to their uſages, opinions, and prejudices.

Is the ſavage then ſo much to be pitied? Are there many of them repining at their fate? Does it become us to deſpiſe the ſtate of nature? Are we not ſurrounded by men who, loathing their exiſtence, deteſt and ſeek to make away with themſelves?

The ſavage limits his cares, his deſires to provide himſelf with things indiſpenſibly neceſſary for his ſubſiſtence; he enjoys peacefully the gifts of nature; he endures
                                    ſilently

filently the ills infeparable from humanity.

The conduct of man in the ftate of civilization is not fo reafonable. Opulence and floth hurry him into thofe vain and falfe enjoyments, which terminate in bringing frefh infirmities upon him. Unbounded paffions, frivolous whims, make him continually deviate from the path of happinefs. He who fells it never finds it; happinefs does not, and cannot exift but within ourfelves, and in the good ufe we make of our reafon.

If the favages were as miferable as we fuppofe, becaufe they are ftrangers to, or defpife all thofe fuperfluities we praife fo much, why fhould they refufe adopting our manners, ufages and laws? *Vander Stel*, Dutch Governor of the Cape of Good Hope, took an infant Hottentot, and brought him up in the practice of European ufages. Rich cloaths were given to him; he learned

C 3   feveral

feveral languages, and the progrefs he made
anfwered the care beftowed on his education.
Vander Stel, conceiving great hopes of the
boy's genius, fent him to India with a
Commiffary General, who employed him
ufefully in the concerns of the Company.
The Commiffary died, and the Hottentot
returned to the Cape. A few days after
his return, on a vifit he paid to fome Hot-
tentots his relatives, he took the refolution
to leave off his European drefs, and wrapped
himfelf up in a fheep-fkin. In this new
raiment he waited on Vander Stel, carrying
a bundle containing his former apparel, and
prefenting it to the Governor, expreffed himfelf thus :—" Pray, Sir, mind that I re-
" nounce for ever this attire; I am deter-
" mined to live and to die faithful to the
" religion, manners and cuftoms of my
" anceftors. The only favour I crave of
" you is, to let me keep the ftock and cut-
" lafs which I wear; I fhall keep them for
" the love of you."—That inftant he took
to his heels, without waiting the Governor's
anfwer,

anfwer, and the Dutch have never feen him fince.

Inftances of this fort are not rare ; and I could adduce feveral exactly fimilar among the Malegafhes.

The ifland of Madagafcar is divided in a great number of tribes. Its population may be reckoned at 4,000,000 of inhabitants, but this calculation is neither precife nor poffible, according to the ftate the ifland is actually in, being divided in focieties diftinct from one another. Each fociety inhabits the canton it likes beft, and is governed by its ufages. A tribe confifts of feveral villages, who all have a particular Chief. This Chief is fome-times elective, but more frequently here-ditary. The land is never parcelled out, and belongs to thofe who take the trouble of cultivating it. Thefe iflanders have neither locks nor bolts, and live in a frugal manner. Want alone regulates the hour of their meals. It is however common to fee them dine at

C 4

ten in the morning, and fup at four in the afternoon. Their repaſt conſiſts of rice beautifully white, very light, and well cooked, over it they pour a fucculent broth of meat or fiſh, feafoned with pimento, ginger, faffron, and fome aromatic herbs. Theſe plain meſſes are ferved on the leaves of the plant raven; of theſe leaves they make ſpoons, plates and diſhes. They are always clean, and never uſed twice.

The Malegaſhes know but two ways of dreſſing their meat; they either make it boil in pots of burnt clay, which they manufacture in a maſterly manner, or let it broil on coals.

They are very dexterous in catching a number of birds unknown in Europe, and as much fought after by naturaliſts for the beauty of their plumage, as by travellers who find them exquiſitely palatable.

The

The pheafant, partridge, quail, wild-duck, five or fix different fpecies of teales, the blue-hen, black-parrot, fpoon-bill, turtle-dove, black-bird, green ring dove, and a fpecies of bat of an enormous fize, afford a delicate and favourite fubfiftence to the people of Europe. It was not without repugnance I ate for the firft time bats of Madagafcar dreffed like a fricaffee of chickens. Thefe animals are fo hideous, that the very look of them frightens a French failor. If people, however, can but get over that kind of repugnancy in-fpired by the mere idea of thefe animals, they will find their flefh more delicate than our beft and tendereft chickens.

The Malegafhes catch an immenfe quan-tity of fifh, both in their rivers and in the fea.

Gold-fifh, thorn-backs of all forts, foles, the largeft pilchards, though lefs fat and good than our own; herrings, mackerels, oyfters, mufcles, lobfters, and turtles, furnifh

nifh with plenty thofe iflanders who inhabit the coaft. The rivers procure them alfo excellent eels, and frefh water mullets, more lufcious than thofe catched in the fea. On this coaft of the ifland feveral kinds of fifh are found, which people fhould not eat without having previoufly put a piece of filver under their tongue; if this filver lofes its colour, and turns black, thofe that would tafte fuch fifh would find them fatal. The fquadron of Admiral Bofcawen fuftained confiderable lofs of men at *Rodrigues*, for not having had recourfe to this ufeful precaution. The French have only vifited the eaftern coaft of Madagafcar. The province of *Carcanoffy*, where Fort Dauphin ftands, is well known to them, as likewife a part of thofe diftricts which include *Foule Pointe*, the bay of Antongil, and the ifland of Noffy Hybrahim.

The

The SOUTHERN PART *of*

MADAGASCAR.

THE diftrict of the ifland about Fort Dauphin is well populated. There is hardly a village but ftands on an eminence, encompaffed with two rows of ftrong palifades. From within reigns a parapet of compreffed earth, four feet in elevation; large and ftout bamboos, placed at the diftance of five feet from each other, and driven deep into the ground, form a kind of fortification, which defends thofe villages, of which fome are rendered ftill ftronger by an additional foffe ten feet broad, and fix feet deep.

The dwelling of the Chief is called the *Donac.* This Donac comprifes three or

four

four large houfes, enclofed by a particular
fence. Here the Chief always refides with
his wives and children. Some flaves watch
and guard, night and day, the doors of the
Donac.

The Chiefs never go without their gun,
and a ftick tipped with iron, the end of
which is ornamented with a tuft of cow-
hair. They wear a cap of red wool, and it
is chiefly the colour of their cap which
diftinguifhes them from their fubjects. The
authority of thefe Chiefs is much circumfcribed. However, in the province of Carcanoffy, the territories are deemed to belong
to the Chiefs, who diftribute them among
their fubjects for cultivation, for this they
expect a fmall return, called in their language *faenfa*. The people of the province
of Carcanoffy are not quite ignorant of the
art of writing; they have even fome hifto-
rical books wrote in the Malegafh language;
but their men of letters, to whom they give
the name of Ombiaffes, only make ufe of
the

the Arabic character. They have treatises
on phyfic, geomancy, and judicial aftrology.
The Ombiaffes are all at once magicians and
phyficians. The moft famous of them come
from the province of Mantatana; it is there
magic has been preferved in all its luftre.
The inhabitants of Mantatana are formidable to all the reft of the iflanders, becaufe
they excel in this art of mendacity. The
Ombiaffes profefs geomancy and aftrology in
public fchools. The art of writing has
doubtlefs been brought to this ifland by the
Arabs, who conquered it three centuries ago.
The paper is manufactured in the valley of
Amboul; it is drawn from the *papyrus nilo-
tica*, called by the natives, *Sanga Sanga*.
The fecond rind of this rufh is fkillfully
taken off, divided in very thin flices, be-
fprinkled with water; being afterwards laid
in various crofs-ways, they are preffed down
very hard; then they are put to boil in a
ftrong lye of wood afhes, and reduced to a
pafte in a large wooden mortar. This pafte
is wafhed with large quantities of water.

upon

upon great frames of bamboo, made in form
of a grate. When by dint of throwing water on the paſte, all the impure particles are
waſhed from it, the ſheet is put to dry in
the ſun, and glued with a decoction of rice-
water, called by the natives *ranou pan*. This
paper is a little yellowiſh, but if glued well
will not blot. The pens uſed by the iſlanders
are made of bamboo.

Their ink is prepared of a decoction in
boiling water of the bark of a tree called
arandrato. This ink is not quite ſo black as
ours, but it has a finer gloſs.

The Arabic has made ſome progreſs
in the north-weſt of Madagaſcar ; the
Arabian princes have formed great ſtates
along the coaſt of Africa, which, according
to our geographers, are the kingdoms of
Monomotapa and Mono-Emugi ; they ſeized
on the iſland of Comora. The princes who
went over to Africa and the iſlands adjacent,
did not forget their mother-country. Their
com-

commerce is indeed not inconfiderable with Eden, Mafcata, and the coafts of Abyffinia. They have a ftaple on the river Bombetoque in Madagafcar, which makes them known in that ifland, where they carry on commerce ; it is hereby they fucceeded in introducing with their language and learning among the natives, fome traces of Mahometifm. There was formerly an inveterate enmity between the Arabs and the Portuguefe in India, an hatred only founded on the zeal which each of thefe nations feels for her religion. The Arabs of Comora and Madagafcar have made feveral incurfions into the Portuguefe fettlements on the coaft of Africa, but with the greateft lofs ; they however deftroyed feveral of thefe fettlements. Finally, this odium vanifhed when the declenfion of the power of the Portuguefe rendered rare the opportunities of hurting them.

Twenty years ago, the Portuguefe at Goa were agoing to avail themfelves of this ceffation of hoftilities, to eftablifh a colony

at

at Madagafcar at the cape of St. Sebaftian. The purpofe of this eftablifhment was merely religious ; the Portuguefe thought more of founding a miflion than a factory, but in this project they failed.

It is furprifing that Mahometifm fhould not have made more progrefs in this ifland, fo often frequented by the Arabs : however if we do not except circumcifion, abftinence from pork, and fome little practices, the influence of which is fo infinitely moderate upon the conduct of thefe people, the defcendants of the Arabs themfelves have loft fight of the fundamental principles of their religious opinions. They do not believe there is an exiftence in another life ; they, like the Manichæans, admit too principles, the one fupremely good, and the other fuperlatively bad. They never offer their prayers to the former, but are terribly afraid of the latter. They inceffantly bring it oblations of homage and facrifices.

The

The contiguity of Madagafcar to the coaft of Africa, makes it natural to afcribe its population to that vaft continent; but the different races of inhabitants are now fo much confounded, as to render it a vain attempt to enumerate them.

The race of the real negroes is eafily dif-cerned here; thofe defcending from the whites are more difficult to diftinguifh. The whites who inhabit the provinces of Anoffy and Carcanoffy, pretend to trace their de-fcent from *Imina*, the mother of Mahomet. They have taken the name of Zafferahimini. The whites of Tamatava Foule-Pointe, Voffy-Ibrahim, and of the bay of Antongil, are defcended partly from the ancient pirates, and partly from Jews. On this account they call themfelves Zaffe-Ibrahim, which means, defcendents of Abraham. There is a race of whites who pretend to have been fent to Madagafcar by the Caliph of Mecca, to in-ftruct the natives in the Mahometan faith and in the fecrets of nature. Thefe impoftors feized

D   the

the province of Mantatana, having previoufly
expelled, or murdered the Zafferamini who
governed it. They are called Zaffe-Cafimam-
bou ; their complexion is more fwarthy than
that of the other whites, and their profeſſion
is to teach to read and write the Arabic.

In the provinces of Anoſſy and Carcanoſſy
the Zafferamini fay they come from the
fandy deferts of Mecca : it is for this reafon
they are called *Ontampaſſemaca*. They are
divided in three claſſes, the Rhoandrians,
Anacandrians, and the Ontzatfi. The Rhoandrians are the firſt and moſt diſtinguiſhed
claſs. The people of this claſs have arrogated to themfelves the privilege of killing
beaſts—a bufinefs almoſt univerfally honor-
able among the favages, and thofe who fub-
fiſt on the chace. The Rhoandrians are the
great of the iſland, and among them they
choofe their fovereigns.

The Anacandrians draw their defcent from
a Rhoandrian and a woman of an inferior
clafs ;

clafs; for this reafon they participate with the Rhoandrians, in the honor and profit of killing fuch beafts for the reft of the iflanders, as are conducive to their fupport.

The Ontzatfi conftitute the laft clafs of the Ontampaffemaca, but they enjoy no particular diftinction ; they are, in general, brave foldiers, who will fight well, and fling ftones, or dart a lance fo as feldom to mifs their mark. They fpend their time dancing, finging, playing, fleeping and making merry. From their tender infancy they learn fongs containing leffons of morality, or fables about their origin.

The indigenous blacks comprife four claffes : the *Voadziri,* the *Lahavohits,* the *Ontzoa,* and *Ondeves.*

The *Voadziri* are faid to trace their genealogy from the ancient fovereigns of the ifland. Their wealth in flaves and cattle is altogether confiderable ; they are

D 2 allowed

allowed the poffeffion of feveral villages.
The Voadziri muft be highly regarded,
fince notwithftanding the defpotifm of
thofe Arabs, who have conquered the ifland,
they have the privilege of killing the
animals belonging to their fubjeƈts, provided they are before a Rhoandrian, or an
Anacandrian. The Lohavohits have much
lefs power than the Voadziri. They can
never hold more than one village, and how
great foever their wealth in cattle may be,
they are indifpenfibly bound to go and feek
a Rhoandrian to kill the animals which ferve
as food to themfelves and their fubjeƈts.

The tribe of the Ontzoa follows immediately the Lohavohits, to whom they are
nearly related ; but they are abfolutely without any privilege or authority. The Ondeves
are flaves by extraƈtion : their name means
in the Malegafh language, *A man undone!*

The Malegafhes have a fable on their
origin, which is not a little confonant with
the

the fubdivifion we have juft made of their different tribes.   Thofe among them who have a little fmatter of erudition, relate that the Creator of heaven and earth drew from the body of the firft man, while he was afleep, feven women, which are the mothers of the different tribes.

The tribe of the Rhoandrians took its iffue from the firft man, and from the firft woman who was taken out of his brain. Lefs noble is the origin of the mother of the Anacandrians, who was extracted from the neck.

The tribe of the Voadziri owes its birth to the firft man and to the woman who came out of his right fide, while he had fallen deeply afleep.

The mother of the Lohavohits and the Ontzoa fprung from the thigh and the calf of the leg of the firft man.

The

The extraction of the Ondeves is the moſt ignoble ; they are ſaid to deſcend from the ſole of the foot.

It certainly is a melancholy conſideration to find, among the people who inhabit the great province of Anoſſi, fables ſo ridiculous upon the inequality of conditions. Savages diſdaining fraternity, ſpurning a common origin— what a deplorable abſurdity ! This kind of phenominon cannot be cleared up otherwiſe than by the conqueſt which the Arabs, the anceſtors of the Rhoandrians made of Madagaſcar. This foreign race left, wherever they ſettled, traces of the moſt pitiful ſuperſtition. The Rhoandrians are actually reduced to about twenty families. They only exiſt in the province of Anoſſy, and there is reaſon to hope, that Madagaſcar will at leaſt get rid of the yoke and government of thoſe conquerors, who have deſolated that iſland, and infected it by ſome practices of Mahometan impoſture.

The

The Malegaſhes are only ſubject to the Rhoandrians as free individuals. We ſee them change chiefs whenever they pleaſe; they may commit themſelves to any one who ſecures to them happineſs and tranquility. Theſe iſlanders are too brave to bend beneath an onerous yoke; but their exceſſive credulity frequently proves pernicious to their liberty, and the ſucceſs in their enterpriſes, without their thinking of it.

How ſhould this people, wrapped up in the thickeſt darkneſs, defend themſelves from the impoſtures of the Ombiaſſes, while nations the moſt enlightened are ſtill daily the dupes of impoſtors and quacks. It ſeems as if it were expedient for a man to ſuffer himſelf to be ſubdued by chimeras : rarely his reaſon is ſtrong enough to preſerve him to a certain point, from that love of prodigies, which oftentimes hurries him away into the moſt ridiculous illuſions; and, if among civilized nations, he conceals artfully

D 4   that

that fatal inclination, it is only becaufe he is
afhamed of his own weaknefs.

The Malegafhes of Anoffy are lively,
gay, fenfible, and grateful; they are not
deftitute of genius and clevernefs. They are
paffionately fond of their women; they are
never downcaft in their prefence, and to pleafe
them engroffes their chief care. In this country the fair-fex have more regard and complai-
fance fhewn them than in any other, duties
equally juft and neceffary to the happinefs
of fociety. Here man never commands as a
defpot, nor woman obeys as a flave; here is
the empire of grace, gentlenefs, and beauty;
for, excepting the complexion, the women
of Madagafcar are handfome, their fhape is
flender, their features are pleafant and delicate; they are remarkable for a foft fkin,
and their teeth emulate the brighteft enamel,
the ground of their eyes exhibits a beautiful
azure, and the apple is of a brilliant brown.

The

The plurality of women is common to the rich and the chiefs; but they only marry one in a legal mode; the reft are deemed concubines. This ufage has not the leaft inconvenience at Madagafcar; all thefe women live and agree well with each other; in other refpects divorce takes place whenever it pleafes the wife or the hufband; but this mutual repudiation is followed by a reciprocal reftitution of the dowery. Adultery is looked upon and punifhed at Madagafcar like theft; the natives have therefore the moft unbounded refpect for the conjugal ftate. They warn ftrangers to refpect their wives, but offer them their daughters, thinking it honouarble if they get them with child. The married women are known by their hair, which is twifted, tied, and turned up in form of a bouquet on the crown of the head; the girls let them flow negligently over their fhoulders. The hufbands are always happy near their wives, their prefence cheers them; no fooner do they defcry them from at a diftance, than they begin

to

to caper and fing; they never ceafe to repeat to them that they charm all that is
loathfome in life. The women feem alfo
perfectly happy, and are always in good
humour. Their brifk, blithe, and even
temper, captivates the Europeans in a peculiar manner.

When the men are gone to war, the women fing and dance all day long, and even
during a great part of the night; they believe that thofe inceffant dances animate their
hufbands, and add ftrength to their courage.
They will hardly take time to fwallow their
meals. When there is no war they affemble
at fun-fet; the fongs and dances always begin in a loud and noify manner, accompanied
with the found of feveral inftruments. Their
fongs are either encomiums or fatires, and
always, feemed to me to intereft the fpecta-
tors. Thefe diverfions are ufeful leffons,
celebrate fine exploits, and ftigmatize bad
ones. As foon as a Malegafh woman finds
her health injured by her connection with

an

an European, she flies from these joyous affemblies, to avoid the farcaftic jefts of her
companions, and to be treated by the Obi-
affes, or phyficians of the ifland. She never
appears in company till she is radically cured.
This cuftom prevents the progrefs of the
venereal difeafe from becoming as rapid as in
Europe. Furthermore the Ombiaffes have
difcovered a fpecific remedy which foon de-
ftroys that dreadful infection, and is faid to
be infinitely fanative; I do not recollect the
name of the plant they make ufe of, but I
know that its leaf refembles that of the
philaria. Thefe phyficians prefcribe to the
patient to chew and fwallow it, lying down
in full length, upon the back, and the belly
alternately, in an horizontal pofture; the
patient muft not be loaded with blankets, and
that the perfpiration may be uninterrupted,
she muft be furrounded by a brifk and quick
fire during all the time the remedy performs
its operation. The diftemper ufually fettles
on the foot-fole; the abfcefs which forms
itfelf there is rarely attended with bad confequences.

fequences.   Care is taken that the great heat
of the fire do not incommode the patient too
much.   Thus thefe favages have a method
of ridding themfelves more fortunately, and
in lefs time, from this fcourge which we
have brought among them, and which has
made fo great an havoc among us.

The greateſt part of travellers, inſtead of
pitying the favages for having ever known
the Europeans, feem to take delight in over-
whelming them with all kind of invectives;
this has always been the reward of the hofpitality which they have ever fo generoufly
and gratuitoufly granted.

He that reads Flacourt, will find a Malegaſh reprefented as the moſt corrupted, the
moſt knaviſh, and the moſt deceitful of all
beings.   He dares affure the reader that,
among thefe iſlanders, vengeance and treafon
pafs for virtues; compaffion and gratitude
for weaknefs; but thefe abfurd declamations
can only make impreffion on thofe who have
not,

not, like Rouſſeau, ſtudied man in his pri-
mitive ſtate. How can he who follows ſpon-
taneouſly natural inſtinct be villainous and
corrupted ? When a violent paſſion takes an
imperious ſway over a civilized man, his deſires more irritated than gratified, plunge
him into an abyſs, whence all the powers of
his reaſon cannot extricate him. But the
ſavage feels no ſuch thing when he follows in
his pleaſure the impulſe of his ſenſes. In
every country where man is free, and the
inequality of conditions without any remarkable perception, the wealth of individuals
conſiſts in the ſoil ; and the ſoil belongs to
every body. The difficulty of quelling paſ-
ſions makes man ſtray from the path traced
out for him by nature ; an education ill-
conducted, examples pernicious, intereſts
various, whims frivolous, wants factitious,
degrade human nature in our ſight to ſuch
a point, as to perſuade certain metaphyſicians
that we are born with a natural bias to vice.
Man in his natural ſtate, ſays Hobbes, is a
wicked child. Let us baniſh ſo fatal an
idea,

idea, and behold in our equals good and sympathising beings. I have studied the character of the Malegashes with some attention; I have frequently been present at meetings where they transact affairs of importance, and have followed them in their dances, their games, their diversions, and ever found in them that prudent reserve which keeps them free from those melancholy excesses, those vices so common among the civilized nations.

If the Malegashes had sometimes recourse to treachery, they were forced to it by the tyranny of the Europeans. The weak have no other weapon against the powerful. Could these islanders have another expedient to resist our bayonets and cannons? They are destitute of knowledge and means, and we abuse their weakness to make them yield to our caprices; their generous hospitality is requited by the most tyrannical treatment on our part; yet we call them traitors and cowards, when we force them to break the

yoke

yoke which it pleafes us to impofe on them.

Thefe melancholy truths are but too well attefted by the downfal of the different fettlements made by the Europeans at Madagafcar.

The King of France granted, in the year 1642, to Capt. Picault, and his affociates, the exclufive privilege of trading to Madagafcar.

One Pronis received orders to take poffeffion of Madagafcar in the King's name, and to form an eftablifhment on a fpot fertile, fufceptible of being fortified, and of an eafy and a fecure accefs. He chofe the village of Manghefia, latitude 24 deg. 30 min. at the extremity of the province of Carcanoffy. This place feemed to him fufficient to anfwer the projected defigns; the numerous herds and droves of cattle which furround this diftrict, and the rice-fields and other vegetable

getable produce, promifed a moft plenteous fubfiftence. A navigable river, which takes its fource at the foot of Mount Silvia, traverfes and moiftens plains of a vaft extent; timber abounds in the proximity of commodious dock-yards; the harbour is quite fafe againft heavy gales, on account of the little ifland of St. Lucius.

Pronis had fcarcely arrived with his colonifts at Manghefia, but Capt. Refimont brought over 70 men from France, to reinforce the little fettlement; but the unhealthinefs of the air carried off, in the fpace of one month, the third part of the new fettlers. Pronis was forced to give up this infant colony, notwithftanding its peculiar advantages of locality. He retired precipitately with the furviving fettlers, to the peninfula of Tholangar, where the air is more falubrious.

Tholangar lies in the 25th degree of latitude. This peninfula widens imperceptibly;

it

it may eafily be blocked up with redoubts
and pallifades, to fcreen it from any in-
curfion on the part of the iflanders. The
fort which has been erected here commands
the road; its elevation is 150 feet above the
level of the fea; an enemy who would come
to anchor here, could not long hold out the
fire from the batteries which command the
road. A fteep declivity furrounded by rocks,
render the landing difficult, and to approach
the fort would be quite impracticable, if
fome ftrong works were added to it. This
fort, called Fort Dauphin, is a long fquare,
encompaffed with good walls of lime and
gravel, and extremely well cemented; it
was thought ufelefs to fhut it from the fide
of the road. The anchorage is excellent;
a fhip would fooner break her cables, than
tofs about when at anchor; but the gales
blowing from the main, and the fteep, latent
rocks fituate north-eaft, wear out the veffels
moored in this foreign part, whofe mouth
is bounded fouthward by Cape Ravenata,
and northward by the point of Itapera.
E   The

The fine river of Fanfhere, which takes its fource on the foot of the high mountains of Manghabey, flows into the fea at two leagues from Fort Dauphin, and very near Cape Ravenata. The waters of this river refrefh a great pond denominated the lake of Amboul : which has 10,000 fathoms in circumference, to a moderate depth of 40 feet.

The lake of Amboul would make an excellent harbour, were not the canal which unites it with the fea, frequently ftopped up by quick-fands.

There are times when large fhips might enter this vaft bafon, but thefe times are very rare ; a fudden fwell of the river ought to bear ftrongly againft the bar of fand which wind and tide accumulate daily at the mouth of the lake. Thefe obftacles ufually rife on fpots where the current bears an equilibrium to the force of the tide. It is not perhaps impoffible to clear away the bar which prevents the fhips entering this fine harbour.

For

For this purpofe fome old hulks, loaden with ballaft, fhould be funk at a proper diftance, and in a direction which obferva-tions carefully made on the fpot can alone indicate. Thefe cumbers would ferve as a mould to the bank, which would not fail forming itfelf by the diurnal fettling of the fea. After this preliminary operation, time fhould be given to that fettling to confolidate, previous to its fuftaining the fhock of the river, fo that it may produce the effect of a grand fluice, when a large and fubitaneous fwell augments its force. The dike ufed to fupport the waves, muft be fo conftructed as to break by itfelf; then the violence of the current will certainly lave and clear the mouth of the river, and render the entrance of the canal practicable.

All the means to contrive a mole in the fea, are good for the object we propofe; and if we have given the preference to old hulks, it is becaufe this expedient appeared to me the moft commodious, the moft expeditious,

E 2   and

and the leaſt expenſive. Beſides, an experiment of this nature cannot but prove uſeful
and inſtructive, whatever may be its ſucceſs.
Ships ſunk to the bottom, are maſſes ſo
enormous, ſo ſolid, through the care taken
to faſten all the parts, that it appears to me
impoſſible to ſubſtitute to them, in conſtruct-
ing banks, moles, and other works calculated
to refiſt the violence of the waves, any better
contrivance. The river Fanſhere can carry
veſſels to the length of 15 to 20 leagues.
The works required to perfect its navigation
are very inconſiderable.

The point of Itapera, to the north of
Fort Dauphin, encloſes ſouthward the great
bay of Loucar. The iſle of St. Clair ſcreens
it from the heavy ſea-gales. This iſland
prevents every obſtruction in the little river
of Itapera, ſo common in that of Fanſhere.
The harbour lies leeward to the iſland ; the
mariners ſeldom come to anchor here, becauſe the bay of Loucar is full of ſteep
rocks.

The

The peninfula of Tholangar was fo much more favourable to the fuccefs of the fettlement of Pronis than the rich and fertile valley of Amboul, and the proximity of feveral navigable rivers, difcarded every apprehenfion of not finding means of fubfiftence; mines of iron and good fteel, flax, rofins, pitch, tar, and timber, were articles the utility of which no wife and enlightened government could have difregarded. But Pronis was a man void of induftry, void of abilities. His indolence, and that of his followers, brought all its natural bad confequences upon the infant colony. The fpirit of rebellion fucceeded licentioufnefs; foon thofe who owed fubmiffion and obedience to their leader, gave him irons. His captivity lafted fix months; Pronis had hardly been liberated by a French fhip, which brought him provifions, than he rendered himfelf guilty of a frefh nefarious deed, by felling publicly to Vander Mefter, Governor of Mauritius, the unfortunate Malegafhes in the fervice of the colony; but what completely fired the inha-

E 3   bitants

bitants with indignation was, that among thofe flaves, there were fixteen women of the race of the Lohavohits.

The moment the company were informed of a conduct fo reprehenfible, they cafhiered Pronis; Flacourt was appointed in his room, but he did not reach Fort Dauphin till the latter end of December, 1648. Flacourt has given us minute details of every thing that happened under his adminiftration. Thus I may well difpenfe with retracing the truly afflictive picture of the injuftice and violence exercifed by this Governor over the unfortunate natives. In the year 1661 he fent 40 Frenchmen, attended by armed blacks, to lay wafte and fet on fire the fertile diftrict of Fanfhere. The manner in which this Chief violated hofpitality accorded to him with fo much generofity, can find no champion in our enlightened age. I am de-lighted with the thought that hereafter every man bleft with the fmalleft fhare of juftice and humanity, will fly a foreign land, re-

nounce

nounce all commercial advantages, rather than imitate the barbarous conduct of this Governor. Nations wrapped up in darknefs, intimidated by the fuperiority of our arms, cannot avoid the yoke to which it may pleafe us to make them bend; but is there a right more iniquitous than that of violence? And how durft we now impute perfidy to favages who, loath of our tyranny, made bold to avenge their dignity. If Flacourt knew better than Pronis, to make obedient the French under his command, he did not fhow himfelf more verfed than the latter in the principles of natural right; he was unjuft and cruel to-wards the people, who being lawful pro-prietors of the country, ought to have dic-tated laws, inftead of receiving them from him.   Let us leave the hiftory which Fla-court has given of Madagafcar, to them that fhall have the heart to read it, and fee if his fucceffors have been lefs inhuman.

Fort Dauphin was burnt down in the year 1655; and not rebuilt till 1663.

Chamargou, who was then Governor, sent one La Cafe to explore that part of the island situate to the north of Mantatana. This man acquitted himself very honourably of his charge. It may be useful to travellers to give them a sketch of the character of La Cafe, whose memory is still revered among the natives of Madagascar. La Cafe was his travelling name, that of his family Le Vacher; his native place Rochelles. When La Cafe arrived at Fort Dauphin, the islanders had no regard for the French, and the colony at Fort Dauphin was, after vast expences, reduced to the most deplorable state of languor. La Cafe undertook to revive the reputation of the French name; he succeeded. From the great number of victories he gained, the natives called him Dian Poufs. No appellation could have been more honourable; for Dian Poufs was the name of a chief who formerly conquered the island, and whose memory is still highly revered by the Malegashes.

The

The French were the only people who did not do that juftice to La Cafe, which his valour and good conduct entitled him to. The Governor of Fort Dauphin, jealous of the fame he had acquired, in difcharging fo ably the difficult negociations he had en- trufted him with, denied him all reward and promotion. The Prince of the province of Amboul, Dian Raffitat, profited by the juft difcontentment of La Cafe, to draw him near his perfon. Five Frenchmen followed him, and quitted Fort Dauphin. Dian Nong, the daughter of Dian Raffitat, having deeply fallen in love with La Cafe, offered him her hand with the confent of her father. This old and infirm chief had the pleafure, on the brink of his grave, to fecure the hap- pinefs of his fubjects, by making his fon-in- law abfolute mafter of the rich and fertile province of Amboul. La Cafe, after his marriage with Dian Nong, refufed the title and honours annexed in this country to the fovereign power; he only wifhed to be con- fidered as the firft fubject of his confort, who

was

was proclaimed fovereign Princefs of Amboul, upon her father's death. La Cafe, cherifhed by Dian Nong, who to the lovelieft features, joined a great fpirit, and the rareft qualities, could only form unavailing wifhes for the profperity of the French fettlement at Fort Dauphin.

He could not go to relieve his countrymen, whom he knew to be in the greateft diftrefs. Chamargou, the Governor, had offered a reward for his head, and for thofe of the five Frenchmen who had followed him to Amboul. The Chiefs in the neighbourhood of the fort, highly provoked at feeing a plot concerted againft the life of a man whom they held in the higheft veneration, refufed unanimoufly to fupply the French with provifions. A complete famine, fucceeded by fevers and multifarious diforders, had now reduced the French fettlers to 80 men.

The colony was on the brink of ruin, when the arrival of a frigate, commanded by by Capt. Kercadio, refpited the fufferers for a while.

Trouble and confufion had feized on the French, from the moment they firft landed at Madagafcar. The natives hated them, their hatred was followed by fovereign contempt. Our tyranny excited them to revolt, but our inteftine divifions had wakened within them the fentiment of terror firft infpired by the fuperiority of our arms. Capt. Kercadio was fenfible that the relief he had brought from France could not be of any long duration. This brave officer, free from the prejudices and rigours of his profeffion, found it expedient to effect a reconciliation between La Cafe and the Governor. He reprefented to the latter that he could no longer confider as his fubaltern a man, whofe marriage with *Dian Nong* had not only made him abfolute mafter of the province of Amboul, but fovereign of the whole ifland of Madagafcar. Kercadio defpairing of the influence, which his forcible arguments

ought

ought to have had over the prejudice and refentment of Chamargou, applied to an able
barrifter, who had embarked on board the
frigate he commanded, and intreated him as
a friend, to exert all his talents to open the
Governor's eyes upon his real intereft, and
upon that of the fettlement intrufted to his
adminiftration.

If this barrifter fucceeded in his enterprife,
he owed his fuccefs lefs to his eloquence,
than to the honor of being known to, and
protected by *Marfhal Meilleraye*.   He no
fooner intimated to the Governor, that he
would find it incumbent on himfelf to give
an account to the *Marfhal* of the diftreffes of
the colony, and perhaps of the lofs of Fort
Dauphin, than this Governor, thus far
haughty and intractable, bidding defiance to
famine and death, and ready to facrifice to
implacable refentment the fad remains of
the ill-fated colony, became timid and appre-
henfive. The very name of the *Marfhal*,
ftruck him with terror. He intreated Kercadio

cadio to pardon his obſtinacy, and made uſe
of the moſt abject perſuaſives to prevail on
him to effect their conciliation with La Caſe.
Kercadio ſet out for Amboul, in company
with the barriſter; his negociation ſuffered
no retard nor difficulty. La Caſe deſpiſed
the vain machinations of his enemies : this
reſpectable man's deareſt wiſh was to be uſeful to his countrymen, he obtained permiſſion to fly to their relief, and peace and
abundance followed him to Fort Dauphin; as
long as the ſettlement was ruled by his coun-
ſels, it remained happy and flouriſhing.

Dian Nong ſhewed herſelf not leſs generous than her huſband.

La Caſe remained no longer at Fort
Dauphin than was abſolutely neceſſary.
Dian Nong was far from being fond of this
new reſidence, and her own private affairs
required her preſence at Amboul; beſides
Chamargou, more jealous of the ſucceſs of
La Caſe than grateful for his ſervices, would

not

not have failed to difguft him.   Of this La
Cafe could the lefs be doubtful, fince the Governor would not condefcend to join his intreaties to the reft of the colony, to engage
him to prolong his ftay at the Fort.   But the
very moment the French, to the number of
200, levied confiderable imports in the fertile province of Carcanoffy, and dictated laws
to the iflanders, a frefh war broke out in
thefe fine regions which rendered the fervices
of La Cafe urgent and neceffary.

This war more fatal to the French than
the Malegafhes, was occafioned through the
inconfiderate zeal of a miffionary.   Dian
Manangue, fovereign of the province of
Mandrarey, a powerful, courageous and fpi-
rited Chief, and faithful ally of the French,
gave a moft diftinguifhed reception in his
donac to a certain Father Stephen, of the
order of St. Lazar, a fuperior of the miffion
at Madagafcar.

This

This father, charmed with the excellent qualities and good nature of the Chief, fancied it would be an eafy matter to convert him : As foon as Dian Manangue could perceive his defign, he thought he owed to the friend-fhip he had vowed to the French, and above all to the recomendation of his friend La Cafe, to inform the zealous mif-fionary that his efforts would be ufelefs. The Chiefs like to declaim and to make fpeeches in public. Dian Manangue af-fembled his wives and the people belonging to his houfhold, to let Father Stephen know publicly that nothing could make him re-linquifh his ufages.

" I pity thy folly, faid Dian Manangue, in defiring that at my age I fhould facrifice to thy difcretion my happinefs and the plea-fures which furround me in the middle of my donac. I pity thee for being deprived of that which charms the tedious, melan-choly hours of life : thou doft permit me to live with one woman ; but if the poffeffion

of

of one woman is a bleſſing, why ſhould the poſſeſſion of a numerous ſeraglio be an evil, when peace and concord ſubſiſt among them that compoſe it ?   Doſt thou ſee among us any ſymptoms of jealouſy, any ſhoots of hatred ?   No ; all our women are good, all ſtrive to make me happy, and I am more their ſlave than their maſter.

" But if thy maxims are ſo uſeful, ſo in-diſpenſible, why do not thy brothers in the fort follow them ?   Why doſt thou not compel to obſerve thy doctrine thoſe who ought to know better the merit of thy words ? Believe me, good friend, I would not have thee deceived ; I find it impoſſible to re-nounce my habits, I ſhall never relinquiſh them but with my life ; I give thee leave to exert thy zeal upon my ſubjects.   And the ſame power I give thee over my family, over my children : but thou wilt not derive much benefit from this conceſſion, unleſs thou art able to blend thy precepts with our manners and uſages."

All

All the anfwer which father Stephen made
to this difcourfe, was the abfolute command
he gave the Chief to divorce inftantly all
his wives, and to keep only one. The father even forgot himfelf fo far, as to threaten
him to have his wives forcibly carried off
by the French, in cafe his orders fhould
fuffer the leaft delay. It may be eafily
imagined, that fo unforefeen a rancour muft
have excited a general indignation and com-
motion in the donac. The women fell
upon the miffionary, loaded him with in-
juries and blows; and would infallibly have
ftifled him in their rage, if Dian Manangue,
notwithftanding his perturbation, had not
immediately haftened to his relief. An ex-
ertion of his whole authority alone was
wanted to obtain him permiffion to remain a
fingle moment alone with the monk, whom
he difmiffed with rich prefents, he even went
farther, and begged the miffionary to grant
him the fpace of fifteen days, that he might
take a refolution with refpect to the momentous bufinefs of his converfion. But his

F   view

view in requefting this delay tended only to
gain time to quit the province of Mandrarey,
in cafe he fhould be purfued by the French,
and the moment he thought himfelf fafe, he
departed with his wives and flaves to feek
refuge in the country of Mafhicores, fituate
at the diftance of twenty-five leagues from
Fort Dauphin.

His departure was not fecret enough to be
unknown to father Stephen; he had his
fpies even in the donac: it was in vain for
Chamargou to try to detain him, the prieft
only confulting his zeal, took the refolution
to follow Dian Manangue to the province
of Mafhicores.   A brother of the the order
of St. Lazar, another Frenchman, and, fix
fervants loaded with facerdotal habits, attended him in his dangerous miffion.

It was in the firft week in Lent he over-
took Dian Manangue, after a world of fatigue.   The Chief rather furprifed than intimidated at the boldnefs of the father, received

ceived him with profound refpect. In vain
did he intreat him to renounce the project of
converfion, Father Stephen only anfwered
him, by tearing from him his *Olis* or amulets,
threw them in the fire, and concluded his
violence with a declaration of war. It cannot be a matter of furprife, that fo barbarous
a conduct was inftantly atoned for by the
life of Stephen and his attendants. Dian
Manangue ordered them to be ftruck dead
on the fpot, and fwore, at the fame time,
the entire deftruction of the French. To
perform the better this fatal oath, the Chief
fent his fon, who had been baptized, to his
fon-in-law La Vantangue, to impart to him
the motives which induced him to fhake off
the tyrannical yoke of the French, whofe
guilty defigns had no other tendency than
the fubverfion of the ufages, manners, and
religion of the country, he added that his
Oli or amulet had commanded him to defend
them, even at the peril of his life; he affured
La Vantangue, that it was not in the power
of the French to vanquifh, fince they had

F 2

dared

dared to commit fuch criminal exceffes. The provoked Chief likewife intimated to his brother in-law, that Chamargou had fent 40 Frenchmen to the weftern coaft, whom he could eafily furprife and put to death. " I fend thee, my fon, (faid he at the conclufion of his letter) " to be at the head of the army, which thou art to fend to attack and exterminate the French ; it is my *Oli* that infpires me, and thou well knoweft the ills that fhall overwhelm us, if we do not faithfully obey its call. My fon will give thee all the particulars of what hath happened ; thou wilt hear indignantly the perfidious proceedings of thofe foreigners towards their moft faithful ally." La Vantangue was very fortunate to get intelligence of the excurfion of the 40 Frenchmen ; he had hardly time to put himfelf upon his guard, for two days after the arrival of his nephew, his fpies brought him tidings that the French had pitched their camp at the diftance of one league from his village.

The

The Chief offered them rice, honey, and four bullocks, praying them to acquaint him with the motive of their journey, having never feen fo great a number of Europeans in the interior parts of the ifland. *La Forge* who commanded the detachment, fent word to La Vantangue that he was commanded to fubject his country to the French domination. The Chief terrified at fo unexpected an enterprize, demanded peace, and propofed 400 bullocks, reprefenting that his country was too diftant from Fort Dauphin, to have incurred the hatred of the French. La Forge rejected thefe propofals with difdain, and fixed the price of the peace at 20,000 bullocks. La Vantangue returned no anfwer to this exorbitant demand; but while the adventurers were laying wafte a plantation of fugar canes, he caufed them to be maffacred.

The tidings of the defeat of the 40 Frenchmen, fent by Chamargou to the weftern coaft, were brought to Fort Dauphin by a Portuguefe, who alone efcaped with his life,

F 3   by

by feeking refuge in a marfhy fpot, covered
with reeds and ftagnant water.   Here he remained concealed two days in water and
mud up to his neck.   The iflanders afraid to
wade through it, fet fire to the reeds, to
make the Portuguefe come forth, but the
thicknefs of the fmoke made him elude their
purfuit.   The iflanders felt the greateft concern to deitroy this man, left Chamargou
fhould come and attack them before the
arrival of Dian Manangue, who was ftill
with his army in the province of Mafhicores.

The Portugufe reported to the Governor
that their journey had been very fuccefsful,
till they had encountered with La Vantangue.   Their number had fpread confternation in every village, and the chiefs had been
glad to pay whatever contributions they had
chofen to raife : in fhort they were touching
the moment of enjoying the fruits of a long
and difficult march, when the rapacity of
their commander brought upon them a complete

plete overthrow, and the loſs of all their rich
booty.

The Governor ought to have ſeen nothing
in this report but the deſerved puniſhment
of thoſe wretched vagabonds, who went to
ravage countries to which they had not the
leaſt right or pretenſion; but his implacable
ſoul inſtead of taking warning by this ſalutary leſſon, took the fatal reſolution of carrying fire and ſword into the country of the
oppreſſed natives. He puts himſelf at the
head of 30 Frenchmen, followed by a little
army of Manam-Coulians; he ſheds the
blood of women and children, deſtroys every
village he paſſes by fire, and takes the donac
of Dian Manangue. Father Manier, the
only ſurviving miſſionary, carried the bloody
banners. The details of this expedition are
too cruel, too barbarous to bear relation.

Chamargou was ultimately forced, through
an abſolute want of proviſions, to ſeek a retreat at Fort Dauphin; it was at this epoch
F 4   he

he endeavoured to pafs the great river of
Mandrarey, when Dian Manangue, who
watched his motions, appeared on the oppofite fhore with an army of 6000 men, to
oppofe his paffage. Dian Manangue wearing the furplice and hood of Father Stephen
the miffionary, braved, at the head of his
army, the French then bordering on the
brink of deftruction. At this critical moment La Cafe arrived, accompanied by ten
Frenehmen and 3000 Androfaces, his fubjects, or rather the fubjects of Dian Nong,
his wife; he inftantly plunges himfelf into
the river, fires upon the enemy, and more
by the terror of his name, than the fuperiority of arms, diflodges Dian Manangue
from his ftation, and puts him to flight.
La Cafe purfued him, though the approach
of night ought to have prevented him. He
recognizes Dian Manangue amidft a numerous troop of iflanders, and is preparing to
fall upon him; but Rabazee, the friend and
favourite of Dian, courageoufly ftops him
and makes a facrifice of his own life to preferve

ferve his fovereign ; night alone could inter-
rupt the flaughter. At the termination *of*
this bloody war, Fort Dauphin was again in
the moft deplorable ftate, the Chiefs would
fend no more provifions, and intercepted
thofe fupplies which were procured from
diftant parts. Dian Manangue who could
pretend to the fovereignty of a great part of
Madagafcar, threatened the French fettlement with a formidable army, and its fole
prefence muft have ftarved out the colony,
without a fupply of 5000 bullocks, which
La Cafe found means to throw into the Fort.
All the expeditions of this extraordinary man
were full of fuccefs : with ten Frenchmen
and two thoufand Androfaces he defeated
Dian Ravaras at the head of an army of
eighteen thoufand men, took from him
twenty thoufand bullocks and five thoufand
flaves. La Cafe finally convinced the council of the late French Eaft-India company of
the neceffity they were under to employ him,
and to reward his fignal fervices.

They

They fent him a lieutenant's commiffion, made him a prefent of a fword, and congratulated him on his fuccefles.

La Cafe returned thanks to the company for this frefh inftance of their favor, adding that he would pledge himfelf to conquer the whole ifland, with two hundred Frenchmen, and to execute many other advantageous projects, if they would make him give a direct account of his conduct to no other perfon or perfons but themfelves. The company rejected this plan, which was undoubtedly more the project of a brave foldier, than of an enlightened agent, becaufe a juft man knows how to refpect the rights of hofpitality and heaves the figh of pity, when he fees the fentiments of equality and humanity violated for the fake of vile commercial intereft.

In 1666 the Marquis de Mondevergue was appointed by the King to the general command of the French fettlements, fituated beyond

beyond the equinoctial line. La Fage and
Caron were then directors of the trade to the
Eaft-Indies. The Marquis reached Fort
Dauphin, March 10th, 1667, in a frigate
of 36 guns, followed by a fleet of nine veffels, having on board the two directors, an
attorney-general, four companies of infantry,
ten chiefs of colonies, eight merchants, and
thirty-two women.

Mondevergue caufed himfelf to be acknowledged Admiral and Governor-General of the
French territories in the eaft. He was
obliged to have recourfe to La Cafe for the
victualling of the fleet. La Cafe did all that
could be wifhed for, and brought matters fo
far as to effect a reconciliation between the
French and Dian Manangue, whofe bravery
and talents are not to be defpifed. This
Chief fwore obedience and fidelity to the
Governor-General.

Caron, who was a Dutchman, did not
remain long at Fort Dauphin, but failed with
a great

a great part of the fleet, to take upon him the adminiſtration of *Surata*.

La Fage remained at Fort Dauphin. Another fleet of ten veſſels, under the orders of Monſ. La Haye, who commanded the Navarre man of war of 56 guns, arrived in November 1670. All theſe veſſels belonged to the king, and were fitted out for war. La Haye cauſed himſelf to be acknowledged Admiral and General, with the authority of Vice-Roy. He made Chamargou ſecond in command, and La Caſe Major of the iſland. At this period the company had ceded to the King the poſſeſſion of the iſland of Madagaſcar.

The Marquis de Mondevergue had it left to his choice either to remain governor of Madagaſcar, or to return to France. He no ſooner arrived at Fort Louis in France, than a commiſſary demanded an account of his conduct, the company being much provoked at him, owing to the malignant reports
                                                                    thrown

thrown out againſt him by La Haye.
Though the public voice was in favour of
the Marquis, who, as a brave officer, had
governed with wiſdom, and reſtored peace
to the iſland, yet he fell a victim to the
credit of his adverſary ; he died a priſoner in
the caſtle of Saumur.

La Haye, whoſe authority was unlimited,
reſolved to get rid of the Chiefs who gave
him umbrage: he propoſed to Chamargou
and La Cafe, to declare war againſt Dian
Ramouſay, who had not come to do him
homage; this Chief was the neareſt neighbour of the French. He was ſummoned to
ſend to the Fort all the arms he had got of
the French. This demand met with an
abſolute refuſal. La Haye ordered La Cafe
and Chamargou to beſiege Dian Ramouſay in his village : they had the command of 700 Frenchmen and 600 Malegaſhes. The attack proved unſuccefsful,
and Dian Ramouſay made ſo gallant and
vigorous a defence, that the French were
obliged

obliged to retire This check did not appear
to be natural: it was thought that Chamargou, diffatisfied with being the fecond
in a country where he had always been the
firft, had not a little contributed to make
the expedition mifcarry. La Haye was however fo much humbled and affected by the
fmall fuccefs of his firft enterprife, that he
took the refolution to abandon Fort Dauphin,
and to repair with his forces to Surata, having
previoufly vifited the ifland of Mafcarenhas,
fince called *Ifle de Bourbon*.

The felf-love of this general, was greatly
hurt, when he perceived that his whole authority was infufficient to hinder Chamargou
from making mifcarry at his pleafure the
operations he fhould undertake.

The departure of La Haye was followed
by the death of the brave La Cafe; it was
obvious that the lofs of this celebrated man
would infallibly be followed by that of the
French colony.

It

It was well known that the iflanders were
eager to be revenged of the injuftice and oppreffion they had fuffered from the French.
Their yoke had become odious and infup-
portable to them; hiftorians fhould for the
honor of civilized nations, oury in oblivion
the grievous particulars of atrocities committed upon thofe people whom they call
barbarians, cheats and traitors, becaufe they
have revolted againft fome European adventurers, whofe fmalleft crime is to have violated the faered rights of hofpitality.

If the fettlement of Fort Dauphin has fo
long held out againft the deteftable admini-
niftration of its chiefs, it was the mere name
of La Cafe which retained the Malegafhes
in a kind of dependence on fo vicic s a conftitution.

Chamargou did not long furvive La Cafe,
and was fucceeded in the command of the
colony by La Bretefche, his fon-in-law.
This man was neither endowed with the
                                        talents,

talents, nor enjoyed the refpect of his father-in-law. He found it impoffible to maintain his authority amidft the trouble and confufion which divided the French and the natives, he embarked in a fhip for Surata ; his family feveral miffionaries and fome Frenchmen followed his example. The fhip had no fooner left the road than the crew perceived a fignal of diftrefs given on fhore. The captain immediately fent off his boats, who took up the few unhappy individuals who had efcaped the maffacre of the French. This maffacre had been ordained by Dian Ramoufay and other neighbouring Chiefs.

Now-a-days there is no confiderable fettlement at Madagafcar, except one of modern date formed in the fouth, by Monf de Modave, and another in the north, formed by Count de Beniowfki.   I was at Ifle de France when Monf. de Modave took poffeffion in the King's name of Fort Dauphin (1768).   If the fuccefs of this new enterprife did not anfwer the hopes of government, it is becaufe
every

every colony that fhall not be founded upon the happinefs and inftruction of the people, among whom we feek to fettle, will never flourifh long. It is not foldiers, but artifans, farmers, laborious and induftrious men, men of knowledge that ought to be fent among them. It ought to be remembered that the contracts or conventions which the favages make with the Europeans are fimilar to thofe which children might make with enlightened men; and fince the treaties made till now with the Malegafhes, are evidently of that nature, it would be extremely unjuft to avail ourfelves of them againft the interefts of thofe iflanders. They can be but ftupid or faithlefs men who would give validity to contracts fo ridicuoufly illufory. You have obtained by ftratagem; you have violently torn confeffions from the natives of thofe foreign regions, and becaufe they did not forefee the danger to which they expofed themfelves in receiving you with bounty and generofity, you will turn againft them, even their benefits, you will make thefe a due, a right to opprefs and enflave

G   thofe

thofe unfortunate tribes. If great commercial interefts call you to Madagafcar, adopt principles the moft juft, the moft humane.

Choofe artifans and agriculturifts to form your fettlement. Thofe who know the character of the Malegafhes, will not doubt of the good reception which thefe iflanders will give to men whofe frugal and active courfe of life wafts abundance and banifhes vice.

The tillage of the ground with the plough, and many other ufeful practices, would infpire the natives with gratitude and reverence. India offers a vaft number of able weavers, who can drefs and give to cottons that brilliant glofs, thofe folid colours, which make them fo valuable to commercial nations.

The colouring fubftances extracted from vegetables, have not in our cold climates, the fame luftre, the fame quality as under the burning regions of the torrid zone.

The

The fruits of our gardens raifed againft a wall or fence, or by efpaliers, do not colour but on the part expofed to the direct beams of the fun.

We have no acid which fixes the colours and impregnates them in cottons in fo folid and unalterable a manner, as the juice extracted from a tree called by the natives of Madagafcar, *the fig-tree of Adam*, and by us the Banana-tree.

The Indians likewife excel in the manufacturing of filk ftuffs. Several provinces of Madagafcar would furnifh abunftant quantities of that precious fubftance. A branch of commerce of fuch importance is the lefs to be neglected, fince the natives of the fouth of Madagafcar can prepare and weave it for garments.

In the environs of the bay of Antongil I have difcovered four claffes of filkworm-cods, which yield a good quality of filk.

The

The Malegashes give them the four following denominations. The *Andeve* is a cod similar to that which yields the finest silk in the south of France.

A tree called by the inhabitants *Anacou*, is covered in a certain season of the year with little cods, which adhere to its leaves and branches, by little filaments or threads. The silk drawn from these cods is extremely strong and fine; but in order to put it into skeins and render it fit for use, the cods ought to be preserved from the dust and ordure which drops from the leaves and branches. These cods are called *andee anacau*. The third species of the cod is the *andee vontaqua*, which produces silk quite as beautiful and superior in finenefs to that of China.

The fourth species of cods cannot be put into skeins. The Malegashes call it *andeeiaraha*, its form refembles a bag containing feveral hundreds of little cods.

The

The wools of Madagafcar are fine, and not made ufe of by the inhabitants. The Indians might learn to card and prepare them, and we fhould foon owe them a frefh branch of commerce of the greateft importance. There is no traveller but knows thofe fine woollen ftuffs which the people of Bengal call fhawls, the Mahometans make turbans of them. This ftuff cofts not lefs than one hundred piftoles the yard, if the fuperfine wool of the fheep of Cachemire is ufed in its fabrication.

So great a price muft aftonifh thofe who know but little of the value of raw productions, and the low price of workmanfhip in India. It is however, with grofs tools the Indian, more dexterous and more patient than the European, fucceeds in weaving thofe precious ftuffs.

If France did choofe in courfe of time, to fhare with India and China the rich commerce in filk ftuffs, wool, and painted linens,

G 3   fuch

fuch as calico, chintz, &c. I think, and many
learned men are of my opinion, that fuch
an enterprize would not be impoffible, by
forming at Madagafcar upon folid pinciples,
a colony of Indian weavers, who fhould be
under the protection of the ifles of France
and Bourbon.   But at the fame time it
would be neceffary to introdcuce the celebrated machines of Manchefter, to card and
fpin both coarfe and fine, the wools and cottons, for then the art of manufacturing ftuffs
and linen cloths would be folely confined to
the weaving bufinefs, and certainly the
Indian weavers maintain a decided fuperiority
over the Europeans.   Such an affertion does
not tend to depreciate our induftry. I am fenfible it would be abfurd to compare our great
manufactures, with thofe of the inhabitants
on the banks of the Ganges; it would be
comparing the productions of dexterity and
patience with thofe of genius.

The induftry of the Indian is not only
confined to weaving, he is pretty well verfed
in

in the art of agriculture, he underſtands the preparation of ſugar and indigo. His hand ſhapes the clay into the moſt ſingular and variegated forms, and the earthen wares of India are even eſteemed and ſought after in Europe.

The Indian is as good a lapidary as the Chineſe, he makes uſe of adamantine ſpath pulverized and imbibed in oil, to cut and pierce the hardeſt ſtones; he employs that ſubſtance of no great value in India, and but little known in Europe, to ſerve all the purpoſes of diamond powder. The Indian is likewiſe very clever in working bamboos, he makes paper, houſhold furniture, palanquins and utenſils of them. This tree is a kind of large reed, from its knots trickles a kind of ſugary liquor, much eſteemed by the orientals. This reed riſes to the elevation of an hundred feet, the hardneſs and lightneſs of its wood makes it fit for a thouſand different uſes.

G 4

Thoſe

Thofe Europeans who profefs the mechanical arts with fome diftinction, might learn feveral proceffes from the people of Afia, which would be highly beneficial to them. We are not well acquainted with the origin of borax. I was informed at Pondicherry, that this falt, fo neceffary to facilitate the fufion of metals, was not factitious, but drawn from the mines of Aurengabad. The late Monf. de Lafonne, firft phyfician to the King of the French, and member of the academy of fciences, requefted me in a very particular manner to make enquiries on that fubject. However all my endeavours proved unfuccefsful. The gold and filver works cut out in philigrams, ftill prove to our ableft artifts, that the Indians are very dexterous in the working of metals. But without enlarging more upon the induftry of thefe nations, what I have faid is enough to prove that a colony of Indians eftablifhed at Madagafcar would be an enterprize worthy of an enlightened people.

The

The Indian will prefer Madagafcar to his native foil : he doubtlefs will rather choofe to work for himfelf under a climate analogous to his own, in a fertile ifland, where he will enjoy in peace the plenitude of liberty, than to till for the profit of the Mogul, the field which has been taken from his anceftors by the moft deteftable depredation, he will train up, by his example, the docile native to work, and raife the colony to the higheft pitch of perfection and profperity.

The wealth of a nation can never be but the produce of work, thus every laborious citizen only remains in a ftate of inactivity and indolence, but becaufe the nation miftakes or neglects her true intereft. A brifk trade gives not only birth to many ufeful and various occupations but even renders neceffary works, the advantages of which are paft calculation ; thefe chiefly are roads and caufeways, the improvement of the navigation of rivers, the canals of junction, the draining of marfhes and fens, and the plantations on the
                                          fummits

fummits and declivities of mountains. It is
upon arid and elevated grounds (I cannot
repeat it too often) the woods become moft
ufeful, becaufe in that pofition they prevent
the earth's ftripping itfelf, they hinder the
formation of torrents, and the encumbering
of rivers.

But if you wifh to bring your fettlements
to fpeedy perfection, put a great deal of
economy in your works, fubftitute the
ftrength of animals to that of men ; make
ufe of air-currents, of water-falls ; neglect
none of thofe motive powers fcattered profufely over the furface of the globe. Re-
gardlefs of that kind of indifference and difdain which moft men affect refpecting the
mechanical arts, the fcience which forms
their bafis is neverthelefs all at once fublime
and neceffary. Should we prefer to that
fcience, the futile declamations, or the idle
chimeras of the man who, through pride,
lofes himfelf in enquiries unconnected with
his

his wants, and above the reach of his frail conception ?

If the utility of the mechanical arts is inconteftable ; if the ufe of thofe ingenious machines which put economy in the greateft part of works, is a fertile fource of riches and profperity, why do we fee in fome civilized countries, people blind to the great benefit derived from them ? Why do they fometimes confider them as the inftruments of their mifery ? Is not this the token which fhews that the commerce of a nation has no energy ? It is a token which bears no equivoque, and if the proceedings which tend to put economy in manual labour occafion popular troubles, we muft conclude hence that thofe who govern are void of knowledge and capability.

However, the evil which refults from the economy in all labours is merely tranfitory, and the benefits which accrue therefrom permanent. If a nation were fo blind to her

intereft

intereſt as to reject under this pretence, the diſcoveries by which the mechanical arts have enriched themſelves, it would be the only way to impoveriſh herſelf; for how could ſhe maintain her competition with other neighbouring nations, whoſe conduct is guided by oppoſite principles ? Beſides, we only ſpeak here of colonies, and thoſe inconveniences are not to be feared in countries branded with ſlavery. The ſlave will not break thoſe ingenious machines equivalent to a great number of hands; he will not reject what tends to render lighter the load of his chains. Surely if ſlavery does not ſtifle all ſentiment, he will conſider as a celeſtial favor every invention, every proceſs that brings ſolace to his miſery.

May then the friends of humanity introduce and countenance in colonies all kinds of induſtry ! May they never be afraid to multiply the machines, to employ all theſe powerful agents, of which the genius of man is become maſter. Thoſe who complain

plain in free and civilized countries, that these great means are even endowed with the power of rendering a vaſt number of hands uſeleſs, muſt at leaſt own their ſovereign influence over the colonies where they render the arms of the ſlave leſs uſeful to his maſter; then they muſt likewiſe own that powerful agents, vigorous animals, with the aid of a machine, may in a beneficial manner, become the ſubſtitute of ſlavery. In this manner the private intereſt of the colonists may be conciliated with the principles of juſtice and humanity, to favour induſtry in their ſettlement. This new order of things muſt no doubt, in a farther ſtage of progreſs, aboliſh ſervitude; but ſuch a revolution will be wiſe, well meaſured, and ſuch, in fine, as is to be wiſhed for.

Among the different machines which ought to be introduced in colonies, the vapor engines, call our attention.

Theſe

These engines, such as they are still used in the mines, consist of a copper which may be heated with all sorts of combustibles. The vapor of the boiling water which comes out of the copper introduces itself under the sucker of the pump, and rises by force of its expansive power; when the sucker has reached its highest degree of elevation, then the communication between the vapor which rises from the copper and the cylinder, or body of the pump is cut off; but at the same time an injection of cold water works the hollow part, in condensating suddenly the vapor which fills the capacity of the cylinder, and at this instant the weight of the external air forces the sucker to descend. We know that the play of the suckers and cocks which open and shut the communication with the vapor and the water of injection, is always performed by the motion of the sucker of the pump. The Marquis of Worster was the first who announced in the year 1663, that water might be raised to a great elevation, by means of the vapor or steam of boiling

boiling water, in turning two cocks alternately. From this hint Monſ. Savery publiſhed in 1700, a vapor-engine, the invention of which he attributed to himſelf. This machine is deſcribed in the phyſical treatiſe of Doctor Deſagrulliers. Papin preſented, about the ſame time, a machine producing a ſimilar effect; but Newcomb and Cowley, the former an ironmonger, and the latter a glazier, added new degrees of perfection to the invention of Savery. Newcomb's machine was uſed in ſeveral mines for the draining of waters, and is ſtill uſed for the ſame purpoſe. The celebrated mechanic, *Walt*, has quite recently ſucceeded in bringing the ſteam or vapor engine, to the higheſt degree of perfection.

The body of his machine is formed of a cylinder of caſt iron, a woolen wrapper covers the exterior part of the cylinder, which is covered hermetically in the upper part, with a perforated lid to let in the end of the ſucker.

That

This end of the fucker moves in a neck edged with hemp, preffed clofe with fcrews, and encompaffed with a vapor-ring, to prevent the external air introducing itfelf in the body of the pump.

When the vapor which rifes from the copper fills the capacity of the cylinder and bears with equal force upon the upper and lower part of the fucker in that ftate of equilibrium of the expanfive power of the vapor, the fucker maintains its reft of elevation; but the elaftic fluid fucceffively lofes its energy, whether in the upper or lower part of the fucker, in the fhorteft fpace of time. In this excellent contrivance, the action of the vapor and its effluxion, are continual; for as foon as the interception of the vapor takes place under the inferior part of the fucker, and the injection of cold water operates the hollow or void under the fucker, the expanfive force of the vapor preffing on the fucker, makes it defcend, and fince the communication of the vapor with the upper

part

part is intercepted afterwards, and the lower re-eftablifhed, the fucker cannot fail rifing again with the fame force, if the hollow or void is made by the injection of cold water in the upper part of the fucker. This is the recent improvement made in the fire engines by Meffrs. *Walt* and *Bolton*; thofe we have in France, after the firft improvement of thefe ingenious mechanics, only operate the hollow void in the lower and not in the upper part of the fucker. In this contrivance Meffrs. *Walt* and *Bolton* made it their chief object to prevent the body of the pump which receives the vapour, growing cold, for this reafon they have preferred the action of the vapor to that of weight of the external air, and in order that the injection might not chill the cylinder in operating the void, they have made ufe of a particular pipe, which communicates to the cylinder, and that pipe they called the condenfator; it is in this part the water of injection is brought. To facilitate ftill more the reduction of the vapour at the moment of injection, they

H have

have added a little pump folely deftined to operate the hollow in the condenfator.

It is alfo by a very fimple and well known mechanifm, we regulate the effect of the fire engine, and procure it the circular motion. We make ufe for this purpofe of a wheel of a large diameter, of confiderable weight, to which the fucker of the engine communicates the circular motion by curbed levers, in a manner very much like that which makes turn a fpinning-wheel by the motion of the foot. In the common engines the wheel which ferves as regulator ought to have twenty feet in diameter, and to weigh four or five thoufand pounds. The major part of this enormous weight is brought to the circumference, to render the action of the balancer the more uniform.

If I have entered into all thefe details, it is becaufe of the importance of making known the laft improvements made in thefe ufeful machines, in order to fpread the ufe

of

of them, not only among us, but likewife
in the colonies. If this motive power were
adopted by the planters in the mills which
ferve to prefs the fugar-cane, how many
thoufands of flaves, devoted to the utmoft
fatigues, would by this means find themfelves eafed and comforted !

The fugar-cane is a kind of reed, which
rifes ten feet high ; its moft common thicknefs is three inches ; it is covered with a
bark which contains a fpongy fubftance ; it
is interfected with knots by the interval of
five inches, and its ftem bears flowers fimilar to thofe of the common reed.

This plant is cultivated in feveral parts of
Africa, Afia and America ; it does not thrive
equally well on all grounds, and a light and
deep foil is the moft genial to its nature.

The fugar plantations do not require fo
very much hard labour ; it is enough to
make furrows at the diftance of three feet

from one another, thefe furrows fhould not exceed fix inches in depth and one foot in breadth. The canes are laid down in their full length, and covered with mould, and at each knot they bring forth the fprigs, and at the expiration of eighteen months thefe fprigs come to maturity, and ought then to be cut off. During the firft months of their growth, the weeds ought to be cleared off the field; but this labour ceafes as foon as the cane is formed.

When the canes have once been cut, they bring forth new fprigs, which yield a fecond crop at the end of fifteen months, whofe produce makes no more than one half of the firft crop. Nothing but the want of hands to re-plant his field can induce a planter to wifh for more than two crops in his plantation.

The preffing of the canes follows immediately after the crop. This operation requires long nightly labours; for the juice of the cane turns four if it remain longer than

than twenty-four hours in the refervoir which ferves to lead it into the firft copper of evaporation; from this, it is fucceffively poured in other coppers, and no time is loft to finifh its boiling. The fugar is cleared from that honey-like juice, which takes away its whitenefs and folidity, by pouring in the laft copper a ftrong lye of wood-afhes and quick-lime. It may be eafily conceived, that what contributes moft towards comforting the flaves employed in this procefs, depends chiefly upon the produce from the mill. The quicker the juice is extracted, the lefs will laft thofe nocturnal toils fo prejudicial to the health of the poor wretches. Nothing, therefore, ought to be neglected, to give to the fugar-mills all the force and action of which they can poffibly be rendered fufceptible; and it is certainly not by mules and weak water-falls, an end fo defirable can be attained. In this cafe the views of intereft fhould be blended with the principles of humanity, to induce the planters to employ the fire-engine in their mills.

The

The woody part of the fugar-cane is more than a fufficient fuel to keep up the ebullition of the copper of the fire-engines, and of all the coppers which ferve in the operations of the boiling-houfe.

In order to convince planters in a fuller manner of the utility of the fire-engine, I fhall demonftrate that it is of great economy, even at Paris, in the moft common works. When, in that capital, the price of a cart-load of charcoal, of twenty-feven hundred weight, cofts fifty-four livres, Monfieur Perrier, of the Royal Academy of Sciences, reckons only at fix fols * the confumption of coals neceffary to produce a motive power equivalent to that of a horfe working eight hours, and making a conftant effort of about feventy-five pounds. Now, the work of a man being but a feventh part of that of the horfe, it refults therefrom that his daily labour is reprefented by the comfumption of ten deniers of coals; but in moft colonies where

* Three-pence Englifh.

where wood and other combuftibles are of no value, why fhould the introduction of a machine of fuch high importance be neglected? The fire-engine, if it be well conftructed, is not fufceptible of derangement, it may be eafily transferred to any place where it may be wanted; the expence of fetting it up is very moderate, and it requires no more than common care and attention in thofe who wifh to make ufe of it. It is not expofed to the danger of ftanding ftill, or of interrupting the works, an inconvenience frequently attended with confiderable loffes. It will alfo be found of great fervice in places where the waters are infalubrious, in procuring plenty of diftilled water, which is known to be wholefome and potable, if impregnated with air.

If we reflect a little on the produce and advantages of the fire-engine, we are no longer furprifed at the preference given of late, by able mechanics, to its motive power, notwithftanding the high price of combufti-

H 4   bles.

bles, a preference generally and unjuftly granted by moft people to the changeable and fatal expedient of currents and water-falls. Currents of water are indeed fubjeft to continual variations, caufed by drought and rain. The water-falls require ftore-houfes and fluices, which often-times ob-ftruct navigable rivers, and overflow fields or fpots of ground infinitely precious for the purpofe of cultivation; the pools or ponds fpread at the fame time over the country, by their ftagnant waters, the germins of pefti-lential difeafes, which make fuch havock among the inhabitants in fummer and autumn.

If to all thefe inconveniences we add the frequent and expenfive repairs of caufeways, fluices, and works under water, and if we comprife the danger ever imminent of feeing the moft expenfive contrivances deftroyed in an inftant, by a fudden inundation or fhoals of ice, we muft be fully aware of the judi-dicious motives which could ftimulate Meffrs. Bolton

Bolton and Walt, the moſt celebrated mechanics in Europe, to ſubſtitute the motive
power of the fire-engine to that of currents
and water-falls, even for the grinding of
corn.

It was on the banks of the Thames, near
Blackfriars Bridge, where we ſaw that famous ſtructure the Albion Mills, where two
fire-engines put in motion day and night
ſixteen pair of mill-ſtones, having ſix feet in
diameter. A thouſand ſacks of flour were the
daily produce of thoſe mills ; an immenſe produce, ſufficient to maintain one-third of the inhabitants of London ! This ſtupendous contrivance, now deſtroyed by accidental or villainous conflagration, ought to have been crowned
with all the ſuccefs for which it is ſo well
calculated, and it muſt be of great benefit to
mankind, by inviting us ſuccefſively, and by
intereſt, to abandon thoſe water-mills, which
ſpread ſicknefs and deſolation throughout a
country.   Monſieur Perier was eager to imitate in France the invention of Meſſrs. Walt
and

and Bolton, by erecting near the arfenal at Paris, a mill of the fame kind. It was no fooner completed, than that metropolis felt the moft beneficial effects annexed to that contrivance; but what rendered its utility fo confpicuous, was the ftanding ftill of the greateft part of the mills, occafioned by the ice, and the long duration of the exceffive froft, at the conclufion of the year 1788. It was much regretted by the Parifians, that that able mechanic confined his undertaking to the play of one millftone only; but he could not then forefee the invaluable advantages which were to refult from the natural circumftances of the contrivance of a machine, the mere object of which was to know and afcertain the degree of utility of the enterprife of Meffrs. Walt and Bolton.

It is but in moments of diftrefs fuperficial men become at laft fenfible of the merit of induftry; at all other times, the moft important objects are moft frequently facrificed to frivolous caprice; it muft be an imperious

want

want that can command their attention. But why do thefe very men, who have at the fame time fo great an influence over the public opinion, fofter a fecret inclination of praifing indiftinctly, and without knowledge of caufe, all that comes from abroad, and overwhelm, by ill-timed and indifcreet eulogiums, with difmay, thofe able artifts fufficient to maintain to advantage the rivalfhip and concurrence with foreign artifts? Have the French, for inftance, no manufacture, no kind of induftry that is commendable? Do not the tapeftry of the Goblins, the carpets of Savonerie, the rich ftuffs of Lyons, the fine cloths of Louviers, the glofs, brilliancy, and duration of our dyes, the drawings, the exquifite tafte which characterizes the works of our artifts, the fine porcelain of Seves, the great pier-glaffes of St. Gobin, and a vaft number of other manufactures, more or lefs important, prove in a moft palpable manner, that France is not quite divefted of induftry To filence thofe mercilefs depreciators of the native arts, only afk
them

them what would be their progreſs, if they were free and encouraged, and if an abſurd prejudice did not forbid thoſe men, who by their education are the moſt proper, to apply to them.

The enlightened man only diſdains what is pernicious or uſeleſs; he reſpeꞔts every profeſſion beneficial to ſociety; he knows that idleneſs is the only ſource of vice and miſery; he is grieved at ſeeing a number of hands kept inaꞔtive, through this ridiculous prejudice, which riſes againſt a certain claſs of beings, only becauſe they can find in their perſonal faculties, means of ſubſiſting and enriching their country. But this prejudice which, among moſt civilized nations, deprives commerce of the principal part of its aꞔtivity, and which is, beyond all doubt, the true cauſe of our ills and miſeries, fortunately exiſts not in the colonies, we may therefore expeꞔt to reap prodigious benefits, if we can bring it about to diſſeminate our knowledge in diſtant regions. The fertile

ſoil

foil of Madagaſcar, the productions infinitely
precious contained in the womb of that celebrated iſland, would not fail furniſhing induſtry with means of eſtabliſhing a commerce, whoſe activity and extent would have
no limits.   It is in this light, we ought to
conſider ſettlements that might hereafter be
formed at Madagaſcar.   Though Monſieur
de Modave has in this reſpect excelled all
his countrymen who preceded him, in eſtabliſhing colonies at Madagaſcar, yet the
foundation of his plan was not ſupported by
thoſe principles of ſolidity which could alone
have rendered his ſettlement of a long flouriſhing duration.   Such was the opinion of
Monſieur Poivre; this man, ſo juſtly celebrated, had governed for ſeveral years, with
wiſdom and true judgment, the French ſettlements beyond the Cape of Good Hope;
he reſided a great many years at Madagaſcar,
to ſtudy the moſt uſeful of its productions.
Monſieur Poivre was Intendant of the Iſles
of France and Bourbon at the epoch when
Mr. de Modave firſt formed his colony at
Madagaſcar;

Madagafcar; and it is obvious to reafon, how momentous and confequent muft be the opinion of a man fo egregious in knowledge and virtue. It is to his indefatigable zeal France will foon ftand indebted for fharing with Holland the rich trade in fpices. If this benefit will not be forgotten by future generations, the misfortunes of that virtuous citizen will only render his memory the more refpeQed. Always eager for the progrefs of knowledge and ufeful enquiries, he never let pafs an opportunity to fpread inftruQion; he confidered it as one of the principal duties of a governor to make ufe of and to excite the emulation of all thofe whom he knew to be poffeffed of talents truly ufeful. He, above all, turned to advantage thofe of the celebrated Commerfon. This learned naturalift had accompanied Monfieur de Bougainville in his voyage round the world; he had gathered a colleQion of plants, and of all the objeQs of natural hiftory he met with in the countries where he landed. The narrative of his voyage prefented a
multitude

multitude of interesting labours. Monsieur de Commerson was very sure that in sailing directly to France, his painful and valuable labours would not remain unrewarded. But all those views of interest were banished from his mind, as soon as he came to know, that Monsieur Poivre wished to employ him in the acquisition of fresh knowledge. After having exhausted the natural history of Isle de France and Isle de Bourbon, he sailed to Madagascar, in 1769, where Monsieur de Modave furnished him with great means of rendering fresh services in the fields of science. How much regret must it cause to the learned world, that labours so precious have been either lost or dispersed after the death of this excellent man, who was snatched from the bosom of science the very moment he was going to enjoy in peace the fruits of his useful enquiries! I have been an ocular witness to the prodigious assiduity of Monsieur de Commerson, who used to pass away almost every night in sorting and preparing the plants, and other

natural

natural productions, which he had collected under a fiery, fcorching fun. I doubt whether any other naturalift has ever difplayed more zeal, or knowledge more extenfive. But what remains now of that immenfe collection, which he ufed to fhow at Ifle de France with fo much more fatisfaction, as it had coft him the more trouble and labour? Nothing, or next to nothing. For the truth of this, I appeal to Monfieur de Juffieu, who has been fo good as to deliver to me all that could be procured from the relics of thofe vaft enquiries. Thefe fad remains of the arduous labours of a great genius confift only of commentaries, of little importance, relative to fome plants defcribed by Flacourt, in his Hiftory of Madagafcar. The only remaining part of his manufcripts that is really interefting, treats of the Kimoffes or Quimoffes. I fhall therefore gratify the reader with the whole of its contents, and fubjoin another written by Monfieur de Modave, on the fame fubject.

" The

" The lovers of the wonderful (fays Monfieur de Commerfon) who would doubt-lefs have been difpleafed, had I reduced the pretended gigantic fize of the Patagonians to the height of fix feet, will perhaps accept, by way of indemnification, a race of Pigmies, which fall into the oppofite extreme. I mean to fpeak here of thofe half men, who inhabit the heart of the great ifland of Madagafcar, and form there a confiderable national body, called in the language of the country, Kimoffes or Quimoffes. The natural and diftinctive character of thofe little men is to be white, or, at leaft, of a paler complexion than all the different blacks ever known, to have very long arms, fo that their hands reach below the knee, without bending the body; and that of the women, to leave hardly any mark of their fex by their breafts or bubbies, except at the time they nurfe their infant offspring; many of them are even obliged to have recourfe to cow's milk, to feed their new-born infants. In point of intellectual faculties, the Kimoffes furpafs

I   all

all the reft of the Malegafhes, who are
known to be very ingenious and adroit,
though abandoned to the greateft indolence ;
but the Kimoffes more active, are likewife
more warlike ; fo that their courage being,
as it were, double in proportion to their
fize, they could never be oppreffed by their
neighbours, who have often attacked them
ten to one. Attacked as they were with
unequal weapons (for they do not ufe gunpowder and mufkets, like their enemies),
they have always fought courageoufly, and
fupported their independence amidft their
rocks, which being difficult to approach,
muft, without doubt, have greatly contributed to their prefervation. There they
live upon rice, different fruits, vegetables,
and roots, and rear a great deal of cattle,
(bullocks with bunches on their backs, and
fheep with long, broad, and fat tails) which
afford them likewife a part of their food.
They have no kind of intercourfe with the
different tribes of Malegafhes who furround
them, neither by trade, nor by any other
method,

method, becaufe they draw all they want from the land they inhabit. As all the little fkirmifhes or wars which take place between them and the other inhabitants of the ifland, have no other objeét than to carry off reciprocally fome cattle or flaves, the littlenefs of the Kimoffes exempts them from the latter injury ; for the love of peace they can bear the former to a certain point, that is to fay, when they defcry from the fummit of their mountains, fome formidable preparations of war going forward in the plain, they take, from their own accord, all the fuperfluous cattle they can fpare, which they tie to the mouth of the defiles which muft be paffed to penetrate into their coun- try, of which, they fay, they make a volun- tary facrifice to the indigence of their elder brothers, but they at the fame time proteft to fight to the laft drop of blood, if they fhould penetrate farther into their terrÍtories by force of arms; a proof that it is not a fentiment of weaknefs, and lefs ftill of cow- ardice, which makes them firft give prefents.

Their

Their arms are the lance and the arrow, which they dart in the moſt maſterly manner; it is ſaid, that if they could, as they much deſire, confer with the Europeans, and obtain from them guns and warlike ſtores, they would prefer offenſive to defenſive action againſt their neighbours, who would perhaps then find themſelves but too fortunate to preſerve peace.

" At three days march from Fort Dauphin, the natives ſhow, with a great deal of complaiſance, little elevations of the ground reſembling graves, which they aſſure to owe their origin to a great maſſacre of the Kimoſſes, who were defeated in the open field by their anceſtors *   Be as it will, this conſtant tradition, as likewiſe a notion generally prevalent all over Madagaſcar, reſpecting the preſent exiſtence of the Kimoſſes, permits us not to doubt that at leaſt a part of this hiſtory be true.   It is aſtoniſhing, that
                                                    all

* I am ſurpriſed that M. de Commerſon did not try to verify this fact, by digging deep into thuſe graves.

all we know of that nation is only collected from them who are their neighbours, that we have no obfervations made on the fpot, and that, either the Governor of Ifle de France and Ifle de Bourbon, or the Governors of the different fettlements which the French had formed on the coafts of Madagafcar, fhould not have undertaken to penetrate in the interior parts of the country, with a defign of adding this difcovery to ever fo many more, which might have been made at the fame time. This matter has been tried lately, but without fuccefs.

" To return to the Kimoffes. I can certify, as an ocular witnefs, that in the voyage I have juft made to Fort Dauphin (about the latter end of 1770) Count de Modave, the late Governor, who had already communicated to me a part of thefe obfervations, finally gave me the fatisfaction of fhewing me among his flaves a Kimofs woman, about thirty years of age, three feet feven inches high, whofe complexion was indeed

I 3   one

one of the cleareft and brighteft I ever faw
among the natives of this ifland; I remarked,
that notwithftanding her fhortnefs, fhe was
very ftrong limbed, not refembling a little
flender diminutive perfon, but rather a
woman of common proportion in part, but
only fhorter in point of height; her arms
were very long indeed, and reached, without ftooping, the knee-pan; her hair was
fhort and woolly; her phyfiognomy tole-
rably good, and more like that of the
Europeans than of the people of Madagafcar;
fhe feemed to fmile conftantly, her temper
was fweet and complaifant, and fhe feemed
from her tenor of conduct to be poffeffed of
much good fenfe. As to the breafts, nothing
but the pap could be found; but this obfervation by itfelf is far from being fufficient
to eftablifh an exception from the general
law of nature.

" Finally, a little before our departure
from Madagafcar, the defire of recovering
her liberty, as much as the fear of inftant
embarkation,

embarkation, made the little flave get off by flying in the woods.

" Upon mature confideration (fays Monfieur de Commerfon) I conclude by believing ftrongly in this new degradation of the human race, which has its characteriftic fign of refemblance, as well as its peculiar manners.

" This fhortnefs of fize, in proportion to that of the Laplander, is pretty near graduate in both; the Laplander and the Kimofs inhabit the moft frigid zones, and the moft elevated mountains on earth. Thofe which form the retreat of the Kimoffes at Madagafcar, are fixteen to eighteen hundred fathoms above the level of the fea The productions of the vegetable reign, which grow naturally on thofe high mountains, feem to be quite abortive; for inftance, the pine, the birch, and fo many other trees, appear like creeping bufhes or fhrubs, only becaufe they are become Alpine, that is

I 4   to

to fay, inhabitants of the higheft mountains."

To this paffage from the MSS. of Monfieur de Commerfon, I fhall add another on the fame fubject, written by Monfieur de Modave.

" When I arrived at Fort Dauphin (fays that gentleman) in September, 1768, I received a piece of writing, containing a particular account of a fingular race of people, called Kimoffes, in the language of the country, who inhabit the centre of the ifland of Madagafcar, in the 22d degree of latitude. I had heard of them feveral times before, but with fo much confufion, as could hardly induce me to beftow the fmalleft attention on a fact which deferves to be cleared up.

" The queftion is here about a nation of dwarfs, who live in fociety together, are governed by a Chief, and protected by civil laws.

" I had

" I had certainly read a paſſage relating to this nation in Flacourt's Voyage, but that paſſage had made no impreſſion on me, becauſe Flacourt rejects the hiſtory of theſe dwarfs, as a fable invented by the players of Herraou; theſe players of Herraou are the Hiſtrios and real Merry Andrews of Madagaſcar, who ſpend their life in ſinging abſurd ballads, or telling ridiculous tales.

" Flacourt calls thoſe little men Pigmies, and mixes their hiſtory with that of a pre-tended race of giants, which the ancient tra-dition of Madagaſcar aſſures to have, in times of yore, made great havock in this iſland. Flacourt relates after the players of Herraou, that theſe little men made once an invaſion in the province of Anoſſy, where they were replaced by the Etanos, or aborigines of the country. The Etanos encompaſſed and hemmed in the pigmies on the banks of the river Itapera, and maſſacred them to a man; they erected afterwards on the ſpot a great number of ſtones, to cover the bodies of
their

their enemies, and to ſerve as a monument of the victory which they had obtained over them.

" Having taken all poſſible information that could be obtained at Port Dauphin and in its environs, I (Monſ. de Modave ſpeaks) reſolved two months after, to ſend to diſcover the country of the pigmies. This enterpriſe however turned out unſucceſsful on account of the falſe and daſtardly conduct of my guides. But the only advantage which I have derived from my expedition, is to have convinced myſelf that there really is a nation of dwarfs who inhabit a diſtrict of this iſland.

" This nation call themſelves *Kimoſſes* or *Quimoſſes* : the middling ſize of the men is three feet five inches, they wear a long round beard : the ſize of the women is ſome inches ſhorter than that of the men. The Kimoſſes are thick and ſtrong limbed ; the colour of their ſkin is leſs tawny than that of the other

other natives, and their hair fhort and woolly. They forge iron and fteel of which they make lances and arrows. They are the only arms they make ufe of to defend themfelves againft their enemies, who fometimes try to carry off their cattle. As foon as they perceive troops of travellers wifhing to pafs through their country, they tie bullocks to the trees, and add to thefe other provifions, that thefe ftrangers may find means of fubfiftence on their frontiers. But if the latter fhould not be prudent enough to let them be in peace, and to be fatisfied with the prefents ufual in fimilar circumftances, the little Kimoffes will defend themfelves with great vigor, and repel by force of arms, thofe who have the audacity to feek, in defpite of them, to penetrate into the valley which they inhabit, and which is difficult of accefs.

" Dian Ramoufay who had followed, as captain, the father of Dian Maimboo, in the two unfortunate expeditions which were
undertaken

undertaken againſt thoſe dwarfs, to carry off
ſome of their droves of cattle, and to ſell
them afterwards at Fort Dauphin, has told
me that he only owed his life to his peculiar
knowledge of the high and ſteep mountains
which encompaſs their valley. Ramouſay
had been ſeveral times in the country of the
Kimoſſes; Maimboo's father had taken him
for his guide, when he ventured to attack
them. The firſt incurſion was quite unſucceſsful; but the ſecond much more fatal.
Maimboo's brother was killed, his little army
put to flight, and the number of thoſe who
eſcaped the purſuit of theſe pigmies, was
very inconſiderable.

" Maimboo, with whom I had great connections to ſupply Fort Dauphin with proviſions, was not old enough to follow his
father on this expedition, but ſo great was
the averſion he preſerved againſt the Kimoſſes, that he ſeemed quite enraged and
furious when I ſpoke of them. He did all
he could to perſuade me to exterminate that
race

race of monkies (for he always gave them this opprobrious appellation). A Chief of Mahafalley, who came to pay a vifit to a Chief in the neighbourhood of Fort Dauphin, to barter filk and other commodities for bullocks, faid before one of my officers, that he had been feveral times in the country of the Kimoffes, and had even made war upon them. He added, that for feveral years they had been much troubled by the tribes in their vicinage, who had burnt feveral of their villages. This Chief boafted of having in his country a male and female Kimofs, very nearly of the fame age, which he faid was between 20 to 25 years, and I hope he will keep the promife he made to my officers, of fending them to me.

" From the accounts I had from Ramoufay and that Chief, I have reafon to believe, that the valley of the Kimoffes is rich in cattle and other provifions. Thefe dwarfs are laborious, and very good hufbandmen. The Chief of the Kimoffes has an authority more
abfolute

abſolute and more reſpected than that of the other Chiefs of the different diſtricts of Madagaſcar. I have not been able to aſcertain the extent of the valley they inhabit; all I know is its being ſurrounded by very high mountains, and that its ſituation is ſixty leagues north-weſt from Fort Dauphin. Weſtward it is bounded by the country of Mantatana. Their villages are erected on little eminences, whoſe ſteep ſides are the more inacceſſible, ſince they have multiplied the obſtacles which forbid the approach.

" The Chief of Mahafalley and Ramouſay do not agree about two facts which merit a particular inveſtigation. It is the general opinion of the Malegaſhes, that the Kimoſs women have no breaſts, and nurſe their infants with cow's milk. It is added, that they are not ſubject to the menſtrual flux, but that at this epoch the ſkin of their body aſſumes a blood-red colour. Ramouſay aſſured me, that this aſſertion was perfectly true; but the Chief of Mahafalley proteſted againſt

againſt it. One ſhould therefore ſuſpend
one's judgment, and be very circumſpect
about the belief to be granted to phenomena
which ſeem ſo very remote from general
rules, if they are confined to a certain number of individuals.

  " I got a Kimoſs woman into my poſſeſſion, who had been taken in the war a few
years ago, by a Chief of the province of Mandrarey; that woman is tall in compariſon to
the common ſtature of the reſt of her countrymen, for ſhe is three feet ſeven inches
high; between 30 and 32 years, her arms
are very long, her hands are like the
paws of a monkey; the pap of her boſom
ſticks as cloſe to her breaſt as that of the
leaneſt man, without leaving the leaſt trace
of bubbies. My little Kimoſs was amazingly
lean when ſhe firſt arrived at Fort Dauphin;
but ſince ſhe can indulge her voracious ap
petite, ſhe begins to be plump, and I believe,
if ſhe once gets in her natural ſtate, her
features will be worth great notice. The
                                    Chief,

Chief, of whom I bought her, told me, that a friend of his had a Kimoís man, and he would do all he could to ſend him to me.

" If the enterpriſe in which I embarked two months ago, had been attended with ſucceſs, I would certainly not have foregone that opportunity of ſending a male and female pigmy to France. Perhaps I ſhall be luckier in future. It is indeed no great wonder to meet with dwarfs in a country of ſuch vaſt extent as the iſland of Madagaſcar, whoſe ſurface compriſes ſeveral climates, and the moſt variegated productions ; but a real race of Pigmies living in ſociety, is a phenomenon that ought not to be conſigned to ſilence."

To this account of Count de Modave and Monſieur Commerſon, we ſhall join that of an officer who had one of thoſe male dwarfs, whom he aſſured me, he would have ſent to France, had not Monſieur de Surville, who commanded the ſhip in which he embarked, refuſed him permiſſion. After

After atteftations fo unequivocal, fhould we not be furprifed to fee Flacourt treat the exiftence of that race as a mere fiction? We ought then no longer to quote the mere authority of that writer to refute matters of fact; he was a man deferving miftruft in every point, on account of his implacable hatred towards the people of Madagafcar. Thefe iflanders are not corrupted and fenfelefs men, becaufe their manners are oppofite to ours, becaufe they are fond of tracing fantaftical figures over the different parts of their body. Manners and ufages change according to climates; everywhere men like to disfigure themfelves in a thoufand divers ways; the Indian lengthens his ears; the Chinefe crufhes his nofe, and flattens the forehead; and if we were to lay any great conftruction upon thefe puerile trifles, our civilized people would perhaps appear lefs wife than the favage.

The iflanders of Madagafcar are neither cheats nor ruffians, becaufe we find them

K   victims

victims of the moft fatal prejudices, of the
moft fhocking fuperftitions. There is no
inhabited country on the furface of the globe,
but has its fables and chimeras; everywhere
you fee man invoke fpirits, confide in the
power of charms, and grant ridiculous belief
to the reveries of judiciary aftrology. It is
certainly not in civilized countries where
this fpirit of illufion has been productive of
the leaft mifchiefs; when fuperftition is once
blended with the multifarious vices of great
affociations, its venom only acquires a greater
degree of rapidity. Let us confign to Flacourt the poor care of tracing the afflictive
picture of the fuperftitious practices of the
Malegafhes; that fubject offers no ufeful
leffon to the enlightened reader. Should we
be furprifed that a frail, fufceptible being,
overwhelmed from its cradle with a great
deal of infirmities, fwerves during the fhort
duration of its inconceivable exiftence, from
the caufes of its calamities, fhould we be furprifed that, amidft the delirium of a troubled
imagination, the favage has recourfe to all
kinds

kinds of chimeras, to fcreen himfelf from dangers that encompafs him from every fide. Hurricanes ravage the field he cultivates; lightning ftrikes the manfion which he has chofen for his afylum; the earth opens her jaws under his footfteps, and by convulfive and terrible motions, fwallows in an inftant vaft diftricts of land. Amidft fo many difafters, fhall the Malegafh remain an impaffive and ftupid fpectator of thofe fcourges? Undoubtedly not; the lefs enlightened, the more will his imagination be ftruck with terror; he will attribute the great cataftrophes, which feem to menace the whole earth with deftruction, to the wrath of an invifible being that governs it; he will feek to appeafe that wrath by prayers and facrifices, and miftaking the nature of the worfhip due to Divinity, invent in his delirium all kind of practices abfurd, puerile, and oftentimes fanguinary. It is folely owing to this fpirit of illufion, from which no nation is quite exempted, that the people of Madagafcar appear to us more criminal than the cannibals,

when,

when, through the moſt iniquitous ſuper-ſtition, they throw their new-born infants into the teeth of ferocious beaſts of prey, after the magic deciſion of the Ombiaſſes. Theſe impoſtors feign to conſult the planets, and pronounce ſentence of death upon thoſe children, if they chooſe to conceive the moment of their birth ominous and ill-boding. The months of March and April, the laſt week of every month, every Wedneſday and Friday of the year are days of pro-ſcription, conſequently the population of Madagaſcar is almoſt one-half of the year attacked in its very ſource. The barbarous ſentence of the Ombiaſſes is however not always executed, ſome parents leſs ſuper-ſtitious and more tender, cauſe ſometimes theſe unfortunate and innocent victims, openly expoſed in the woods, to be taken up by faithful ſervants; they have them ſe-cretly educated, endeavouring by ſacrifices to leſſen or remove the malignity of the ſtar which preſided over the birth of their ill-fated offspring.

But

But let us draw a deep veil over thofe horrors which revolt human nature! O could I, for the honour of humanity, varnifh over a ufage fo criminal, fo nefarious! What irregularities are not annexed to the ignorant and credulous part of mankind? The meafure of our errors is, if I am allowed the expreffion, that of our miferies; they are aggravated by ignorance, or diffipated by the light of knowledge. Man is either a very new being on the earth he inhabits, or that earth has undergone very great revolutions; for let us reflect never fo little upon the fmall degree of light which fhines even upon thofe nations whom we confider as the moft illumined, can we diffemble our profound ignorance, and not own that we are fcarcely emerged from the chaos? What the ableft of men knows, is fo very little, that indeed it is only permitted to fuperficial minds to glory in it. At the fame time the apprehenfion of exaggerating our progrefs in the moral and phyfical fciences ought not to render us unjuft towards the age we live

K 3   in.

in.   The rights of man are now better underftood; the caufes of the moft alarming
phenomena are no longer a myftery; our
progrefs in the exact fciences has unravelled
fecrets, which nature feemed to have put
above the reach of our feeble underftanding
Henceforth the march we are to follow in
our enquiries is defcribed, the obferver will
no longer be afraid of going aftray; the
limits of probability, doubt, and certainty,
repofe on foundations that cannot be fhaken.
Truth is not, like error, fufceptible of a
multitude of fhapes, nor does fhe efcape any
being whofe heart is upright, and whofe
mind is juft; but fhe flies from thofe frivolous men who fet value upon things that
have none in them.   Thofe degraded minds
praife only the fuperfluities which ferve to
feed luxury and pride; of courfe they can
only efteem and feek after thofe fophiftic
refources calculated to conceal from the eyes
of the multitude the fatal fequels of their
dangerous and depraved inclinations.   Thofe
corrupted men, replete with prejudices, the
abfurdity

abfurdity of which is only hidden by the falfe luftre which environs them, fubftitute the contempt to the love of humanity. Abandoned reafon has no command over their actions; with falfe appearances, eafy manners, apparent affability, a fcrupulous attention in following fafhions, ufages and opinions, they dare every thing in fociety; they attack moft fuccefsfully what is moft facred among men, they cry up luxury, debauchery, and bondage. Who of us has not frequently witneffed that nefarious fophiftry, which changes, as it were, prejudices and vices into virtues? Surely hearts thus corrupted, minds thus deceitful, are for ever banifhed the fanctuary of the exact fciences! The favage is lefs remote from it. He that frankly owns he is ignorant, is nearer to inftruction than moft of thofe prefumptuous minds who, hardly knowing the furface of things, fpeak and decide upon the moft difficult, the moft complicated fubjects, without being reftrained by the conviction of their infufficiency. During my refidence

K 4

at

at Madagafcar, I never ceafed to try experiments on the natives, the refult of which
proved to me how eafy it would be to give
them juft notions of our fciences.   I had occafion to be furprifed at their aftonifhing
facility of becoming fenfible of the general
caufes of the principal phenomena which
could moft furprife or alarm them.   Little
verfed as we may be in the ftudy of the
exact fciences, we know the march to be
followed in diffeminating them; was it not
by obferving this march that Europe emerged
fuddenly from a ftate worfe than ignorance?
It is to this falutary march we owe the fall
of that vain inftruction, which only teaches
us errors and futility.   But in order to reap
from it ftill greater advantages, fear, the
daughter of ignorance, and the inexhauftible
fource of illufion, ought to be banifhed from
the furface of the earth; it ought to be reduced to that ftate of nullity whence it only
fprung to the misfortune of the human race.
Has fhe then taken fuch deep roots in all the
minds, that it is become impoffible to pluck

                                                her

her out? Is it thought to be fo difficult a
tafk to perfuade favages that great difafters
are the neceffary confequences of the laws
of motion? Shall the natural phyfician
lead at his pleafure the heavenly fire by
means of conductors? fhall he draw the
electric matter from the clouds without the
eye-witneffes to thefe decifive experiments
acknowledging the utility of the ftudy of
nature? From that only period of knowledge
the favage will ceafe to be terrified at the
awful clapping of thunder; from that moment, were he even not to know the caufe,
he will judge that it is known to the lover of
phyfical knowledge who found means to ac-
quire it—and from that moment all his fears
will be at an end. The fame effect will
have over his reafon the volcanoes, the earth-
quakes, if we demonftrate to him in fubftances which he is well acquainted with
fpontaneous inflammations, convulfive motions and effects analogous in every degree.
We fhould not think man's underftanding is
fo narrow and confined, that he cannot follow

low arguments even of an intricate nature, if they are founded on experience. I am senfible, that in civilized countries, a vaft number of people, folely occupied with getting their livelihood by continual labour, and compulfive exercife, have not leifure to diveft themfelves of thofe erroneous opinions inculcated in their minds from their tendereft infancy; but favage tribes, who inhabit fertile countries, are of a quite different difpofition; they are eager to be inftructed, they have leifure, and we certainly cannot difpute them that advantage.

The

The NORTH-EASTERN PART of

MADAGASCAR.

———————

THE North Eaſtern part of the iſland
of Madagaſcar is the rich ſtaple of the
colonies of the iſles of *France* and *Bourbon.*
The moſt frequented harbours are *Foule
Pointe*, St. Mary's and the Bay of Antongil.
In theſe three places the French have endeavoured to form colonies. A ſoldier in
the ſervice of the late Eaſt-India Company,
whoſe ſurname was Bigorne, gave me ſeveral
uſeful inſtructions reſpecting the piratical
ſettlements in this quarter. This man had
ingratiated himſelf with the inhabitants, and
by a long reſidence, acquired a kind of influence over them, the beneficial conſequences of which were long felt by *Iſle de
France*

France and *Bourbon*. It was near him, I have acquired some feeble notions of the nature, usages, and productions of the North-Eastern part of Madagascar.

The natives of this coast are still better and humaner than those of the province of Carcanossy; these good people use neither locks nor bolts, and think it sufficient to shut the entrance of their houses with thorns and branches; were they even full of gold, they would not be afraid of being robbed; yet their dwellings are but a heap of leaves and mats, which may be broke into without any effort of strength. The pirates who infested the Indian Seas, being alarmed at the preparations that were carrying on to put an end to their depredations, took refuge in the North-East of Madagascar. It appears that their first settlement was in the island of Nossy-Ibraim, now called St. Mary's. One extremity of that island lies at the distance of eleven leagues from *Foule Pointe*, the other extends in Northern direction, as far as the mouth of the bay of Antongil.

The pirates infinuated themfelves in the confidence and favour of the iflanders, by contracting alliances with them. The reader is perhaps furprized that people of fo infamous a profeffion fhould not have left behind them a more degraded memory: this foreign land was become for them and their children, a fecond native country, they catched the manners and adopted its cuftoms. In other refpects, in thofe fertile and rich countries, it is almoft impoffible to derive any benefit by invading private property, fince the fole wealth of the inhabitants confifts in the foil, and this belongs to all of them without any particular diftinction. It is therefore no wonder that the pirates, who returned continually to this place of refuge, to repair and victual their fhips, met always with a favourable reception from the natives, fince they fhared their opulence without fufpecting their rapines. They compared the conduct of thofe wretches with that of feveral European veffels, and the comparifon was far indeed from being in favour of the

latter,

latter, who had more than once employed
violence by feizing provifions, by commit-
ting unheard of atrocities, burning and facking villages, or thundering upon them with
their artillery, whenever they found the natives not forward enough in fupplying them
with bullocks, poultry, and rice. Hence we
may conclude, that the fight of a fhip bearing European colours, was to the Malegafhes
a fignal of terror and calamity. The inhabitants of *Foule Pointe* ftill recollect, that in
the beginning of the prefent century, a European fhip, decoyed a great number of the
natives into a large tent, which was no
fooner full than the floor funk under their
feet; and by this execrable artifice, the Europeans found it very eafy to bind and drag
away into flavery a great number of thofe
poor, defencelefs wretches. Were we even
juftified to pafs over in filence thofe faci-
nerious deeds, we ftill fhould think ourfelves
ferviceable to mention them, to fhow how
many ills and atrocities our European predeceffors have left to be atoned for.

The

The pirates continued their depredations with fuccefs till the year 1721, but at this epoch feveral nations, alarmed at the enormous loffes fuftained by their commerce, united with one another, to fcour the Indian Ocean from the oppreffion of thofe formidable tyrants, who had feized a large Portuguefe man of war, which had on board of her Count *Receira* and the Archbifhop of Goa, and on the fame day another fhip, carrying thirty guns. Thefe two rich prizes were taken off the ifle of Bourbon.

Thefe pirates, inflated with and proud of their fucceffes, made a long and defperate refiftance. Confiderable fquadrons were required to oppofe them, they were only to be intimidated by the moft rigorous and exemplary punifhments. The Europeans, amidft the moft imminent dangers, were obliged to purfue them to the very receffes of their nefts, and there to force them to burn their fhips.

Thefe

These were the means made ufe of to purge the Indian Seas from thofe pirates who infected them ever fince *Vafco de Gama* had firft opened the route to India to European fhips. The abfolute lofs of the maritime forces of the pirates, would fuffer them no longer to opprefs commerce, and to leave the miferable den of a fettlement they had made at St. Mary's, an ifland adjacent to, and dependent on Madagafcar.——Thofe wretches, forced to give up their erring and vagabond courfe of life, rendered themfelves egregious by frefh villainy. Finding it no longer beneficial to follow their infamous profeffion in fertile diftricts, where all property is common, too weak in numbers to conquer the natives, one would have thought there had been no other means of being pernicious left to them but that of fpreading among the natives the flames of difcord ; but if they had folely confined themfelves to excite wars and divifions among the Malegafhes, the flames would in all probability have been ftifled, and as foon as calm would have

opened

opened the eyes of thefe iflanders, they would certainly not have failed to revenge themfelves of the perfidy of the pirates. It was therefore neceffary to the fuccefs of their pernicious defigns, to render war ferviceable to thofe people. The fale of prifoners, that is to fay, the Slave Trade, anfwered doubly their views of foftering and perpetuating divifions among the Malegafhes, and procuring to themfelves frefh means of growing rich, and of being courted and protected by thofe Europeans who favour that abominable traffic. By this frefh atrocity, the pirates concluded their depredations, an atrocity which to this very hour depopulates, defolates the ifland of Madagafcar. This deftructive fcourge, from the moment of its birth, has never ceafed an inftant to increafe in rapidity. It is not a lefs arduous tafk to forefee its termination, than to calculate its ravages Of all the crimes, of all the horrors caufed by the pirates, the introduction of the Slave Trade at Madagafcar, is doubtlefs the greateft, and at the fame time

L   I fhould

I fhould think it polluting my pen, were I
to draw the fhocking picture, of the violent
atrocities they have committed, and of the
abominable ftratagems they had recourfe to.
The Slave Trade is an inftitution the more
deteftable, fince the ills it occafions are
fcarcely felt by thofe who enjoy the profits
which acrue from it.   It feems as if it required a long feries of reflections to difcover,
that liberty is quite natural to the effence
and dignity of man, and that it is the higheft
degree of injuftice to have converted it, if I
am permitted to fay fo, into an article of
traffic or trade.   If this truth does not make
fufficient impreffion upon enlightened nations to induce them to abolifh flavery, how
can we expect that it fhould be felt by favages deeply wrapped up in the fhades of
ignorance ? Our furprize muft therefore ceafe
at feeing that the natives of Madagafcar, fenfible of the advantages they continually derive from the Slave Trade, preferve even
fentiments of gratitude for thofe infamous
monfters to whom they think themfelves
                                    indebted

indebted for the beft part of their wealth. Before thofe depredators fettled among the Malegafhes, horned cattle, fheep and goats were of no value; rice and other provifions had no price but that which the navigators chofe to put upon them; it even appears that during their piratical depredations, they fpent in drunkennefs and whoredom, the pro- fits arifing from their cruizes.

Want of forecaft is not rare among men habituated to a vagabond and difolute courfe of life; the extreme profufion of thofe wretches has nothing in it of a furprifing nature; but always greater hypocrites than fpendthrifts, it is no wonder that they took care to conceal fo carefully from the natives, the impure fource whence they drew their opulence. This is perhaps the only point which they were obliged to be prudent in, for fear of incurring the hatred of the people of Madagafcar, with whom it was fo much their intereft to preferve a good under- ftanding.

The

The baneful and ufelefs account of their
fhameful depredations would have fpread
horror and alarm all over the ifland, where
death is the punifhment of the fmalleft
crimes. The people of Madagafcar would,
I dare fay, have exterminated thofe dangerous guefts, if they had been acquainted with
their perverfe inclinations; but fince their
memory is not held in deteftation, and has
not left in the mind of thofe iflanders, traces
of their infamy, they certainly muft have
deceived them by a profound diffimulation,
and by feigned outward appearances of affection and confidence. And how could thofe
favages have been penetrating enough to
know and unmafk thofe villains, trained from
their tendereft age to impofture and artifice—
thofe dangerous villains, who found it con-
fiftent with their fordid views of intereft and
rapine, to conceal from the poor Malegafhes
the greateft part of their vices?

We confefs that the expofition of thefe
reafons alone can give us full fatisfaction,
after

after the vain efforts we made on the fpot,
with a defign of difcovering the true caufe
of that kind of affection, nay, I dare call it
veneration, of the Malegafhes, for the memory of thofe infamous pirates.

It was not at a time when the pirates were
folely occupied with defolating and ravaging
the Eaftern Seas, they could foment great
troubles at Madagafcar, their ftay in this
ifland was always of a very fhort duration ;
befides, being under neceffity of getting their
fhips fpeedily repaired and victualled, they
could not think of fpreading troubles and divifions among thofe iflanders, who could
have avenged themfelves, in their abfence,
on their wives and children, and deftroyed
their fettlements ; and it was only at times
they could indulge themfelves in all the exceffes of drunkennefs and debauchery.   But
once compelled to renounce their infamous
profeffion, they adopted a quite different plan
of life ; they fixed their eyes upon the means
of recovering part of that wealth they had fo

L 3   imprudently

imprudently fpent, and of gaining the protection of the Europeans, by opening to
them a branch of commerce, the extent and
importance of which they were no ftrangers
to. It is thofe wretches who firft brought up
the Slave Trade in the North-Eaftern part of
Madagafcar. All the traditions of the country, and the teftimony of *Bigorne* confirmed
to me the truth of this affertion. It was
only by dint of trouble and confufion thefe
pirates finally fucceeded, about the year
1722, to furmount the averfion of the Malegafhes for that abominable traffic. Previous to that epoch, feveral European fhips
had vainly endeavoured to perfuade them to
fell their prifoners and malefactors. Their
negociations in this refpect, very far from
being attended with fucceis, were rejected
with all the pride of noble indignation, and
if fometimes they dared to make ufe of violence or artifice, punifhed in a moft dreadful
manner. The pirates were too well acquainted with the courageous fpirit of the
Malegafhes to have recourfe to fimilar means;
they

they knew themfelves to be too inferior in numbers to conquer them, or feek to tyranize over their opinion refpecting a fhocking, diabolical traffic. The leaft violent ftep on their part, would inevitably have been followed by their ruin, and by that of their wives and children. The fureft means of gaining their end was, to kindle among thofe iflanders the torch of difcord, and to profit by their inteftine wars, to induce them to difpofe of their prifoners, who, by their number, could not fail becoming burdenfome to them. But amidft all thefe troubles, it was infinitely important to their defigns and fafety, to preferve a friendly intercourfe with both parties, and to act the part of mediators. They were ftill obliged to wait an opportunity, or at leaft a plaufible pretence, to put in execution that odious plot. They did not, however, remain long in that expectation.

The *Bethalimenians*, who inhabit the interior parts of the ifland, had left their vil-

L 4 lages,

lages, and reforted in great crowds to the fettlements of the pirates, with a view of procuring to themfelves feveral articles of commerce, whofe utility and convenience they confulted. They fought above all, very eagerly after fine Indian calicoes, the handkerchiefs of *Mazulipatam*, muflins, and other goods more or lefs valuable. The inhabitants of the fea-fhore, known by the name of Antaverians and Manivoolians, faw them with pleafure; they would have thought to be wanting at once in the duty of hofpitality, and in their affection to the pirates, had they caufed the leaft interruption in the trade of cattle and provifions of all forts, requifite for the victualling of their fhips.

The Bethalimenians are a more frugal and more courageous people than the Antaverians and Manivoolians; they no fooner faw that the fource of the wealth of the pirates was exhaufted, by the abfolute deftruction of their fhipping, than they prepared to return

to

to their villages, with the rich booty they
had amaffed. The Antaverians and Manivoolians would not have oppofed their departure, had not the pirates tried every effort
to make them rife, by making them believe
that thofe valuable goods, the fruit of their
labours and attachment, would be for ever
loft to them, if they fuffered them to be
carried into the inland parts of the ifland.
It is thus that after a long refiftance, folely
founded upon the refpect due to hofpitality,
the Antaverians and Manivoolians fuffered
themfelves to be vanquifhed and involved in
an unjuft war. That cruel war was the ftem
of all thofe which ftain the North-Eaft of
Madagafcar with blood to this very hour.
Before that period, the natives lived in peace,
and their little divifions, infeparable from
focial life, never lafted long, nor left any
traces of refentment behind them. The
pirates were fo cunning as to avoid appearing
in the armies of the Antaverians and Manivoolians, without wifhing to appear to obferve neutrality. For they fold at a very high
price

price arms and warlike ſtores to their friends the Antaverians and Manivoolians; but refuſing the ſame aſſiſtance to the Bethalimenians they ſecretly adviſed them to barter with an European ſhip juſt arrived at *Foule Pointe,* their priſoners for fire-arms and ammunition. The Bethalimenians, provoked by the exceſſive violence of the Antaverians and Manivoolians, followed eagerly that perfidious counſel. Defending themſelves with gallant bravery, they had taken a great number of priſoners; theſe priſoners now incumbered them, and by diſpoſing of them by ſale, they obtained what arms they wanted to combat their enemies. The Bethalimenians were much obliged to the pirates, for having pointed out to them the means of making the Antaverians and Manivoolians repent their injuſtice. Having once obtained a ſufficient quantity of warlike ammunition, they found themſelves capable to awe their enemies. They ſoon found themſelves better ſupplied than the latter, who could then no longer oppoſe their departure. Thoſe ſelf-

ſame

fame Malegafhes, who had always fhewn the moſt invincible repugnancy to the ſale of priſoners, ſuddenly changed their principles on that ſcore. At the ſame time thoſe people believed us to be man-eaters. The inceſſant efforts made by the Europeans to procure themſelves ſlaves by artifice or violence, had not a little contributed to confirm them in that injurious opinion. The enemies of the whites, who were not a few in number, delighted in gaining proſelytes to that odious aſperſion, and I can aſſure the world that that calumny has been propagated from generation to generation in ſuch a manner, as to be preſerved to this day. There are certainly means to eradicate that diſgraceful imputation, by bringing up in Europe with a quite peculiar care ſome young Malegaſhes, and ſending them back to their country — Beſides, it would be the greateſt ſervice that can be rendered to thoſe regions. However, little reflection we may beſtow on the ſalutary conſequences of ſuch an expedient, we

fhall

fhall find caufe of furprize at its having been fo long neglected.

If we pafs over in filence that long feries of wars, which, from that epoch, has never ceafed to defolate the Northern part of Madagafcar, we cannot help obferving, that the pirates alone have kindled the torch of difcord among thofe favages, conciliating at the fame time the affection of the Antaverians, Manivoolians and Bethalimenians.

From that moment the Europeans difdained no longer courting their protection. The public fale of the prifoners ferved as a fuel to the fire of hatred and vengeance; thofe two combined fcourges left no other bounds to their ravages than the entire depopulation of an ifland celebrated for its extent and prodigious fertility. How many victims immolated to the infatiable cupidity of a handful of maritime robbers!

Ye

Ye men that are juſt and compaſſionate, ſee how much blood and crimes it coſt, to raiſe your colonies to that climax of proſperity, the advantages of which are daily exaggerated, as if that proſperity, ever precarious, were not more apparent than real, ſince the opulence of the ſmall number has no other foundation than the ſweat, blood, ſervitude, and miſery of the multitude !

After the Slave-Trade had eſtabliſhed the power of the pirates, it has not proved leſs ſerviceable to their progeny.

Tamſimalo, whoſe mother was the daughter of a powerful chief, and the father an old Corſair, notorious for cunning and plunder, aſſumed the reins of ſovereignty after his father's demiſe : no extraordinary event diſtinguiſhed his reign. Neverthelefs his memory is ſtill revered among the iſlanders, and his reſpected aſhes are depoſited at St. Mary's, ever ſince the year 1745, the epoch of his death.

John

John Harr, his fon, fucceeded him ; but his power was more circumfcribed, and his mifconduct brought upon him the contempt of his fubjects. He made *Foule Pointe* his place of refidence, leaving the government of St. Mary's to his mother and to a fifter, known by the name of *Bettie.* Shortly after the death of Tamfimalo, the French Eaft-India Company formed a fettlement at St. Mary's. Monf. *Goffe* was ordered to take poffeffion of the ifland in the Company's name. This officer was accompanied in this ceremony by *Bettie,* the daughter of Tamfimalo. This honour, according to the cuftom of the country, belonged to the relict of Tamfimalo, whofe fovereignty was generally acknowledged. This haughty and imperious woman, taking offence at the kind of flight and inattention which Goffe affected to throw by that ceremony upon her dignity, fwore to be revenged. Goffe difregarded for a long while the anger of that woman : this conduct was not prudent, and could, foon or late, have brought great difafters upon the

colony

colony entrufted to his care. Epidemical
diforders, obftinate fevers and agues plunged
his fettlement into a ftate of languor and
weaknefs, during the latter end of the year.
The government of *Ifle de France* were
obliged to fend him annually frefh men to
compenfate the confiderable loffes which he
fuftained from the unhealthinefs of the ifland.
Mortality made fuch havock in the courfe of
autumn, that it obtained the name of *The
Churchyard of the French*. It is true however, that the people who were fent to that
place were of fuch a defcription, that their
lofs could excite no kind of regret.

If Goffe was deficient in point of refpect
to the widow of Tamfimalo, he, on the
other hand, neglected nothing to infinuate
himfelf in the affections of *Bettie*. That
charming woman, joined to a pleafant countenance, a great deal of natural fweetnefs
and amenity. The natives were much more
attached to her than to the mother. *Bettie*,
fully fenfible of the progrefs fhe had made in
Goffe's

Goffe's heart, made many times prove abortive, the fatal projects of her mother against the French : at laft her zeal was confined to bounds which fhe durft not tranfgrefs. The widow of Tamfimalo accuffed Goffe of having attempted to difturb the facred afhes of her hufband, and of having taken from his tomb the riches which it contained.

This accufation, true or falfe, excited fuch a ferment among the natives, that the deftruction of the French was irrevocably refolved. They furioufly poured upon the colony, fet fire to it, and maffacred all the French. When this fatal news was brought to *Ifle de France*, on Chriftmas-Eve, 1754, a fhip fitted out for war received orders to block up the entrance of St. Mary's harbour, and to chaftife the inhabitants in the fevereft manner. Their punifhment was dreadful accordingly ; a vaft number of villages were deftroyed by fire, feveral large canoes full of natives funk to the bottom, and the people on board of them were drowned ; that which
carried

carried the widow of Tamfimalo ftrove with many efforts to reach the bay of Antongil, and to efcape the floops of war that gave her chace. Soon the fire of the great guns reached her; the widow was killed; feveral of her companions fhared the fame fate, the reft were made prifoners, and *Bettie* was among the latter. She was carried to *Ifle de France*, and juftified herfelf before the Great Council : fhe made it appear, that her con-nection with Goffe had put her life in dan-ger, and that fhe would no longer be fafe at St. Mary's, having forfeited, through her at-tachment to the French and the efforts fhe had made to fave them, all the confidence and affection of the people. The council, ftrongly convinced of her innocence, fent her back to *Foule Pointe*, to her brother *John Harr*, with confiderable prefents. She was requefted to make ufe of all her means and influence to re-eftablifh calm and harmony between the people of Foule Pointe and the French. The former, terrified at the mif-chief done at St. Mary's, had taken refuge

M   in

in the interior parts of the country. All
commerce was at an end, and the exigences
of *Iſle de France* called for the moſt urgent means to revive it ſpeedily. *Bettie*, on
account of her great aſcendency over her
brother, was the propereſt perſon the French
government could pitch upon to attain their
end. She took with her Bigorne, an old
ſoldier in the Company's ſervice, and a
man of a good underſtanding, and an active
diſpoſition.

Bigorne ſoon learnt the language of Madagaſcar, and, by a frank and open behaviour,
won the affection of the iſlanders. By his
care, by his activity alone, commerce and
trade were reſtored. Among all the honourable atteſtations unanimouſly made of his
ſervices, we ſhall diſtinguiſh that of Monſ.
Poivre, who, in the year 1758, became an
eye-witneſs to the excellent conduct of that
brave ſoldier. That celebrated governor,
whoſe approbation cannot be ſuſpected of
prepoſſeſſion or partiality, has frequently
made

made before me the eulogium of that man, whofe memory is ftill dear to the iflanders. The influence he had acquired over them was lefs due to his eloquence than to a natural goodnefs of heart.

The fpeeches which he made before the natives in their great affemblies, called *Palabras*, could not be compared with thofe of their own orators. Monf. *Poivre*, who was prefent at feveral of thofe *palabras*, often told me that the natural eloquence of the Malegafhes had really aftonifhed him. He took delight in relating the moft minute particulars of a great *palabra*, at which all the neighbouring chiefs were prefent, furrounded by numberlefs crowds of their refpective fubjects, to conclude a treaty of commerce with the commiffioners of the French Eaft-India Company.

I fhall prefent the reader, in a few words, with the account he gave me of that *palabra* :

After

After the Speaker had made his obeisance to the Chiefs, he advanced towards the French, and making a profound bow, addressed Bigorne as follows :

" You know, Bigorne, that for up-
" wards of eighty years, the Whites have
" come hither to trade with the Malegashes;
" canst thou say that ever a white man has
" been killed by one of our nation? We
" have always received you, not only as our
" brothers, but as masters of the country.

" When the French demanded bullocks
" and rice, we have never refused them.—
" When they wanted to erect palisades, or
" to build dwellings, have not we been to the
" forests to fetch what wood they required?
" Those, Bigorne, who came before thee,
" and those that are now here, have they
" any subject of complaint against us?—
" have they not drawn the water from our
" wells?—have they not felled the trees of
" our forests, without any man of Foule
                                        Pointe

" Pointe having afked them, *Why doſt thou*
" *that?*—The nations of the South, and
" thofe of the North, and quite recently
" thofe of St. Mary's, have killed French-
" men, and made war upon them! but the
" people of Foule Pointe never ftruck one
" of them: they have, on the contrary,
" given them all kind of fuccour, at all
" times they have fhown them friendfhip
" and benevolence. Should the Chiefs of
" Foule Pointe be lefs powerful than their
" neighbours?—O Bigorne, more powerful
" they are; do they fear to go to war with
" the whites?—*No.* Who durft make war
" upon the illuftrious fon of Tamfimalo,
" upon John Harr, our fovereign and father?
" Who are the Whites fo daring to attack
" thofe formidable, invincible chiefs here
" prefent, *Maroo-at, Ramiſi, Rama-toa?*—
" Would not we fhed the laft drop of our
" blood to fupport them?—It is then only
" to our friendfhip, to our good nature, the
" French owe the excellent treatment they

M 3   " have

" have received at Foule Pointe fince they
" vifit this harbour.

" Let us now examine the conduct of the
" French with regard to us.

" Why, O Bigorne, haft thou planted a
" palifado of large ftakes, much more ex-
" tenfive, much ftronger than that which
" exifted before, without afking permiffion
" of John Harr and the other chiefs ?—Haft
" thou obferved in this the ancient cuftom ?
" Speak, anfwer, haft thou made the fmalleft
" prefent to them ? But thou art filent, thou
" blufheft, thou feeleft thyfelf guilty, thou
" lookeft at them, thou craveft their indul-
" gence. Here I afk pardon for thy im-
" prudence, of thofe generous and invincible
" chiefs; of John Harr, who prefides over
" this auguft affembly. Bigorne, we do love
" thee, but mifufe not henceforth our affec-
" tion towards thee; fwear never to be
" guilty of the like faults gain. Such
" errors would alienate from thee for ever,
                                    " the

" the hearts of the people of Foule Pointe,
" and to preferve it, fwear that our interefts
" will be henceforth thine own.   Only afk
" thofe chiefs here affembled why, fince the
" arrival of the feven laft great fhips, the
" captains have neglected to make the cuf-
" tomary prefents, which ferve to cement
" the good underftanding in the exchange the
" Whites wifh to make with the Malegafhes?
" Why have not thefe fhips brought where-
" withal to pay off the debts which the
" French have contracted a twelvemonth
" ago?

    " In good faith we have fold them all
" forts of provifions, without any other fe-
" curity than fmall flips of paper, which
" contain, thou affureft us, the promife of
" being paid in three moons.   Why has
" that folemn promife remained unfulfilled
" to this day?—Surely you wifh to force
" us to break off all connections with the
" Whites, or at leaft you give the moft fatal

" blow

" blow to the illimited confidence which
" we gave to their word, to their oath.

" A large fhip anchored here laft year,
" fuffering the moft urgent want of provi-
" fions, without having the means neceffary
" to procure them.   The merchants of
" Foule Pointe fupplied her with bullocks
" and rice, at the fame price as if fhe had
" paid ready money for it.

" The captain promifed them payment
" by the firft fhip that fhould come from
" the *Ifle de France:* fince that period,
" twelve fhips came to moor in this port,
" and all twelve refufed to pay off fo law-
" ful a debt.

" Now, O Bigone, canft thou fay that
" the people of Foule Pointe have been
" wanting of good faith toward the
" French ?

" Shalt thou even fay, that by giving a
" gun of exportation for a bullock, thou
" pay'ft too dear for it ?

" Shalt thou fay that a yard of blue linen
" is of the fame value as a meafure of rice
" weighing fifty pounds ?—Either thou be-
" lieveft us very ignorant about the price of
" things at *Ifle de France*, or thou haft
" conceived the foolifh project of dictating
" laws to us, inftead of our dictating to
" thee.

" Do not you wifh (continued the orator,
" addreffing himfelf to the crowd) to deal
" with thefe ftrangers upon the jufteft, the
" moft becoming of principles ?"

Here the affembly fignified their wifhes, by
univerfal fhouts of acclamation.

Bigorne was going to raife his voice, but
the Speaker filenced him, and continued his
fpeech by command of John Harr, and the
other Chiefs.

" Thefe, faid he, are the conditions pre-
" fcribed by the merchants of Foule Pointe :
" The meafure of rice fhall be made fmaller,
" if

" if in meafuring it, the Whites fhall at-
" tempt to tofs the rice, by knocking againft
" the bottom of the meafure to augment
" its contents, they will not fuffer the mea-
" fure to be heaped up at the top, as it has
" been formerly."

This remark made the affembly fmile.—
" They will no more barter a bullock for a
" bad gun of exportation, they will exact a
" good mufket.

" The bamboo of gun-powder fhall be
" augmented in fuch a manner, that three
" bamboos fhall contain enough to charge
" three hundred mufkets.

" The people of Foule Pointe, who are
" fervants to the Whites, fhall receive one
" gun of exportation for thirty days fervice."

The Speaker, turning towards the affembly, afked them " Are not thefe your laft
wifhes ?" That inftant all the air refounded
with *ayes*, fhouts, praifes, and approbations.

When

When the tumult had fubfided, the Speaker exclaimed with a thundering voice:

" Bigorne, thou heareft the will of the
" *palabra*; it is the law of the chiefs, it is
" the wifh of the people who trade with the
" Whites. Explain well to thy mafters what
" I have juft been faying; if they accept of
" thofe conditions, we fhall confirm the
" treaty by a folemn facrifice; if they do
" not, let them be gone, we have nò pro-
" vifions to give them."

Bigorne tranflated this fpeech, word for word, to Monf. Poivre. That gentleman was forced to interpofe his whole authority, to hinder his upbraiding the Speaker with the vehemence of his oration. He was not accuftomed to fo rough a treatment on the part of the people. He thought this leffon the more bitter, as he received it in prefence of the officers honoured with the confidence of the Company.

Mr.

Mr. Poivre faw, on the contrary, with pleafure the energy of thefe favages ; he was ftruck with the power and depth of their arguments ; but, charged with the intereft of the Company, he had it not in his power to alter the ufual price of merchandize. He requefted Bigorne to make this remark to the *palabra,* affuring them at the fame time, that the merchants of Foule Pointe fhould be fpeedily and generoufly paid for the fup-plies they had granted. He willed the aug-mentation of the falary of the Blacks in the fervice of the Whites. He blended all thefe promifes with expreffions the moft obliging, the moft calculated to roufe the fenfibility of the Chiefs. He preached peace and unity, called them brothers and friends, and inti-mated to them, that all the Whites who fhould not entertain for them the fame fenti-ments of efteem and amity, would be univer-fally cenfured. The fpeech of Monf. Poivre, tranflated into Malegafh by Bigorne, feemed to make more impreffion on the fpeaker than on the *palabra,* it was even folely by his advice

advice the treaty was refolved upon by fhouts of acclamation. The conclufion of the treaty was an object of no fmall importance. The fhips were in great want, and required daily three bullocks and a proportionate quanty of rice to feed the company, which confifted of fix hundred men. The treaty was concluded in the moft folemn manner: the fpeaker flaughtered the victim, took up the blood in an earthen pan, mixed it with brine, pimento, pulverized flint, a pinch of earth and gunpowder, over which he poured fome *tafia* or rum. He took two leaden balls, with which he mixed, and reduced thofe different ingredients, of which he finally made a potion or liquor, conjuring the devil to change it in poifon for whofoever fhould drink of it, and afterwards break his oath. He then took two lances and plunged the points in the liquor, while John Harr fprinkled the ground with fome drops of it.

The

The fpeaker was holding a knife in his hand, and firft invoking the god of the Whites, and then the god of the Blacks, he befought them with a loud voice, to inftil in the hearts of both, peace, concord, friend-fhip, and good faith.

Then ftriking with a fudden motion, the points of the two lances plunged in the liquor with the knife, he pronounced curfes and horrid imprecations againft thofe who fhould infringe the treaty.

" If the Whites break their oath, may this " drink be their poifon, may the hurricanes " which fly with rage from the four corners " of the air, fall upon their fhips; may they " be fwallowed by the waves; may the " corpfes of thofe wicked men be torn by " the frightful monfters that dwell in the " abyffes of ocean.

" Hark, John Harr, liften attentively to " the voice of the mighty genius that in-
" fpires

" fpires me; fhould the people of *Foule*
" *Pointe* be fo bafe, fo wicked, as to violate
" this folemn treaty, may this liquor be
" poifon to them, may they fall by the
" fword of their enemies; may their bellies
" burft, and their filthy carcafes be the food
" of crocodiles.

" Ought not the invifible fpirit who pre-
" fides over this affembly to be avenged?
" —Ought he not to punifh the perjurious,
" fince he receives their oaths?—All men,
" white or black, are equal before him;
" all are fubject to his fupreme will; he
" exacts from us all the fame fidelity, the
" fame good faith, under pain of punifh-
" ments as rigorous as terrible."

Rabefin (this is the name of the fpeaker)
repeated thrice thefe horrid imprecations,
with fuch vehemence of gefture and utter-
ance, as made on the palabra an impreffion
which would baffle all the powers of language to defcribe.

It

It was in this ſtate of terror and agitation, John Harr and the reſt of the chiefs took with a trembling hand, and in a leaf of raven, as much as a good ſpoonful of that diſguſting liquor, which they ſwallowed with a thouſand horrid grimaces and diſtortions of their face and body. Their example was followed by moſt of thoſe who were preſent at the palabra. There was but a few Frenchmen who feigned taſting it, notwithſtanding the intreaties of Bigorne, who would have them drink without doubt, from a ſenſe of perſuaſion, that this ridiculous and unpleaſant farce was neceſſary, if not to the ſucceſs, at leaſt to the validity of the treaty.

Rabefin then ſlaughtered the reſt of the victims ; a great feaſt, followed by dances, muſic and games, terminated in a noiſy though very jovial manner, this famous palabra. I have deſcribed it in preference to thoſe where I have aſſiſted in perſon, becauſe the buſineſs decided in the latter cannot cope in point of importance with the former.—
Thus

Thus I have, in my opinion, attained the only end which I ought to have aimed at, in drawing by this defcription a fuccinct and flight fketch of the character and ftrange cuftoms of thefe iflanders.

This fketch is fufficient for the reader who wifhes more to be informed of than amufed with all the miferable and frivolous details which are fometimes annexed to tranf- actions of the moft ferious nature, not only at Madagafcar, but even in countries that boaft of a better and more civilized ftate.

Rabefin was mafter of changing, at plea- fure, the features of his face; his language always confonant with his geftures, bore the appearance of conviction; nor was he a ftranger to the art of moving minds the leaft fufceptible of enthufiafm, and of firing with anger the leaft irrafcible.

Is it not furprifing that Rabefin, as a favage, fhould have poffeffed to an eminent

N   degree,

degree, that fallacious art which is frequently proftituted to the moft dangerous purpofes by our civilized orators?—How could Rabefin know that to create illufion, the language of the heart is always preferable to that of reafon?—How could he learn to profit by that fecret inclination which makes us fo fond of impofture and chimeras?—What an imperious fway is not exercifed over the multitude by thofe perfidious declaimers, or cunning quacks, who either by intereft, or by the rage of making a diftinguifhed figure, ftudy to exhibit in brilliant colours the moft fatal errors and falfehoods. Falfehood, fufceptible by her nature of affuming infinite combinations, may difguife herfelf under all kinds of forms; but truth has no fuch dangerous advantage, her mode of being is quite uniform, and to feek to embellifh her, is degrading her luftre, and attacking her energy. Cato would have thofe famous orators, thofe cunning fophifters, banifhed from Rome. I coincide in opinion with that great man; reafon cannot have more formid-

able

able enemies than them. All effervefcene, all exaltation is never without danger, even when its views are thofe of utility; but if exaltation tends towards objects of a pernicious nature, the ills it may produce are paft calculation. This fentence however, extends only to thofe who, feeking to impofe upon the multitude, difdain no means of feduction to gain their end. The fentence would be too fevere, were it not to pay due homage to genuine eloquence, that fublime talent which conveys all at once conviction and perfuafion to the heart of the enlightened. True eloquence conftitutes the charm of good minds, and is one of the moft powerful incentives to happinefs. Perfpicuity, precifion, elegance and energy of diction are its chief attributes. A man truly eloquent, borrows no foreign aid; he knows that what is not profoundly and forcibly felt, can never be forciby expreffed, he contemns, rejects thofe brilliant acceffaries, adduced with artifices which only ferve to give to error, if not the weight, at leaft the appearance, and

N 2

fometimes

fometimes the eclat of truth. Rabefin enjoyed great reputation, but his moral character did not correfpond with his abilities;
corrupted from his infancy by his intercourfe
with the Europeans, he paffed for the moft
crafty, the moft dangerous knave. Bigorne,
who was better acquainted than any body
elfe with his vices and afcendency over the
inhabitants of *Foule Pointe*, was not only
obliged to fhow him all forts of tokens of
efteem and deference in public, but even to
feek to gain him, in the moft fecret manner,
by confiderable prefents. Thefe were the
only means by which he could come to his
end, all others would have mifcarried and
compromifed him. Men inacceffible to cor-
ruption are not common. Flatter not yourfelves, civilized nations, in this refpect you
are not in the leaft fuperior to the hordes of
favages.

Moft of your orators imitate with more
art, but perhaps with lefs deceitful outward
appearances, our Rabefin, who fold adrortly
and

and for the fake of his own private profit, interefts of which he was fuppofed to be the moft ftrenuous defender. Would not one have thought him totally averfe to the treaty of commerce, which the agents of the Company wifhed to be concluded with the inhabitants of *Foule Pointe?* and from the fudden and unforefeen conclufion of this treaty, one could not reafonably accufe any one but John Harr and the other chiefs, becaufe they received publicly rich prefents. But Bigorne, who was highly provoked at the fpeech of Rabefin, did not fail acquainting Monf. Poivre, that all his efforts would have been fruitlefs, if that fpeaker, brought over by prefents, previous to the palabra, had not formally acceded to the refolutions made without the concurrence of John Harr and the reft of the Chiefs. This fact is well worth remarking, fince it occured among favages, where good faith, and what is more ftill, the fear of breaking folemn oaths, enjoins all individuals a rigorous obfervance of all contracts, under pain of the heavieft punifhments.

N 3   The

The day after the conclufion of the treaty, the markets of *Foule Pointe* were abundantly ftocked with provifions. The fhips were eager to purchafe what they wanted, and got it fpeedily, and at a low price.

Monf. Poivre being arrived in France, recommended Bigorne in the ftrongeft terms to the Eaft-India Company. At that time he was only interpreter at *Foule Pointe*; but upon the recommendation of M. Poivre, he was appointed all over Madagafcar, under the direction of the Government of *Ifle de France*, to manage all that concerned trade and the victualling of fhips. Bigorne filled this truft with great prudence and ability till the year 1762, when he was called to France, for having declared war againft John Harr. He is faid to have taken every care to preferve the peace at *Foule Pointe*, but he could not help giving public aff-ftance to feveral powerful Chiefs, allies of the French, who had reafon to complain of the depredations of

John

John Harr, whose mind became daily more addicted to vice and licentiousness.

The Chiefs, enemies of John Harr, conjointly entreated Bigorne to take upon him the command of their combined armies.—This brave soldier would not yield to their request, but on a condition which must have appeared somewhat strange to savages: he openly declared, that in taking the command, he would also take the wise precaution of never exposing himself to the fire of the enemy, because his loss would infallibly be followed by that of the brave warriors who should fight under his colours. A general who, consulting but his courage, hurries in the thickest of the fray and shares the combat, is no longer master of giving to his forces the most advantages disposition; henceforth the army is absolutely without chief; confusion necessarily seizes the combatants, and chance alone decides the victory.

Whether

Whether the arguments of Bigorne made any impreſſion on the Malegaſhes. I cannot tell. Theſe undiſciplined ſavages, who could not even think of the advantages which always reſult from perfect order and conformity, might have believed that Bigorne had more talents than intripidity: at the ſame time, having expreſſed ſome ſentiments of ſurprize, they came to range themſelves under his colours. Bigorne made them go through ſome very ſimple manœuvres, and finding them ſubmiſſive and determined to obey his orders punctually, he marched againſt the enemy. When the two armies were within mutual reach, Bigorne renewed his orders of not charging the enemy till he ſhould have given the ſignal of battle.

The army of John Harr was much more numerous and ſtronger than his, but the poſition of Bigorne ſecured to him the completeſt victory, if John Harr durſt venture to attack him. John Harr was not able enough to judge of his diſadvantageous poſition ;

tion; he charged the enemy with vigour, but was repulfed in fo terrible a manner, that he could only find fafety in flight.— Thus John Harr, who fo far was called invincible, was vanquifhed by the mere pofition of a man who did not mix in the battle, and was even at fome diftance from the field.

John Harr being informed afterwards that Bigorne had directed the motions of the victorious army, anfwered—How could I defend myfelf againft the invincible fpirit of a white man that attacked me?—but to be revenged, I am going to leave *Foule Pointe*, to retire to the bay of Antongil. My quitting this port will alarm the merchants of *Foule Pointe*, the markets will no more be fupplied, commerce will linger, the Chiefs of Bigorne will recal him to *Ifle de France;* thus my leaving *Foule Pointe* promifes me a fpeedy deliverance from the moft formidable enemy.

The

The prediction of John Harr was soon realized. *Foule Pointe* was in the utmost consternation, and his absence put an end to all commerce. Some Chiefs, friends of Bigorne, did all in their power to supply the markets with provisions, but the merchants of *Foule Pointe* opposed them. The French ships, which came to take in fresh provisions, after having vainly endeavoured to restore peace and harmony among the people, were forced to set sail to *Isle de France*, in the most deplorable condition, and destitute of articles of the first necessity. At their common complaint, Bigorne was recalled and turned out of office; meanwhile we are told he was innocent, and few men in his place could have suffered so long the unjust vexations of John Harr. Fain would I credit this story, but his conduct must always appear reprehensible to those who are of opinion that we ought not to prescribe rules and dictate laws in a foreign land,

Be

Be it as it may, the departure of Bigorne made John Harr return to *Foule Pointe*, where he was infinitely better received than he could have hoped, and commerce foon reaffumed its wonted brifknefs. This immoderate joy was of no long duration. The flame of difcord was not extinguifhed, it was foftered by hatred and divifion. Finally, after a long feries of wars, Madagafcar got rid of that dread and turbulent oppreffor, who could not live in peace either with his allies, or with his fubjects. John Harr was flain by the Manivoolians in 1767, and his fpoils ferved to enrich his enemies, and to augment their power.

Yavi, his fon, inherited but a flender part of his territories, he was too young not to be fatisfied with what the people left him.— The reign of this Chief deferves no more than the bare mention of his name.

At the death of John Harr, the iflands of France and Bourbon belonged no more to

the

the Eaft-India Company. The King of France appointed Monf. Poivre director of thefe colonies. From that period, Bigorne found no obftacle which could prevent his return to *Foule Pointe*, where his prefence was of the utmoft utility. Upon his arrival, the inhabitants gave him the moft flattering marks of their friendfhip and regard. His great renown of talents and integrity among the natives, made him the umpire of all their difputes; he reftored peace to the North of Madagafcar, and Monf. Poivre could only beftow encomiums on his good conduct.——— I can certify his merit, having been intimately connected with him in a voyage to Madagafcar in the year 1768. Monf. Poivre wifhed for a collection of the rareft and moft ufeful plants of Madagafcar, for his celebrated garden of *Montplaifir*, now known by the name of the *Royal Botanical Garden* at *Ifle de France.* This gentleman, who honoured me with his frindfhip and confidence, pitched upon me to gather that valuable treafure. He certainly could not have made a finer prefent

prefent to the colony over which he commanded. This able governor never fuffered
a fhip to fail without charging the captain,
or fome learned officers, to bring him the
different productions of the countries whither they were bound. His requeft was always attended with inftructions. Thus he
made the garden of *Montplaifir* the richeft
nurfery ever known, fince it contains the
moft valuable plants of the four quarters of
the globe.

At my arrival at *Foule Pointe*, I was forry
not to find Bigorne, whofe affiftance I wanted, to get the means that could enable me
to fulfill the object of my miffion. Having
vifited the environs of *Foule Pointe*, I fet out
to join him at *Mananharr*, a village fituate at
the entrance of the great bay of Antongil.
In my way I landed at St. Mary's, where I
remained all the time neceffary to ftudy its
various productions: I reached *Mananharr*
on the eighth day after my departure from
Foule Pointe. Bigorne received me in the
                                    moft

moſt cordial manner, and gave me many uſeful hints and inſtructions. It is with him I
viſited the moſt intereſting ſpots in the vicinity of the great bay of Antongil; it is with
him I have ſeen thoſe ſtupendous quarries
of rock chryſtal, whoſe enormous maſſes almoſt ſeem to border upon fiction.

We ſhall now proceed to give an account
of the French ſettlements in the North of
Madagaſcar.

We ſhall terminate what we thought remarkable on this head, by the great colony
entruſted to the care of Count *Benyowſki,*
which coſt enormous ſums, turned out unſucceſsful, and had a very tragical end.

The notorious celebrity of that nobleman
is too great for us not to gratify the reader
with the intereſting narrative of his principal
adventures, written by himſelf, and recently
remitted to me, in a MS. copy, by the governor

vernor of *Iſle de France.* All the remarks
I have to make is, that the notoriety of
that audacious man coſt France whole
millions, and brought upon Madagaſcar freſh
calamities.

A LETTER

A LETTER

From BARON ALADAR, now *known by the name of* COUNT BENYOWSKI, *Governor of* ISLE DE FRANCE.

" IT is with the utmost plea-
" sure and eagerness flowing from the zeal
" and affection I feel in serving you, I am
" induced to comply with your commands.

" Born in Hungary, descendant of the
" illustrious house of the barons of *Be-*
" *nyowski*, I am a general in the service of the
" armies of the Empress our Sovereign.—
" My father descended from *Aladar* XIII,
" and my mother from the family of Reray;
" I am therefore of Polish extraction.

" In 1765, the King of Poland, Elector
" of Saxony, being dead, and his kingdom
" invaded,

" invaded, I retired to Warfaw, to efpoufe
" the caufe of a prince furrounded with
" troubles, and the overthrow of the cele-
" brated Conftitution of the firft members
" of the ftate. By a fecret warrant the
" grandees of the kingdom were feized, a
" partifan of the Prince Bifhop of *Cracaw*,
" and other great men ; I was to be fecured
" by order of Prince Repnin, minifter of
" Ruffia. Having dived into this defign,
" and being at a lofs how to act, I fled with
" the utmoft precipitation to a friend of
" Prince *Radzivil*, whofe protection I foli-
" cited. There I remained till the con-
" federation of Bar iffued their declaration,
" being invited to it by Marfhal Pulawfky,
" I immediately lifted in that of *Cracaw*,
" commanded by Marfhal Czarnowfky.—
" Being received as an officer in the regi-
" ment of Caftres, I was taken prifoner by
" the Mufcovites, who had feized upon
" Cracaw. I paid a ranfom of 2,000 ducats,
" joined again the confederation of Bar, and
" being appointed Colonel, with the title of

O   " General,

" General, I took up arms againſt the
" Muſcovites, under the command of For-
" tality Swaniecz, and fought againſt the
" enemies (as it is proved by the acts of
" confederation.) The enemies having been
" put to flight, I was ordered to the Turkiſh
" territories, with Marſhal Pulawſky.   The
" Pacha of Natolia gave me a kind recep-
" tion, with ſupplies of money and men,
" wherewith I returned to Poland, and gave
" battle to the Muſcovites, near the river
" Pruth, where I was wounded and made
" priſoner.   I was carried to Riow, where
" I found Marſhal Czarnowſky, Count Po-
" toſki, and young Pulawſky, with three
" thouſand men.   Being finally removed to
" Caſſan, I paſſed through Nezi and Tuta,
" and by means of a German ſurgeon, con-
" veyed a letter to his eminence the Prince
" Biſhop of Cracow, then at Kaluga, in
" which I appriſed him of my misfortune.
" The governor of Caſſan, Monſ. Guaſnin
" Samarini, ſuffered me to be at large in the
" town.

" On

" On the 15th of Auguſt 1769, a Ruſſian
" officer came to my houſe, and delivered
" me, ſecretly, letters from the Princes
" priſoners, with orders to carry them to
" Kaluga. After ſome conſultations with
" thoſe who were moſt concered, I made
" my eſcape from Caſſan, pretending before
" the governor, a deſire of ſeeing the copper-
" mines, and fortunately reached Kaluga,
" aſſiſted by Colonel Batchimetriewſky, go-
" vernor of Fortality, who was one of the
" party of the princes. I had been appoint-
" ed to conſult perſonally with the princes
" and grandees. It was reſolved that I
" ſhould ſet out to Peterſburgh. I repaired
" without delay to Quorſum, and taking up
" my quarters in the houſe of Colonel
" Soaceſky, I fulfilled my engagement. On
" the point of returning to Caſſan, I was
" arreſted by order of the Empreſs of Ruſſia,
" and nothing having tranſpired about my
" ſecret evaſion, I was ſent priſoner to
" Kaluga, where I had been ſent by the
" princes.

" Having

" Having contracted a great friendship
" with the governor, we made an agree-
" ment, in virtue of which, assisted by
" Tuga, we were to return to Poland. The
" governor had already taken every measure
" to facilitate our escape, when on the 18th
" of October 1769, an officer of the guards
" arrived from Petersburgh with orders to
" put the governor under arrest, the latter
" got the start of the officer by killing him,
" and sought safety in flight, leaving us all
" prisoners. That same day we were loaded
" with irons and conducted to Petersburgh,
" where I found it impossible to get the least
" intelligence of my companions of wretch-
" edness. I was crammed up in the prison
" of Fortality. Being finally obliged on the
" fourth day to appear before Count Orlow
" and Czernichew, I was examined upon
" different points.

" Being unable to collect any thing from
" the answers I made, and still less from
" their threats; they promised me pardon,
" in

" in the name of the Emprefs, if I would
" fwear fidelity to her, and difcover the
" fecrets entrufted to me. As I did not
" relifh this offer, I was remanded to prifon,
" where, by means of an officer, I wrote to
" Prince Lobkowitz, lieutenant of the King
" of Poland ; but I received no anfwer. A
" few days after, being again brought be-
" fore the commiffioners, violent means
" were made ufe of to make me write and
" fign what follows :

" *I, the underfigned, do acknowledge,*
" *that I have not only broke my engagements,*
" *but even committed murder, and became*
" *guilty of blafphemy againft her Imperial*
" *Majefty ; and fhould my fentence be mitigated*
" *through the natural clemency of her Majefty,*
" *I do hereby bind myfelf, after having re-*
" *covered my liberty, never to put my foot on*
" *the territories fubjeƐt to her Majefty, and*
" *lefs ftill to carry arms againft her.*

" RARON MAURICE-AUGUSTUS
" ALADAR DE BENYOWSKY,
" *General of the firft Confederation.*"

Peterfburgh, Nov.
22d, 1769.

" After having drawn up and figned
" this piece of writing, I was again put
" under arreft, and finally on the 24th of
" November, at midnight, an offier came
" at the head of twenty-eight men, and
" threw me into a carriage. We took the
" road of Mufcow. One Major Winblat
" was the companion of my misfortune.
" Without any other allowance than bread
" and water, we paffed through Niezneifki,
" Kuzmodemfkoi, and Janitzkoi and Soli-
" chantzki, where we halted a few days,
" on account of an indifpofition which had
" feized the officer who had orders to con-
" duct us. On the 28th of December of the
" fame year, a foldier informed me, that
" five pofts further, fome horfemen had
" conducted people, who had been ftopped
" at a certain diftance from us. As they
" were fo near us they were extremely de-
" firous of feeing perfons as unfortunate as
" themfelves, and they perfuaded their of-
" ficer to conduct them to us at night. I
" then recognized the moft Serene Prince
" Bifhop

" Bifhop of Cracaw, his tears prevented his
" fpeaking, we were only permitted to be
" together for a little while, and then fepa-
" rated. We travelled together, but in dif-
" ferent carriages, as far as *Tobolfki*, the
" capital of Siberia. We made but a very
" fhort ftay in this town. We were dragged
" by dogs acrofs the defarts of Tartary,
" without hearing any thing from other
" quarters of the earth. We fuffered much
" from hunger, and having traverfed Siberia,
" we met with exiled officers of different
" nations. Finally, on the 2d of May 1770,
" we arrived at the port of Ochozk. The
" governor received us kindly. A few days
" after two Ruffian officers arrived, who
" called themfelves guards of their High-
" neffes the Princes detained at Kaluga. I
" became intimate with them. On the 3d
" of September we embarked and failed to
" the harbour of Bolfao. On the 24th of
" December I received, by a merchant, a
" letter from the Bifhop of Cracaw. I
" learned from the contents, that the cap-

O 4 " tive

" tive princes had been removed to the
" North of Tartary, towards Anadyo, and
" that a troop of Ruffian foldiers were pre-
" paring to rife and fet them at liberty. I
" gave to Major Winblat written inftructions
" how to behave, fo that we both might
" recover our liberty. For my own part, I
" got very intimate with Monf. Gurefinim,
" the officer who was conftantly with me,
" he not only facilitated to me all means of
" efcaping, but even made me an offer of his
" purfe. Whilft matters were in this fitua-
" tion, we were joined by two exiled Ruf-
" fian officers, who told me, that there was
" a prifoner quite near us narrowly guarded,
" who was fuppofed to be a man of great
" diftinction, and had been in irons feven
" years. No body could give us any fatif-
" factory account about him, we were only
" told that for ten or eleven years he had
" been in the cuftody of an old officer, who
" much wifhed for his deliverance. From
" that moment I endeavoured to ingratiate
" myfelf with that officer, who very readily
                                    " liftened

" liftened to my propofals. He told me the
" prifoner's name, who was accordingly of
" an illuftrious birth : we concerted mutu-
" ally the plan of our efcape, and bound
" ourfelves by oath to do every thing to
" make it fucceed. It was on the 25th
" of March when, with the help of Al-
" mighty God, we were to recover our
" liberty at the expence of our blood. Being
" the only perfon that underftood how to
" manage a fhip, I was made chief of the
" enterprize.

" The plot was difcovered on the 21ft of
" April, the governor gave orders to a de-
" tachment to carry me off a fecond time by
" night, to another place. My affociates,
" frightened at the ftroke, came to me on
" the 26th, imploring my affiftance. It was
" an eafy matter. The lieutenant upon duty
" about me, had fecretly conveyed fome
" arms to his houfe, which he diftributed
" among my companions, at the head of
" whom I rendered myfelf mafter of the
                                    " fort

" fort in the night of the 27th.   In the
" beginning of this action, the governor and
" feveral officers and privates were killed.
" There was but a few of my party flightly
" wounded.   The next morning the foldiers
" and Coffacks attempted, arms in hand, to
" enter the town of Bolfao, when the inha-
" bitants, frightened at the firft and fecond
" difcharge of our mufquetry, furrendered
" on the 29th of April.   I entered in triumph
" the town of Kamfchatka, and found not
" the fmalleft oppofition.   I fent inftantly
" people to feize the fhips in the harbour,
" and marched with the reft of the men to
" Zamiecka, where I took prifoner the fe-
" cretary of the Senate, arrived from Peterf-
" burgh, and forced him to deliver up all
" the letters of Chancery.   Having taken
" all that belonged to me, and to two hun-
" dred inhabitants of Kamfchatka. I entered
" the harbour, where I feized three fhips,
" I took the ftrongeft for myfelf, and dif-
" mafted the reft.   I caufed the ice to be
" cleared from the fhip St. Peter, and hav-
                                    " ing

" ing provided myfelf with all neceffaries,
" fet fail on the 12th of May 1771. The
" crew of my fhip corififted of fixty-feven
" perfons, viz. Eight officers, eight married
" women and a girl furnamed the Princefs;
" the reft were all mariners. I left the
" harbour of Kamfchatka, paffed under the
" 52d degree 52 minutes, and failed down
" the canal of the iflands called Jedfo.——
" Steering my rout North-eaft, I landed at
" the ifland of Bernighiana, fituate in the
" 55th degree of Eaftern latitude, and in
" the 9th meridian from the harbour whence
" I had failed. Here I found Monf. Ocho-
" tinfky with eighty men. This Polifh of-
" ficer told me he had effected his efcape in a
" manner very fimilar to mine, and fettled
" with his crew in the American iflands,
" called Alentis. He had entered into an
" alliance with the natives, and rivetted that
" alliance by marrying fome of their wo-
" men. I left him three of my men, and
" he gave me letters to produce wherever it
" fhould be neceffary. On the 26th of May,
" fteering

" fteering my courfe far from that ifland, I
" found the fea covered with ice; I found
" myfelf obliged to land at the ifland of
" Aladar, fituated under the 61ft degree of
" latitude, and the 22d meridian from Kam-
" fchatka. I left that ifland on the 9th of
" June, and failed South-eaft. I defcried,
" in my opinion, the point of the continent
" of America, under the 60th degree of
" latitude, and the 26th meridian from
" Kamfchatka; and failing afterwards to-
" wards the 51ft degree of latitude, on ac-
" count of a heavy gale, I changed my
" direction, and fteered again South-eaft.—
" On the 20th of June I faw myfelf off an
" ifland known to the Ruffians by the name
" of Urum Sir, or the ifland of Chrifti, fituate
" in the 53d degree 45 minutes latitude,
" and diftant 15 degrees 38 minutes longi-
" tude from Kamfchatka. I had a great
" deal of friendly intercourfe with the Ame-
" ricans, who perfuaded me to make fome
" ftay among them. Finally, on the 27th
" of June, I fet fail Weft-fouth, and kept at
" fea

" fea till the 30th of the fame month. I
" difcovered in the 46th degree 6 minutes
" of latitude, and 10 degrees longitude from
" Kamfchatka, a country likewife occupied
" by the Ruffians, where I could not land,
" on account of contrary winds, which bore
" me far away. Having, therefore, taken
" the refolution of fteering my former courfe,
" after having fuffered a great deal from the
" inconftancy of the winds, having feen all
" our frefh water exhaufted, and been oblig-
" ed to drink the brine, which may be ren-
" dered potable with fpermaceti and flour,
" we landed on the 15th of July, at an ifland
" in the 32d degree 45 minutes of latitude,
" and 354 degrees 45 minutes longitude of
" Kamfchatka. Its beautiful fcite, and o-
" ther natural amenities, induced me to give
" it the name of *Liquoris*. It is inhabited. I
" heaved anchor on the 22d, and fteering
" to the weftward, I moored on the 28th
" at *Kilingur*, a Japonefe harbour, fituated at
" 34 degrees of latitude and 343 degrees of
" longitude from Kamfchatka. This port
" is

" is joined to a town and citadel, where we
" met with a very good reception from the
" inhabitants, who fupplied us with frefh
" provifions. On the 1ft of Auguft I failed
" from this harbour, and landed on the 3d
" at *Meako*, where the Japonefe became
" very intractable and infulted us. Hence,
" wifhing to feek the Philippine iflands, I
" continued my rout fouthwards, and coaft-
" ing for feveral days the other iflands, I
" went on fhore at *Ufma*, in the 27th degree
" 28 minutes of latitude, and 335 degrees
" of longitude.

" The natives of this ifland received us
" with great hofpitality, and I ftaid for fome
" days among them. They fupplied us
" plentifully with provifions, and after a
" mutual treaty, I fet fail to the ifland of
" *Formofa*. I reached it fortunately, and
" entered the harbour which lies eaftward,
" in the 23d degree 15 minutes of latitude,
" and 223 degrees of longitude. The inha-
" bitants attacked us, and three of my men
" were

" were killed.   Having however avenged
" their death, the winds being always con-
" trary, I was forced to fteer towards the
" continent of China, coafting along the
" little iflands called *Pifcatoria*; at laft all
" our frefh water beind exhaufted, we were
" forced to enter *Tanafoa*, arms in hand, to
" repulfe the Chinefe who would not fuffer
" us to fill our cafks.   I then bore away for
" *Macao*, a town belonging to her moft
" faithful Majefty, where I went on fhore
" September 22, 1771.   *Seignor Salema de*
" *Saldanha*, the governor, received me with
" great friendfhip and cordiality.   He grant-
" ed permiffion to all the fhip's company to
" come on fhore, and I ordered them to
" leave their arms on board, to remove all
" kind of miftruft.   In this town I was in-
" formed, that a treaty of friendfhip and al-
" liance was fubfifting between our auguft
" fovereigns, and wifhing to keep a fecret
" which concerned them, I begged leave to
" hoift the colours of his moft Chriftian
" Majefty, and my requeft was granted.—
                                   " What

" What could I fay farther to your Excel-
" lency, but what is well known to your
" people? Having left my fhip with M. *De*
" *Robieu*, Prefident of the Council, now in
" China, I embarked on the 17th of January
" 1772, with my people, on board fome
" merchantmen, in which I reached fafe
" and well the *Ifle de France*, where I have
" written this narrative. I therefore fup-
" plicate your Excellency, to order my
" fpeedy return to Europe.

" I fhall proclaim this friendly favour
" wherever I go, and preferving an everlaft-
" ing attachment, I have the honour to be

" Your Excellency's

" Moft obedient Servant,

" BARON MAURICE-AUGUSTUS
" ALADAR DE BENYOWSKY,

" *General of the firft Confederation.*"

Done at the Ifle of France,
March 21, 1772.

One

One cannot refift furprife, feeing that Benyowfky has neglected every thing that might have contributed to inftruct the navigator, refpecting the courfe from Kamfchatka to China, by way of Japan. It only required the firft elements of nautical fcience to mark the foundings and anchorage, to indicate the force and direction of the winds, to determine the variations of the compafs, to fix the refpective pofition of the rocks and principal capes. Finally to give, if not the longitude, at leaft the latitude of the principal points.

The logbook of the pilot charged with the care of watching the direction of the courfe of the fhip, ought to have given him fufficient inftruction.

A traveller of any fcholarfhip, or who is only animated with the defire of becoming ufeful, vifiting diftant climates, failing through paflages little frequented by European fhips, could never have neglected

P   particulars

particulars indifpenfible to the fafety and
improvement of navigation. Benyowfky,
however, boafted of his vaft knowledge, and
of having difcovered a new paffage from
Kamfchatka to *China.* The fubftance of his
voyage, which proves that he was ignorant
even of the moft common technical fea-
phrafes, leaves us no document, no certain
trace of the direction of his courfe.

This is not an equivocal accufation; I
appeal to thofe who have, as well as me,
feen him arrive from Canton at *Ifle de France.*
They will all certify, that with a view of
rendering the relation of his adventures the
more romantic, he publicly gave out, that
in a little veffel, ill-armed, ill-equipt, deftitute of provifions, or rather having no other
means of fubfiftance than fifh and flour, he
left, at his departure from Kamfchatka, the
coafts of Afia, and fteered towards thofe of
America. Moreover, that *intrepid* adventurer
was not afraid to repeat before the moft experienced feamen, that he had landed in unknown

known countries to the North of California.
This ftrange affertion was anfwered by a
thoufand objections. The diftreffed ftate of
his fhip rendered his narrative but little probable; befides, the fummary of the journal
which he had the imprudence to publifh,
made no mention of the countries fituated to
the North of California, and lefs ftill of their
productions. It was efpecially on this head,
that Benyowfky found himfelf extremly em-
barraffed. He could at leaft find no other
expedient to get rid of the importunate quef-
tions which were afked him on this fubject,
than by declaring, that he only referved to
the court the homage of his valuable difcoveries.

This evafive would not anfwer; they prefented to him the general map of the globe;
they requefted him to trace on it the line of
his voyage, affuring him that this ftep could
not compromife him. Benyowfky refufed
compliance. Monf Poivre, then Intendant
of the Ifles of France and Bourbon, was very

glad

glad thefe efforts were made in his prefence, to unmafk the impudent gafconades of that ftranger. This enlightened governor wifely avoided taking a direct part in the bufinefs, but he made ufe of this vigorous attack to infpire Monf. de Boyne, the minifter of the French Marine, with a falutary and juft diffidence in the pretended difcoveries of Be-nyowfky. If, as we fhall fee hereafter, his official letter has not been productive of the good effects which he expected, it would be highly unjuft to cenfure him on that fcore: howbeit, the mere narration of the romantic adventures made by Benyowfky, was fuf-ficient to undo in the public opinion, that man who was afraid of laying before a ge-nerous nation, a fhameful declaration, in which he owns himfelf guilty of an abomin-able crime. This ftranger, faid the people, has not loft his fenfes, and wants to perfuade us, that violence and rigour were made ufe of to deprive him of his innocence, and make him fign a deed which degrades, difgraces, and renders him odious and fufpected. Is

there

there in our language an expreffion ftrong enough to characterize the unheard of degree of impudence of a perfon unknown, who could thus permit himfelf to hand about an accufation ftill more opprobrious to himfelf, than injurious to his enemies? Is there a country on earth where the authentic, open avowal of a murder be the means of recovering one's liberty? What can be the end of that fcandalous confeffion? Is it not impoffible to fufpect its very motive?

I am, at this moment, but the faithful interpreter of the general fentiment of indignation, with which this improbable narrative infpired every enlightened citizen at *Ifle de France*. It throws a great light upon the moral character of our adventurer, who is not only condemned by his own writings, but rendered defpicable by grievances of a much more confequential nature.

Benyowfky, having efcaped from the prifons of Kamfchatka, fails to China with thirty

or

or forty fellow-prifoners. No fooner is he arrived at Canton, than he finds among the French, individuals who commiferate his misfortunes. This is matter of fact, and Benyowfky has never denied it; the merchants and officers of the Eaft-India Company granted confiderable fupplies to him and to thofe of whom he called himfelf the chief. The generous French made a ftill greater effort in his behalf, they invite, perfuade Captain *St. Hylaire* to take the chief, Benyowfky, and all his men on board his fhip, and to carry them to *Ifle de France*. Captain *St. Hylaire* being entrufted with a rich cargo belonging to different private individuals, made fome objections in the beginning; he hinted fome apprehenfions in granting hofpitality on board of his fhip to fo great a number of ftrangers, juft broke out from the prifons of Kamfchatka; yet the fentiment of compaffion furmounted in him every other confideration. No fooner had the captain fet fail, than his uneafinefs was revived with more power and reafon: they gave him occafion

cafion to repent his imprudent generofity.——
Thefe adventurers, at the time they embarked, had taken care to conceal their arms;
Captain St. Hylaire, apprifed of this infidious
cunning, was much grieved to fee himfelf
furrounded by men, perhaps more difpofed
to command him than he was to command
them. Thirty or forty goal-birds, armed
in a formidable manner, could well alarm
him about the fate of a cargo worth fome
millions. In a fituation fo delicate, fo difficult what fhall he do? Shall he make ufe of
his authority to difarm thofe ftrangers? confider his crew is weak, his fhip badly armed;
fhould he in this cafe have put at ftake the
fortune of his employers, rifked his life and
liberty with a fet of ftout, refolute, enter-
prizing fellows, who had all to gain and nothing to lofe? The flighteft pretence could
give birth to a quarrel, to an infurrection
which it was prudent to avoid. Captain St.
Hylaire, as a man of prudence, weighs, cal-
culates, forfees the danger, and refolves to
watch fecretly the ways and proceedings of

his

his paffengers. He does more, he feigns to fhow great honours, refpect and deference to Count Benyowfky. From that moment our adventurer gives himfelf all the airs of a great man, he drains every refource of the moft impudent juggling to make himfelf appear greater; and by the moft ridiculous bravadoes, he even dupes the companions of his mifery. He loudly proclaims himfelf their chief; his orders are rigoroufly execut-ed; henceforth he commands as mafter, and the people obey as flaves. He would fuffer no perfon to fpeak to him but a nobleman.

Thefe honours fo adroitly conferred on Benyowfky, by flattering his pride, reftored order and calm in the fhip. Subordination fo neceffary to the fafety of the navigator, was no longer troubled by thofe dangerous men. Finally, after a fhort and fortunate paffage, they were landed at *Ifle de France.* Benyowfky, furrounded by a numerous fuite, waited on the governor of the colony. Their appearance of wretched prifoners, was fuddenly

denly changed into a proceffion of parade,
confifting of a General, decorated with feveral ribbons, followed by a brilliant ftaff of
officers, whofe rich uniforms announced
their bearing high commiffions. What an
aftonifhing metamorphofis! or rather what
a ridiculous farce! Had I not been a fpectator, I fhould be afraid of giving this account. As foon as the real hiftory of thefe
adventurers was known at *Ifle de France,*
the general and his fplendid retinue, became
the objects of derifion of all the fenfible
people of the colony. Enthufiafm is not
the attribute of feamen; it requires cool
blood to mafter the elements, and inftruction
to conduct from one extremity to the other,
thofe floating citadels which fecure and protect the commerce of civilized nations: the
life of feamen, the fafety of a fquadron of
fhips, is not to be committed to the charge
of men too fufceptible of elevation, or to
delirious heads, of a vivid or diforderly caft
of mind; that clafs of men who feek after
and admire what is fabulous and romantic,

5

is only common among indolent and frivolous nations, and in great cities, where its
fatal influence is productive of more irregu-
larity than that of impostors. Those en-
thusiastic men are rare in the colonies where
they always are without credit, without authority.

Benyowsky felt all the bitterness of the
truth of this assertion; he saw at the same
time how much it behoved him to quit
speedily a country where his adventures and
voyages made no sensation, and excited no
enthusiasm : the more he prolonged his stay,
the less consideration was shewn him. At his
departure for old France, he dropped the name
of Baron Aladar, and took that of Count
Beryowsky; but it really deserves notice, that
at that epoch, he gave out publicly, that he
was a going to solicit the Government General of Madagascar at the court of Versailles.
This fresh gasconade afforded a great deal of
diversion, and caused not the smallest alarm.
It

It required fomething more that human forefight to fear, left a hope, fo chimerical in
appearance, fhould one day be realized: I
dare confequently affure the reader, that no
expreffion is ftrong enough to reprefent the
univerfal fentiment of furprife and perplexity
which agitated every mind, when the news
arrived, that Benyowfky had been appointed
to the important place of Governor General
of Madagafcar. I am quite ignorant of the
means of feduction tried by this adventurer
to gain his end; but when Monf. Poivre
gave me this information, he added " We
" have feen fwarms of locufts devouring in
" an inftant abundant harvefts; we have
" feen two terrible hurricanes threaten this
" ifland with total fubverfion; Madagafcar
" always ferved to compenfave the mifchief
" done by thofe awful fcourges : henceforth
" the *Ifle de France* has loft all refources, it
" muft fall and perifh, if fimilar fcourges
" fhould again happen to fpread difolation
" over thefe fields. Under the government
" of

" of Benyowſky, Madagaſcar will no more " be the ſupport of this ſettlement; in our " future misfortunes we muſt only hope for " precarious and diſtant relief. I was much " habituated to the ſuccefs of cheats and " adventurers, but the ſuccefs of Benyow- " ſky overwhelms me with confuſion, the " more ſo, as I have written a letter on his " account to the miniſter. I well know " that oddities are pleaſing, that they amuſe " the multitude and raiſe their credulity " to the higheſt pitch of excefs; but how " could I imagine that a ſtranger juſt broke " loſe from chains and priſons at Kam- " ſchatka, and ſunk into contempt by his " own writings, ſhould obtain an important " charge without my approbation? Strongly " attached, in virtue of my office, to the " welfare of this colony, I ought, the firſt " time he ſpoke to me about Madagaſcar, " to have excited in him a deſire of dethron- " ing the Mogul; his requeſt would un- " doubtedly have been complied with, and " we ſhould thus have got rid of him."

Benyowſky

Benyowſky was permitted to raiſe a company of volunteers; he wiſhed his troop to be cloathed and accoutred in ſuch a manner as to ſpread terror and conſternation among the Malegaſhes. He proved by this how little he knew about the character and diſpoſition of this people. He choſe the bay of Antongil as the chief place of his reſidence, but from the beginning of October to the beginning of May, peſtilential fevers ravage and deſolate that diſtrict. No doubt the murderous vapours which riſe from the marſhes and woods, are the real cauſe of this fatal epidemical ſcourge: the inflammable air, and the putrid particles which riſe copiouſly from the ſtagnant waters corrupted by the decayed parts of vegetation, change, during calms and great heats, the goodneſs of the atmoſpheric air. In that ſeaſon, the air is rarely refreſhed by quick ſea-breezes, and the Northern winds carry thoſe exhalations along the coaſt, and their pernicious effects are completed by calms and a conſtant drought. The natives know but little how

to

to preferve themfelves from this danger; by remaining in their hovels amidft a thick fmoke, the moft robuft, and the moft fober of them frequently fall victims to the violence of the diftemper; it is therefore no wonder that the Europeans, forced to pafs the winter on this coaft, perifh by a contagion which even cuts off thofe who are the moft accuftomed to the climate.

I have feen the entire deftruction of a fmall French fettlement at the clofe of the year 1768, notwithftanding the prompteft and moft extenfive medical aid, not one of thofe unfortunate men efcaped with his life. Every foul of them, ftrong and weak, perifhed in a very fhort time. If we were witnefs to that dreadful contagion, without fharing the fame fate, it was owing to the maritime and falubrious air which furrounded our fhip, and corrected, to a certain point, the fatal effects of the putrid exhalations. Moreover, when the firft fymptoms of the diforder appeared at *Foule Pointe*, all communication
with

with the land that was not indifpenfible, was rigoroufly prohibited. The crew were not permitted to trade with the iflanders, or to let their canoes come along-fide of our fhip; without this precaution, the malady would have broke in upon us: no remedy known could have checked its fatal progrefs. Thofe who come under this latitude, ought not to flight thefe obfervations, the truth of which is confirmed by thoufands of examples. In a word, one muft either perifh, or fly from thofe unwholefome parts as foon as the contagion manifefts itfelf. No fpot in the North of Madagafcar is free from the putrid and epidemical fever. The cruel diforders are not equally fatal every year, their violence and duration feem to depend more particularly on the direction of the wind. When it blows North for any length of time, the fcourge has reached the higheft pitch of fatality. Few are thofe men that are ftrong and robuft enough to refift the influence of that dangerous wind, which is only known

to blow in this latitude from the latter end
of October till the month of May.

Benyowſky's ideas and documents, with
regard to the degree of healthineſs of Madagaſcar, muſt certainly have been very imperfect : meantime it may be preſumed,
that the unhealthineſs of that iſland was not
quite unknown to him, ſince he had reſided
for ſome time at *Iſle de France*, and we have
ſeen that it was at that very epoch he conceived the project of ſoliciting the government of Madagaſcar. But that man, accuſ-
tomed to brave all kinds of danger, could not
think this a competent obſtacle to prevent
the ſucceſs of a permanent ſettlement.

However, Benyowſky arrived in the bay
of Antongil, with a military eſtabliſhment,
calculated to terrify the natives. The ſol-
diers of his legion wore ſabres of an enormous ſize, their girdles were trimmed with
piſtols, and it ſeemed as if their arms, caps,
and uniforms had been purpoſely invented,

to

to frighten the poor favages out of their wits. The moment he landed, he took pof-feffion of the ifland in a moft fole n manner: he caufed himfelf to be acknowledged Go-vernor General; he then drew up plans for feveral forts or ftrong-holds, and refolved to render himfelf formidable to the Malegafhes and to conquer and fubdue them. Juftice was neither the bafis of his project, nor the knowledge of locality his guide. Soon be-came he the detefted tyrant of thefe regions, made war upon the natives, and exercifed all kind of cruelties over them. The terrified favages retired to the innermoft receffes of the country, all commerce was at an end; Benyowfky was forfaken, and all over the ifland they called him the bad White.

It was certainly an eafy matter to forefee that the fettlement of Benyowfky would prove unfuccefsful. The bare relation of thefe facts muft inflict the fevereft cenfure on the imprudent confidence repofed in that adventurer. Let us now hear an officer of

Q the

the higheſt diſtinction, whoſe name I ſhall forbear to mention here. This officer had accompanied Meſſrs. Belcombe and Chevreau, who were ſent out to inſpect the ſettlements of Benyowſky at Madagaſcar.

" I arrived (ſays this officer) at Foule Pointe on the 17th of September 1776. The population of the villages adjacent to the harbour was reduced to one half of the former number; bloody wars had diſolated the whole country : the crops had been deſtroyed, and agriculture was given up to ſuch a degree, that we could ſcarcely obtain three hundred pounds of rice. The want of all other proviſions was equally great and diſtreſſing. My ſurprize could hardly be deſcribed. I had been in the ſame place three years before; trade and agriculture were then flouriſhing, and the markets afforded plenty of every thing; ten large ſhips received a complete cargo of rice, yet this immenſe quantity of an article of the firſt neceſſity made not the ſmalleſt change in its price

price or value. Thefe fhips all failed to Ifle de France, which three fucceffive hurricanes had plunged in the greateft diftrefs. All the crops were loft; a dreadful famine menaced the whole colony; they felt its precurfory calamities, when the fudden arrival of the ten fhips loaded with rice, refcued the inhabitants from mifery and defpair. If in this circumftance, like in many others, Foule Pointe has faved Ifle de France, thefe hopes had now completely vanifhed. The fields laid fallow, all commerce was at an end. The defpotifm of Benyowfky had fpread terror and alarm throughout the ifland.— The natives fled the coaft in confternation, and fought refuge in the heart of the country.

" Monf. Belcombe convened Yavi, the fovereign of Foule Pointe, and feveral neighbouring chiefs; he afked them if they had any complaints to make againft the French, and above all againft the fifteen foldiers of the legion of Benyowfky, who guarded the

harbour

harbour of Foule Pointe. Their anfwer was
not frank, they were doubtlefs afraid, left
their complaint fhould become a pretence for
frefh perfecutions. They confined themfelves to demand freedom of commerce.
Monf. de Belcombe affured Yavi and the
other chiefs, that the French foldiers were
only at Madagafcar to prevent and fecure the
liberty of the natives ; he exhorted them to
cultivate their fields, and to live in peace with
their neighbours. Monf. de Belcombe, previous to his departure to the bay of Antongil,
gave the ftricteft orders to the commanding
officer to keep up difcipline among his men,
and to put fpeedily an end to the fears and
alarms of the natives.

" Since the great object of the miffion of
Monf. de Belcombe concerned the fettlement
of Benyowfky at the bay of Antongil, he
repaired thither, and had himfelf acknowledged Infpector of the French fettlements at
Madagafcar at the head of the troops.

" I followed

" I followed Monf. de Belcombe, being ordered by the Governor of Ifle de France to take cognizance of all the particulars of their infpection.

" The audacity of Benyowfky aftonifhed me to a degree paft expreffion. He firft received Monf. de Belcombe with haughtinefs, and I may fay with impudence.

" That gentleman feemed fatisfied with the military pofition of the place chofen by Benyowfky for his principal fettlement, to which he gave the name of *Louifbourg*. But if the place is eafily to be fortified, there can be none more humid and unwholefome.

" Louifbourg is fituated on a kind of cape, which projects into the fea, to the diftance of three hundred fathoms, the ground on which the houfes and magazines are erected, rife hardly four feet above the level of the waters when the tide is ftrong. It acquired this elevation by heaping one load of rubbifh

Q 3   upon

upon another. All the land adjacent forms a marſh covered by the high water; the fort, which commands and covers Louiſbourg, conſiſts of three baſtions, each of them bearing one piece of artillery. It is built of wooden ſtakes. I dare ſay, that by this time, the ſtore-houſes, the fort and all the dwellings require to be built afreſh, the timber and wood-work being in a quite rotten condition. The cape on which Louiſbourg is erected, joins on one ſide port *Choiſeul.* This harbour is ſpacious, and will hold ſe＋veral large ſhips. A fine large river called *Linguebat* completely gives this cape the form of a peninſula. The river Linguebat has one hundred and eighty fathoms in breadth, near its mouth; it is navigable, I traced its courſe in my boat to the diſtance of ſeven leagues. At that diſtance it is ſtill one hundred and fifty fathoms broad. On the banks of this river, Benyowſky erected ſeveral forts, the moſt conſiderable of which is like that which defends Louiſbourg. In tracing the courſe of this river, I beheld with

with rapture thofe romantic fields, the view of which prefents a moft interefting fpectacle.

" Finally, I arrived with Meffrs. Belcombe and Chevreau on a fpot, which Benyowfky called the *Plain of Health*. We had vifited from Louifbourg to this place feveral fmall forts and fifteen villages. Benyowfky fpoke to us in the higheft praife, of the happy locality of this fpot truly rural, but we found it did not deferve its name. The Plain of Health appeared to us an unwholefome place, encompaffed by mountains, whofe great elevation ftops the clouds, and condenfates them into rain. Monf. de Belcombe pointed out to Benyowfky the difadvantages of its fituation, and however ftriking they were, Benyowfky fcorned to own himfelf convinced. In vain did they fhow him the different inlets of the mountains, the defiles of which could not poffibly be guarded, he obftinately affirmed, that it would be more difficult to attack that place

than

than Louifbourg. He maintained in the
ftrongeft terms, that a little battery, which
he called fort Auguftus, fituated on the fummit of a hill, in the centre of the Plain of
Health, defended his fettlement in fuch a
manner as to difcard all enemies, however
numerous and formidable. I afcended this
fine fortrefs by a bad ftaircafe of one hundred
and fifty fteps. It confifts of a fquare of
eight fathoms, furrounded with a pallifade
entirely rotten and decayed; four three
pounders were the dreadful artillery which,
from one fide, was to protect the navigation
of the Linguebat, and from the other, to command refpect for the great fettlement which he
propofed to make at the foot of the fort; a
fettlement which he had already named the
Town of the Plain of Health.

" This town confifted ther of a magazine
fifty feet to thirty, and of two other houfes
of a fmaller fize; the one defigned for an
hofpital, and the other for the foldiers bar-
racks. Monf. de Belcombe afked Benyowfky
if

if he had nothing elſe to ſhow him. Benyowſky, without being in the leaſt concerted,
anſwered : my forts command the navigation
of the important river Linguebat; the free
courſe of that river makes me abſolute maſter
of the adjacent diſtricts. Is not this a very
great ſervice rendered to France ? Could any
thing better have been wiſhed for, with the
funds and forces which were at my diſpoſal ?
Could any other man in my place have done
more ? Could he have done ſo much ? Monſ.
de Belcombe anſwered ſmiling; My Lord
Governor, you have informed the Miniſter of
the Marine, that you had laid the foundation
of a conſiderable town in this place, which
you have called the *Plain of Health.* Where
is that town ? What is become of it ? Has
it diſappeared ?—I can ſee but a few wretched hovels.

" The reply which Benyowſky made to
this puzzling queſtion was, that he had been
in want of caſh. My citadel, added he, coſt
more than I thought it would; the firſt object

ject of my attention was the safety of the
town, of which I am going to shew you the
plan. This project is no chimera; it shall
be executed as soon as I shall have money
sufficient for that purpose.

" Your citadel, answered Monf. de Belcombe, is a paltry little battery, commanded
on all sides by lofty mountains, which sur-
round it; this battery of four three-pounders
planted on the summit of a hill, will never
answer the object you proposed. In other
respects, I am come from France, by order
of the Minister, to inspect your works, and
I cannot help telling you my mind; permit
me to ask you another question not less interesting : where is your higway from Louis-
bourg to Bombetoque? Pray put it in my
power to make a proper report to the Minister. You have given him the fullest particulars of its advantages; you have demon-
strated in your memorial, that this communication of the Eastern with the Western
coast ought to make you reign, as it were,
over

over the coaft of Africa, becaufe the port
of Bombetoque is only parted from it
by the breadth of the canal of Mozam‑
bique. Thofe wild diftricts, interfected
with high mountains, forefts, rivers, were
no obftacle to your project; this is what
furprifes, what aftonifhes me.

" That road is traced, anfwered Beny‑
owfky, and no perfon will difpute with me
on that head. I will fhew you the itinerary
and the direction to be followed to crofs that
ridge of mountains which feparates the
Eaftern from the Weftern coaft; you leave
the high mountain of Vigagora to the South,
and follow, excepting a few bye-ways, the
road frequented by the natives when they go
from the coaft of Bombetoque to the bay of
Antongil. Some works are, doubtlefs, re‑
quired to make that road more practicable,
the prefent feafon of the year, and what is
worfe ftill, the fituation I am in with regard
to the natives, will not permit me at this
moment, to occupy myfelf with thofe works;
but

but if you will take that road, I will accompany you, and you will be able to judge by yourfelf, of the little difficulty I fhall find in removing its obftacles.

" Monf. de Belcombe had neither time nor defire of making fo long and difficult a journey, by traverfing the ifland of Madagafcar; he was pretty confident that Benyowfky would not have ftarted fuch a propofal without being fure of its being declined. Monf. de Belcombe thought it proper to fignify to him, that the objeƈt of his miffion was to infpeƈt the works completed, and not thofe projeƈted. Paffing immediately to another queftion, he afked him why he had left off fending rice and bullocks to Ifle de France. The wars I was obliged to fuftain againft the natives, anfwered Benyowfky, have deprived me, and ftill deprive me of provifions of the firft neceffity. How could I in fuch a fitua-tion, fend provifions to Ifle de France? You muft be fenfible of the impoffibility. I find it likewife an eafy tafk to juftify the

wars

wars I have carried on.   I convene a Palabra,
I make advantageous propofals to the natives;
they not only reject them, but infolent
chiefs dare to threaten me: they go farther,
the fignal is given to put me to death—feveral mufkets are fired upon me.   I efcape,
miraculoufly as it were, from this imminent
danger, gallantly fupported by my foldiers,
I difperfe the rabble, and frighten them by
the fire of the artillery from the fort.   I
demanded openly the heads of thofe chiefs
who had dared to make an attempt upon my
life, in the middle of a folemn affembly.—
I call the Sambarives who inhabit the banks
of the river Manahar to my affiftance; five
hundred of their warriors come and range
themfelves under my colours, they help me
to punifh and fubdue my dangerous neighbours.   Forced to fue for peace, the conditions of the treaty have been folemnly refolved on and fanctioned in a great *palabra*.
The ufual ceremonies have been obferved;
I rewarded the Sambarives and difmiffed
them; I promifed them protection and fup-

port againſt all the enterprizes of their enemies; I exhorted them to cultivate their
fields, and to compenſate by ſo doing the ills
occaſioned by our diſſentions; theſe ills are
great; the country lies waſte; moſt of the
villages only exhibit to ſight a heap of aſhes;
the fields have ever ſince lain fallow, and
famine was the neceſſary conſequence of all
theſe troubles. But calm and tranquility are
now on the point of being revived; the natives, more fearful than ſubmiſſive, will
apply themſelves again to agriculture; they
will make amends for the misfortunes which
they brought upon themſelves by an atroci-
ous conſpiracy againſt a man that knows
how to make himſelf feared and reſpected.
The power veſted in me ſhall never ſhake in
my hands, it ſhall never be compromiſed, I
will enforce obedience, every man of a military ſpirit will approve of my conduct, and
adopt my principles; the Whites ought
never to confide too much in the good nature
of the Blacks; they ſhould not even con-
deſcend to court it; I am a foreigner, and
this

this is a reafon which induces me the more
to make the French flag refpected. My adminiftration will give it that preponderance
which it loft through the weaknefs of my
predeceffors. This was the fenfe of the
fpeech of Benyowfky. He added to it a
thoufand invectives againft the iflanders, and
painted their character in the blackeft and
moft odious colours.

" We judged that an abfolute want of provifions was the fole motive which had determined him to make peace. The hatred and
refentment of this vindictive man, yielded
only to the moft urgent and compulfory circumftances. Monf. de Belcombe was highly
alarmed at it, and took pains to infpire
Benyowfky with fentiments more juft, more
humane; and though he was convinced of
the inutility of his efforts to render the peace
more lafting, yet he wifhed at his return to
Louifbourg, to make a new treaty, to convince the inhabitants of Madagafcar of his
truly pacific fentiments.

" Benyowfky

" Benyowſky combated ſtrongly the project of Monſ. de Belcombe. He alledged, that
the holding of a new palabra would be a
very inconvenient meaſure. All, however,
he could either ſay or do, was in vain. The
palabra met on the ſecond of October 1776;
it was not numerous, and only attended by
ſix chiefs and one hundred and fifty iſlanders.
Monſ. de Belcombe renewed the treaty of
peace, exhorted them to apply themſelves to
huſbandry, and to avoid every ſubject of
diſſention. The natives ſeemed quite mo-
tionleſs, and inſenſible of all profeſſions of
friendſhip and aſſurances of benevolence.—
Benyowſky ſeemed much diſſatisfied at this
ſilent diſapprobation of his conduct. Before
we left Madagaſcar, I entered upon a diſ-
courſe with Benyowſky, about the ſmall
advantages France could derive from her
ſettlement at the bay of Antongil. You are
right, ſaid Benyowſky, but a leſſon of two
millions is not too dear to teach your nation
that they ought to have given me a marine,
and two millions a year to ſpend; then
                                        ſending

fending me fix hundred recruits every fix years, I would have made it a flourifhing, formidable colony in the courfe of twenty years. I told him the country was fo very unwholefome, that five men perifhed out of fix. He anfwered, that confiderable clearings of the ground, in due feafon, would keep thofe diftempers at bay. All my arguments being thus obftinately contradicted, I finally left Benyowfky, aftonifhed at the degree of confidence granted to the projects of that adventurer.

" Arrived at Ifle de France, we found that colony begin to be diftreffed for want of provifions. The refources from Madagafcar were entirely cut off The government of the ifland was obliged to fend fhips to the Cape of Good Hope, and heavy complaints poured in from all quarters, to open the eyes of minifters refpecting the mifconduct of Benyowfky.

R   Monf.

" *Monf. de Belcombe* being arrived at Paris, made a faithful report refpecting the adminiftration of Benyowfky, who was recalled, and found means of an apparent juftification. His commiffion, however, was withdrawn from him, and the celebrated *Dr. Franklin* unfortunately took our juftly difgraced adventurer under his protection. Benyowfky is fent to America, and from the moment of his arrival, conceives again the project of rendering himfelf mafter of Madagafcar. His project is put in execution, he reaches the bay of Antongil, in an American fhip. I know nothing of the tendency of this expedition, but I know that Monf. de Souillac, governor of Ifle de France, fent, on the 9th of May 1786, the Louifa frigate, commanded by Vifcount *La Croix*, to refift the enterprize of Benyowfky. A detachment of fixty men of the regiment of Pondicherry, under the command of Captain Larcher, received orders to take their departure in the fame fhip.

The

The *Louisa* cast anchor at Foule Pointe, on the 17th of the same month. There intelligence was received, that Benyowsky had seized a magazine belonging to the king, at Angoncy, a village situate to the North of the bay of Antongil.

As soon as Viscount *La Croix* had taken in the necessary provisions at Foule Pointe, he left that harbour and set sail to Angoncy, where he arrived on the 23d of the same month. Captain Larcher made immediately preparations to land his men, several well-armed sloops, bearing two pieces of cannon, made towards a flat shore, where no obstacle seemed to oppose his landing; but at the moment of disembarkation, a discharge of musketry on the part of the troops of Benyowsky, discarded every doubt of the hostile intentions of that adventurer. The French fired off their cannons, which soon dispersed the enemy who fought shelter in the woods. From that instant the Captain made good his landing without the least obstruction.—

Mr.

Mr. Larcher, at the head of his men, marched ſtraight to the ſettlement of Benyowſky.
The natives who became his guide, led him
on an open road, which would have cauſed
invincible obſtacles, had it been well guarded and defended.

He was obliged to wade through five
marſhes and to paſs over an old bridge,
ninety feet long, before he reached the ſettlement of Benyowſky. It may be eaſily
imagined, that the Captain would not have
taken that road, had he known how dangerous it was to paſs it. Having croſſed the
bridge with his artillery, Monſ. Larcher heard
the diſtant noiſe of ſome workmen. Shortly
after the van-guard diſcovered a red flag, the
uſual ſignal of battle. Monſ Larcher immediately ranged his corps in battle array,
and continued his march towards the ſettlement. He deſcried fifty dwellings built in
a regular line, one of which was more ſpa
cious and elevated than the reſt. He took it
to be the houſe of Benyowſky: the fort
                                    could

could not then be perceived, being concealed from fight by a grove. As foon as they defcried the fort, they faw about an hundred men making a precipitate retreat to it.

This fort, fituated on a hill furrounded with a ftrong pallifade, was defended by two four-pounders and fome fmaller pieces of artillery. Benyowfky began to fire upon the French, when he faw them at the diftance of fix hundred yards. The firft cannon fired was loaded with balls, the fecond with old iron, and the third with balls. Thefe difcharges were fupported by a brifk fire of mufketry. The detachment of the regiment of Pondi-cherry advanced in good order, and when they had reached a convenient diftance, the captain ordered them to fire upon Beny-owfky. This firft and only difcharge proved decifive. Benyowfky fell by a cannon-ball which paffed through his heart, the very moment he was going to fire off a cannon charged with old iron. Very fortunately the priming did not catch, which would

R 3 otherwife

otherwife have made great havoc among the French. Their pofition forced them either to conquer or die; they were bereft of all means of fupport, all communication was cut off in fuch a manner, as fruftrated the poffibility of hoping to effect a retreat to their fhip. Immediately after the death of Benyowfky, the fort furrendered at difcretion The greateft part of the natives made their efcape over the pallifades. All meafures of purfuing them were avoided, and Monf. Larcher having fulfilled the object of his miffion, treated the inhabitants with the greateft humanity, agreeable to the orders he had received. Several of the natives followed the examples of the Whites, threw down their arms, and furrendered themfelves prifoners of war. They were inftantly fet at full liberty. Thefe generous proceedings induced the chief of Angoncy to come to demand peace, and to put himfelf under the protection of the French. He prefented to the Captain an old Portuguefe woman and the Baronefs of *Adefchein*, the widow of a

German

German officer, who had followed Benyowfky to Madagafcar. Thefe two women had
fought refuge near the chief, and it was only
at their urgent intreaty, he delivered them
to the French. This chief made the moft
bitter complaints about the tyranny of Benyowfky ; he added, that that adventurer
governed thofe fertile countries with an iron
fceptre, and took by violence, and deftroyed
by fear the fruits of native induftry. He
levied continual contributions, in addition to
the taxes with which he chofe to overwhelm
them. That hateful defpot infringed, in a
moft outrageous manner, the moft refpected
cuftoms and ufages. He rejected with
haughty difdain the juft remonftrances of the
natives. Treating them as flaves, he even
ftrove to deprive them of the hope of ever
regaining their liberty. They were fubject
to all his whims: his unalterable temerity,
his ftratagems, and more ftill, the natural
impetuofity of his temper, had made him
the abfolute mafter of Madagafcar. He had
made every preparation to expel the French

from

from that ifland, and to turn even their generofity and beneficence againft them.

The Malegafhes, exhaufted by inteftine
wars, loft, during the adminiftration of
Benyowfky, almoft all their good qualities;
they were nothing but mean flaves, devoted
to the caprices of a ferocious and intractable
mafter

OBSER-

OBSERVATIONS

ON THE

Northern Part of Madagascar.

THE Northern part of Madagascar is infinitely more fertile in all kinds of provisions than the Southern. For this reason it is much more frequented by European ships; the interior parts of this district have scarce ever been visited, and all the instructions I could gather or collect could not enable me to describe it. The road by which the natives go from Bombetoque to the bay of Antongil, is only remarkable for the numberless obstacles it presents. If the natives surmount them, it is only because they are more trained and inured to fatigue than the greatest part of Europeans. The high mountains of *Vigagora*, over which the traveller must pass, present at every step, obstacles capable to

stop

ſtop men the moſt habituated to brave all kinds of danger. A Perſon that ſhould be obliged to take that difficult road, would do well to provide himſelf with ropes and ſtakes to paſs the ſteepeſt places. I know by experience the utility of ſimilar precautions, and tried them many a time with ſucceſs in travelling through mountains. When I was ſurrounded by precipices, a ſimple ſtrong piece of packthread, held by my guides, facilitated to me the acceſs to the ſteepeſt places. Silken cords are far preferable to hempen ones, becauſe they are ſtronger and lighter. In the fording of rivers, the current of which is rapid, perſons who cannot ſwim may, by means of large bamboos tied to a long rope, croſs the moſt rapid rivers, if they have able and vigorous guides who are good ſwimmers, to drag them from one bank to the other. With prudence and induſtry a man may ſurmount the greateſt obſtacles.

In

In forefts and woods the compafs is his guide, everywhere elfe, the mechanic arts furnifh him with means to extricate himfelf from the greateft dangers and the moft diffi-cult pofitions. Thofe means vary according to circumftances. We fhall, without enter-ing here upon further details, confine our-felves to obferve, that a kind of hammoc, ufed in the colonies to convey women and children, would be of infinite fervice to thofe who travel in favage and wild regions. But this hamock ought to be light and im-penetrable to water. Thefe two conditions may be eafily fulfilled, in making ufe of a ftrong kind of facking varnifhed over with gum elaftic, diffolved in linfeed oil. It is this varnifh which keeps the inflammable gaz in air-balloons. Thus fuch a hammoc will not only anfwer the purpofe of a bed being tied to a tree, but it may likewife be ufed by means of a bamboo, to have one's felf carried from one place to another, in cafe of indifpofition, and fince the facking becomes impenetrable on account of the varnifh, the

hammoc

hammoc anfwers the purpofe of a real canoe, the advantages of which are too obvious to the intelligent reader, for me to demonftrate any farther, its convenience and utility.

In the Northern part of Madagafcar, Foule Pointe, called by the natives *Voolou-voolou*, is the place moft frequented by the Europeans.

The entrance of the port lies in a Northern direction : the breadth of the paffage is about fifty fathoms, the depth of the bafon mea-fures likewife near fifty fathoms ; it will hold ten large fhips, which may be moored all in a line. The riding is very fafe, but between the months of October and June, the entrance is fometimes obftructed and fhut by a bank of quickfand, which difappears as foon as the fouth-eaft winds fucceed the northern gales and calms. The fea only marls four or five feet in time of the greateft tides, when the coral rocks, which form the harbour, and run north-north-eaft are un-covered.

covered. We find upon them fea plants, moffes, black corals, madrepores of value, ftar-wort, fea-infects and fhells, which, by the multiplicity of their form, and the brilliancy of their colours, ferve to decorate the cabinets of the curious. The mouth of the river offers large beds of the moft delicate and palatable oyfters, which form themfelves in bunches of the moft fingular and peculiar configuration : at a fmall diftance from the fpots which are covered by the fea, one finds veins of a fand quite different from that of the flats, and which feems to be half vitrified. This fand is mixed with half broken and triturable ftones, ftrewed with an infinite number of little fragments of natural glafs. The obfervations I have taken at Foule Pointe, give me feventeen degrees forty minutes twenty feconds for its latitude, and forty-feven degrees twenty feconds for its longitude. During my refidence, the thermometer rofe only to the twenty-feventh degree of the divifion of *Reaumur*, and never defcended lower than the fifteenth. The barometer

had

had but a very few variations, and was always between twenty-eight inches two lines, and twenty-eight inches five lines.

The ships take in all sorts of provisions at Foule Pointe, which are equally plentiful and abundant; the markets are well stocked, if the Europeans do not cause any hindrance or constraint. These few years back, the natives have refused to sell pigs and kids. An old man, who lives at the distance of four leagues from the harbour, and who bears the reputation of an able magician, has forbidden them to deal in those useful animals. This Ombiass made them believe, that they would bring upon themselves the greatest misfortunes, if they did not endeavour to destroy the whole race of those impure creatures; this decree however does not prevent the Europeans from catching them in the mountains, where they are found in herds together. The villages inhabited by the tribe of *Voolou-Voolou* are not very considerable. They are fortified with pallisades,

and

and moſt of them erected upon the declivity of hills. A vaſt number of uſeful trees ſpread over them a delightful ſhade. Amidſt the cocoa-trees, the bamboos, wild vines, lemons, oranges and bananas, the fruit of which latter is ſo much ſought after by the Europeans; you likewiſe diſtinguiſh the *Raven*, a kind of palm-tree, only known at Madagaſcar.

This tree riſes to an amazing height; its ſtem is prepared and eaten like the palm-cabbage, its bark is hard, its filandrous and incorruptible wood, ſerves as timber for the dwellings, whoſe partitions and floors conſiſt of the ribs of the leaves, tied and joined together with great ſkill and art; thoſe ribs are as ſolid as wood and as flexible as leather. The leaf ſerves to cover thoſe huts, and laſts longer and is preferable to our roofs thatched with ſtraw or ſtubble.

It is likewiſe of the leaf of *Raven* the Malegaſhes make their diſhes, plates and cups.

Beneath

Beneath the membranaceous cover of the bloom of this palm-tree, we find a gum of a moſt exquiſite taſte, and almoſt as ſweet as honey.

It is not to be wondered that the natives are fond of ſeeing themſelves ſurrounded with a tree which is ſo uſeful to them. It yields very good planks or boards, when ſplit in all its length; the moment after the planks are cut, they ought to be made ſtraight.

The diſtrict of *Voolou-Voolou* contains excellent paſture grounds and a great deal of cattle. In tracing the fertile banks of the fine river Onglebey, one is ſurpriſed at ſeeing that river ſuddenly diſappear, and loſe itſelf in the ſands at the diſtance of four hundred fathoms from its mouth. This fiſhy river, ſwarming with birds of the aquatic kind, is very deep in ſome parts, in others very broad. The canoes row up to a diſtance of more than twenty leagues. It is a pity that

that this, like all other rivers of Madagafcar, is full of monftrous crocodiles. If one goes along the banks, their fight ftrikes with terror even the moft intrepid inhabitant; it requires great precaution to guard one's felf againft being furprifed by thofe amphibious monfters, which rufh both upon men and beafts. I faw a bullock dragged away and devoured by one of them.

The fame thing which makes the delight of the rivers of Madagafcar, conftitutes alfo their danger. The trees which cover the banks, afford a retreat and an afylum to thofe lurking and formidable animals. Leaving at the diftance of fome leagues the harbour of *Foule Pointe*, or *Voolou-voolou*, and advancing towards the lofty mountains of *Ambotifmena*, the profpect of the country changes. The hills fcreen the plains and valleys from the winds and hurricanes. The heat becomes lefs troublefome, becaufe the country is elevated and more covered with wood: the fields lefs cultivated, prefent a

S   wilder

wilder and more rural landfcape to the eye. Here the natives do not guard their herds and flocks, and let them err without guide and without reftraint.

The meadows are at the bottom of the valleys. A multitude of brooks and rivulets take their meandrous courfe through them, and convey the more rapture to the enchanted wanderer, fince they are the moft romantic picture of fimple nature. The enamel of the flowers has more luftre, their colours are more lively and variegated than our plains. Groves of trees, planted without art, without fymetry, render the fpectacle more and more pleafant and interfting. At the diftance of a few leagues farther, the landfcape varies again, and becomes more mountainous.— The ableft painter would find himfelf at a lofs how to fix his choice upon the moft picturefque landfcape; his ftraying, irrefolute fancy would no longer fuffer him the free exercife of his talents, and at every other ftep he would find a fudden, an unforefeen

change

change of perfpective. But if the traveller's attention is not wholly bent upon feizing the *tout enfemble* of thefe paradifiacal regions, and he applies himfelf to ftudy its feparate productions, then an immenfe and truly ufeful career will open before him; an infinite crowd of plants, fcattered profufely, will invite him to make his obfervations and enquiries.

He will diftinguifh fix different claffes of rice; he will fee barley of fuperlative beauty; he will find ten different claffes of *ignamas*, or *yams*, as big as the thigh of a man, which afford excellent food both to men and beafts. But befides thefe roots, which require fome care and cultivation, there are alfo fome of a quite wild or favage kind, which the natives call *fanghits*. The *fanghit* is of the fize and bignefs of a man; it is a moft palatable root, and has a reddifh bark. This admirable root ftills at once hunger, and quenches thirft; it is diuretic and very digeftive.

This

This part of the iſland produces likewiſe, four ſorts of turneps, beſides beans and peas, very recreative to the palate.

The *varvatts* reſemble the caper-tree, and bear the ſame bloſſom. Each huſk contains a little pea as big as a lentil. This leguminous plant riſes to the height of the cherry-tree, and in ſome of the interior diſtricts, its leaves ſerve as food for the ſilk-worms.

If the traveller quits the fields and meadows, to enter thoſe immenſe foreſts, which make the retreat of a vaſt number of wild beaſts, beauties of a different kind delight his imagination. A profound ſolitude, a coolneſs ſurprizing in this burning climate, a ſhade inacceſſible to the beams of the ſun ; echoes reſounding from all ſides, with the lowing and bellowing of the cattle, give him freſh enjoyments ; but enjoyments of this nature, he will always behold with a kind of enthuſiaſm, thoſe numberleſs trees of prodigious ſize and loftineſs, among which, one called *Foſterbee,*

Fofterbee, will attract his notice in a peculiar manner.

Thofe who prefer mineralogy to botany, will find in the high mountains of *Ambotif-mena*, plenty of objects worthy their attention. They will find ftupendous maffes of rock-cryftal ; fome are perfectly cryftallized, others feem to have no regular form, many of them contain fherls and other ftrange bodies : thofe fherls, on which naturalifts fet the higheft value, are not rare in thefe mountains, the fame may be faid of the granites, and feveral traces of tin mines, called by the natives *Voola-footfhefin*. Mines of the beft iron are fcattered with profufion all over the furface of this diftrict. The Malegafhes grind and pound this mineral, put it in heaps between four ftones fmeared with potters earth, and make ufe of a double wooden pump inftead of bellows, to render the fire quicker and more active : one hour is fufficient to melt the mineral ; and the iron which they draw by this procefs is of a ductile and malleable

S 3   quality.

quality. There are no doubt, other mines in this diftrict, but to difcover them neither trouble nor labour ought to be fpared.— Thefe riches are concealed in the bofom of the earth, and it requires fearches and a great deal of hard labour to draw them from thofe fecret receffes. In other refpects, if we may give credit to what the natives affure us, the accefs to the mountains of *Ambotifmena*, is almoft impracticable to the Europeans. Their fummits are equally fteep, and precipices forbid the wanderer to approach. The loftieft of thefe mountains lies one thoufand eight hundred fathoms above the level of the fea, and bears fimilitude to the Table mountain defcribed by all the travellers who have been at the Cape of Good Hope.

We can only give the reader this faint fketch of the rich minerals of Madagafcar; there are treafures more valuable in the other variegated productions of that ifland.

Thefe

Thefe productions are quite genial to the nature and fecundity of the foil.

We fhall now give the curious and interefted reader a defcription of the plants which we have brought to the Royal Botanical Garden at *Ifle de France*, from the ifland of Madagafcar.

S 4 DESCRIP-

DESCRIPTION

Of several non-descript Trees, Shrubs and Plants, which grow in the North of the Island of Madagascar, and are now transplanted in the Royal Botanical Garden at Isle de France.

MALAO-MANGHIT.—Is a great tree, whose bark is brown, the trunk straight, and the wood white. Its sap at first lacteous and white, turns as red as blood if exposed to the air. The fruit is a kind of nutmeg. The natives attribute the same virtues to this nut which we attribute to the real nutmeg. The leaves yield a sweet aromatic odour.

Rarabee.—The Rarabee is a wild nutmeg-tree, loftier and finer than the Malao-manghit. It bears a nutmeg, from which the Malegashes extract a very aromatic oil, with which they anoint their body and hair. This oil

is

is proper to cure and diffipate the fcrophula, being taken inwardly it is an excellent remedy to ftrengthen the ftomach.

Bafhi-bafhi.—This tree refembles the Rarabee, being only a little different in its leaves and fruit. It grows on all elevated fpots. The green of its fhell, the nut' and mace are aromatic.

Rharha-horac.—The Rhara-horac is a real wild nutmeg-tree. Its trunk is big, the boughs bear a very denfe foliage. It loves to grow on humid and marfhy grounds. The *Fooningomena-raboo*, a large blue pigeon, is very fond of the fruit, and having digefted the mace, fows the nut throughout the ifland.

Raven-fara.—Of all the nutmeg-trees at Madagafcar, the Raven-fara deferves moft the attention of botanifts. The united perfume of the clove, cinnamon and nutmeg, differs but little from the fweet odour which

is

is extracted, by diftillation, from the leaves
of the Raven-fara. Thefe leaves yield an
oil or effence, more efteemed than that extracted from cloves. The cooks in India
make ufe of this perfume in ragouts, in preference to all other fpices. The Raven-fara
is a valuable tree. It is fond of humid fpots,
without finding dry and arid ones contrary
to its growth : this tree grows very big and
bufhy ; its pyramidical top is well furnifhed
with thick leaves; its wood is white, inodorous, hard and heavy, but the bark
fpreads a very fweet fcent. The fruit of the
Raven-fara is a real nut flattened at both
ends. The fmell of the nut and green fhell
is lefs ftrong, and lefs fragrant than the
leaves, but, in my opinion, I found it more
delicate.

Haram.—The Haram is the loftieft and
largeft tree in the province of *Voolou-voolou*.
The wood is white, and the heart bears a
red tint. When it has reached the laft ftage
of its growth, it divefts itfelf every year of
                                        its

its external bark, which is grey and thick: the trunk of this tree is even and without boughs as far as the top which bears plenty of leaves, and the tuft which crowns it, prefents a very pleafant afpect. The leaft incifion made in it, procures great abundance of a white and very aromatic rofin. The women of Madagafcar make a pafte of it, with which they rub their face, to preferve the fkin in all its frefhnefs.

If this rofin is burnt, it exhales a perfume like that of frankincenfe. The fruit of the Haram is a nut, of which the fhell alone is aromatic.

Laben.—This tree grows on the fea-coaft in fandy diftricts; it rifes to a great height. Its hard and reddifh wood is good for all kinds of joinery. The fruit of the *Laben* has the form and thicknefs of an olive, it contains a white, oily and very delicate kernel.

Foo-ra-ha.

Foo-ra-ha.—The *Foo-ra-ha* is one of the finest trees, and of the most useful productions of hot climates; after the *Teek*, it is the best timber for building ships that can be got in India; I can only compare it with the *Tacamaca* of the isles of France and Bourbon, it yields, like the latter, a green balm, very efficacious in curing wounds and sores. This tree is big, leafy, has large branches, and is very remarkable for its prodigious height.

Tevartna.—The *Tevartna* offers, in the middle of forests, all the symmetry of art; it seems as if it had been cut out on purpose, in a pyramidal shape, with seven stories; its leafy branches, ranged horizontally round a straight, smooth trunk, make its form appear very singular. This is perhaps the finest tree on earth for decoration.

Hintchy.—This tree, the most common of those observed in the environs of *Voolou-voolou*, is peculiarly well adapted to make covered walks, because its top has a very thick

thick and full foliage. It refembles the plum-tree, and rifes to the fame height; its wood is red and fit for joiners work; the bark is fmooth and white, and the leaves are broad, and of a very beautiful green.

Foterfbee.—The *Foterfbee* is one of the largeft trees of Madagafcar, but its wood is only fit to be burnt.

Tanguem.—This tree grows on the fea-fhore. Its wood is hard and veiny, and fit for the ufe of joiners and for inlaid work; the Malegafhes make but too much ufe of the fruit of this tree, whofe dangerous properties are not unknown to them; it is one of the rankeft and moft formidable poifons.

Antafara.—The *Antafara* is known at Ifle de France by the name of *milkwood*; its bloffom has the form and fmell of the jeffamine; a flight incifion brings out a lacteous juice equally abundant and cauftic.

Affy.

Affy.—This is a beautiful palm-tree; it rifes to the height of ten feet; its trunk bears the mark of the leaves which it drops fucceffively; its top is crowned with two or three rows of leaves, four or five feet long, and one inch and a half broad. Thefe leaves, fimilar to thofe of the lily, have the folidity of the palm, and the form of a fine umbrella?

Tafoumouna.—Is a large and thick leaved tree; its bark is fmooth, the wood white, and the fruit a real acorn, like that of our oak; the kernel has a kind of aromatic tafte and fmells like turpentine.

Hounits.—The wood of the *Hounits* is of a fine yellow colour; the bark is red, and if an incifion is made, a fap as red as coral iffues forth; the natives, by means of common lye, extract a beautiful red tincture from the bark and roots of this tree, which is otherwife very fine and lofty.

Zavin-raven.—Is a tree of a moderate fize, not leafy, and knotty about the trunk; the

bark

bark is grey, the wood white, and it grows.
in the marſhes.

Lingo.—A kind of creeping root, which
twines itſelf up to the top of the talleſt trees.
The *Lingo* has only two inches in diameter ;
its wood is yellow, and ſo is the inſide of the
bark.   The women uſe the bark of this root
to dye their pagnas yellow or red.

Harongan.—Riſes to the height of fifteen
feet, and grows in the ſands. Its leaves
yield a red tint, with which the inhabitants
dye mats and baſkets.

Tancaſſon.—A wild vine of a ſouriſh, unpleaſant taſte.   It riſes to the ſummit of the
higheſt trees.   Its root is very diuretic, and
the natives are very fond of it.

Taco.—Another wild vine, much like the
Tancaſſon.

Voo-a-lomba.—The fruit of a vine, which
the Europeans prefer to all the reſt, they
call

call it the grape of Madagafcar. Its tafte is fomewhat tart; this plant dies every year, and its root is a kind of *Ignama* or *Yam*.

Anakwey.—A great fenfitive plant.

Arefoo.—A kind of elder.

Tougnounan.—Its wood is proper to make the poles of lances; it bears bell-flowers.

Tafomounan.—A fruit in form of an acorn, with little white flowers.

Racoudrit.—A green fruit in form of a grape.

Uvang-biri.—A creeping plant with large fquare hufks; the bean it contains is anti-hemorrhoidal.

Tevarta.—A bufh in form of a pyramid.

Azambou.—A fruit in form of a red nofe-gay.

Ua-he Taitchou.—A good eatable fruit.

Sampan Leva.—A fruit in form of a yellow bead.

Tchinghit.

Tschinghit.—A bean with yellow blossom. A kind of wild bladder-nut.

Lacca.—A little fruit like a pepper. The blossom in form of the collet of a ring.

Vognindosong.
Fanpechorou. } A kind of starry lily. Announces the time to catch whales.

Voua-hintchy.
Filao. } Equisetum arborescens.

Voantlisan.—A thorny tree, having but a few leaves at the top.

Tchuvi-ovi.—A kind of ypecacuanha, seriploca.

Jacuan.—A kind of almond. The tree which has no leaves, yields gum.

Timbalave.—A shrub with white gondola-like flowers.

Anghivi.—Bears a red fruit, which gives a sour though pleasant taste to the drink of the natives.

T *Ampalt.*

Ampalt.—A round leaf, which polifhes iron.

Azon-ranoo.—Bears hufks, the points of which are oppofite to one another.

Farafar.—A plant of the parafitic kind, whofe long red flower has the form of an hand, or of a fork with five branches, or prongs.

Vongo.—A fine tree, whofe fruit is called *Vaafou-voura.* By incifion it yields a yellow gum.

Vua-mitfa-voi.—A fpecies of after.

Tongouna-lein-tein.—A fpecies of mint.

Moulton-rongou.—Refembles the rara. Its leaves are fmall, and the fruit is oblong and angular.

Sanoang-matan-nahanrou.—A kind of rampant afparagus.

Ranga-zaa.—A white flower with onions.

Tchilotoo.

Tchilotoo.—A white tulip.

Fifoutchee.—A tree with leaves like mallows, the bloſſom comes round the trunk.

Schira.—A palm-tree, whoſe bark being burnt, yields a kind of ſalt, which the natives eat at their meals.

Raven-tongharts.—A plant of the balſamic claſs.

Tanroujou.—A fruit with buds. A kind of benjamin.

Azou-ranou.—A buſh, bearing a red fruit, of the cinnamon colour.

Afratrahce.—A ſhrub with a fragrant rind.

Vaing-bare.—A creeping plant, with crinigerous leaves, and white flowers.

Talate.—Bears thick leaves, and a red fruit like the holly-oak.

Jang.—A tree which yields large bunches of flowers.

T 2

Vua-vani.

Vua-vani.—Has flowers like thofe of the *Lihoa* in China.

Vua-Montucung.—A creeping plant, with leaves like the tamarind ; its fruit refembles a horfe-bean.

Vua-tootooc.—A fhrub with a red eatable fruit, which taftes like the ftrawberry.

Vuang-titirang.—A fpecies of nut, whofe fhell is yellow and hairy.

Voua-fourindi.—A great tree, which bears large bunches of little red flowers.

Ampali.—Bears a long leaf, which polifhes wood, and takes the ruft off the iron.

Ioud-ifafal.—Kind of femper vivens.

Vua-fevarantoo.—
Vuang-tae.— } Malum cidonium.

Vua-fatre.—A fpecies of box-tree, whofe aromatic fruit is eatable.

Enghi-panza.—Little indigo.

Enghi-bee.

Enghi-bee.—Little indigo.

Vua-macaliong.—A tree from which they extract oil.

Sacaviro-amboo.—Hog-ginger. A kind of zedoary.

Vua-fao.—A kind of palm-tree.

Chifontfui.—Has fmall leaves, ranged two by two, the flower bears four green leaves in the form of a calix.

Vua-honda.—A fruit in form like the cucumber, and in flavor like the quince.

Sangnamoo.—An herb, which ferves to catch fifh.

Sanga-Sanga.—A triangular rufh ; or the real papyrus.

Vua-toudinga.—A fruit like the *pipar* of China.

Fua-caraboo.—A fpecies of large flat chefnut, which grows on a creeping bufh.

Vouang

Vuang-ping lela —Bears the leaves of the cinnamon-tree, but is not fragrant.

Vua-tingui le-pas.—A fruit of a green colour, which opens and difplays its feed from the infide in a cod, with three round angles.

Anja-oidy.—A fpecies of very tall fweet broom.

Vua-hia-vave.—A creeping plant, with white female flowers.

Vua-namboo-avon.—A red fruit in form of a bouquet, violet flowers, whitifh leaves, ranged two by two. It is of great fervice for cuts and ulcers.

Vua-rha.—A fpecies of fig-tree, which yields good palatable fruit.

Varao.—A fpecies of marfh-mallow.

Lindem.—A fpecies of palm-tree, with leaves like thofe of fcolopendra.

Andouranga.—A little plant with leguminous flowers, and red hufks, like the indigo.

Agnan-

Agnan-ramboo-lahee,
Tongoo-hintchi,
Haramee.
} The rofin of which feems to be the fubftance of ambergris.

Vanguinang-bua.—A fhrub with crinigerous white leaves and white flowers. Its root heals wounds.

Cani-pouti.—An herb with broad leaves, the juice of which is ufed by the natives to draw figures on the different parts of their bodies.

Tottlafs.—A kind of bay-tree, whofe leaves and wood are aromatic.

Azou-minti.—A very curious, pyramidal bufh.

Azou-minti-bee.—A fine tree, with broad leaves,

Tocam-boodi.—A palm-tree, with large leaves divided at the end.

Fouraugdra.—A fpecies of triangular alkekenghi, with parfley leaves; it is a rampant plant.

Voua-

Voua-mandroucou.—A flower in form of a nosegay, issuing from the stem; the petals are spiral.

Vua-mena.—A plant whose fruit is sweet and as red as a coral, the wood and leaves are likewise red.

Mang.—A tree whose leaves are like those of marsh-mallows, but rather larger and stronger. The flowers are hairy like those of the *ketmia*, and of a rose-colour.

Angua-maloo.—A kind of aromatic shrub, whose flowers and buds imitate the yellow of gold.

Volang-bondi-pouni.—A red wood, which turns black in growing older, and is used by the natives for the purpose of dying.

Tzimamasoo.—A kind of creeping plant, whose flower is like the jessamine, except the colour, which is of a beautiful red.

Diti-azou.—A fruit, having the shape and appearance of a little pear.

Manouquibonga.

Manouquibonga ——A bush, which has branches or sprigs like the vine, and whose beautiful red flowers present the form of an *aigrette*.

Tavoutula.—A little bulbous plant, whose flower is as grey as linseed ; it is a species of orchis.

Chetchia.—A species of hieracium, with yellow flowers.

Angan ramboo.——A ditto, with yellow flowers,

Catoubanda.—A species of weed, which cures swellings, sprains and bruises.

Nantoo.—Mat-weed, of two sorts, with great and small leaves.

Amp.-elang-thi-fouhi.——*Gentianella*, with violet flowers.

Campoudi.—A species of *alcinea*.
Veloutir.—*Pithonia.*

DESCRIPTION

DESCRIPTION

O F

COCHINCHINA.

COCHINCHINA is a kingdom of about one hundred and fifty leagues in length, extending from the eleventh degree to the feventeenth and half a degree of Northern latitude.

Its boundaries are the *Tonquin*, from the North; *Ziacpna* and the *Camboge*, from the South; the fea from the Eaft; and from the Weft, the favages called *Hemouy*, and the kingdom of *Laos*.

This

This kingdom has only from twelve to fifteen leagues in its greateſt breadth ; it is divided in eleven provinces, four of them being ſituate to the North, and ſeven to the South.

The four Northern Provinces are :

| DINHEAT, | DINHGNOE, and |
| QUAMBING, | HUE. |

Hue is called the royal province, and the capital of this kingdom bears the ſame name.

The ſeven Southern Provinces are :

CHAM,	FANRIPHANRANG,
QUANGZHIA,	NANLANG,
QUINHIN,	AND
FOUYEN,	BOONAY.

This latter province has quite lately been taken from the *Cambogians.*

Hue, where lies the royal city, is the fineſt of the eleven provinces. It is there the kings of COCHINCHINA have their reſidence.

For

For thefe fixty years paft, fince thefe kings have feparated themfelves from *China*, the royal city cannot boaft of any remarkable buildings but the royal palace and the pagcdas ; the reft of the town is ill-built. It lies near a fine and large river, formerly deep enough to carry the largeft fhips. But fince the dreadful inundation which happened in this country five or fix years ago, feveral fand-banks block up the entrance of the port to great fhips.

The town of *Hue* is interfected by canals, after the Chinefe fafhion, to facilitate the conveyance of goods, and for the convenience of its numerous inhabitants, who could not endure the fcorching heat of the fummer without bathing twice or three times a day.

The king keeps in the environs of his palace, from twelve to fifteen thoufand men, who are his guards and fervants ; and about three hundred very neat galleys, which ferve, in war time, to tranfport the troops from one place

place to another; and in peace, for the ex-
curfions made by the monarch, who never
hardly leaves his palace but in a galley. The
galleys which he ufes to go on board of are
very beautiful, and even very richly gilt;
above all, thofe of his women, fome of
whom do always accompany him whenever
he goes out. This prince keeps alfo upwards
of four hundred elephants, accoutered for
war, and in the number of thefe animals
confifts the ftrength of his kingdom.

The government of Cochinchina is mo-
narchical; the king is fole and abfolute mafter.
He governs his whole kingdom with the
affiftance of his four firft minifters, two of
whom are called his right-hand, or *Tha*;
and two his left-hand, or *Huan*. They
tranfact all important ftate affairs, and make
all civil and military appointments. Every
province has a governor, who is both chief
of the military, and chief-juftice. In *Fanri-
phanrang*, the governor has the title of vice-
roy. All the forces are divided into two
bodies,

bodies, in foldiers and marines. Both are divided in regiments.

The king's guards confift of the fineft men in the kingdom. The fineft company is that called, *the Golden Sabres.* The men of this company are picked out, and felected from all the other companies; they are the ftrongeft and braveft, for which reafon they have likewife a greater fhare of authority.

The king now upon the throne, is the ninth who governs Cochinchina, fince the feparation of *Tonquin.* He is a tall well-looking man. He had only the title of *Chua* or fovereign; but in the fourth moon of the year 1744, he declared himfelf *Vua* or king. What excited him to affume that new title, was the wretched fituation to which he knew Tonquin had been reduced by civil wars. Till then he had been contented with the modeft title of *Chua,* for fear of being involved in a war with *Tonquin,* where the king pretends to the exclufive title of *Vua,* or king of *Cochinchina.*

TAXES.

T A X E S.

The king of Cochichina is very rich in gold and *caches*, of which he has feveral cargoes. His great wealth originates from the tribute which all his fubjects pay him from the age of feventeen to fixty.—— This tribute is more or lefs confiderable, according to the fortune and power of each individual. Every three years, the governor of each province caufes a frefh lift to be made of thofe who have attained the age prefcribed by law, to pay the tribute. The chief of every village makes an exact lift, and carries a copy to the governor of the province, who makes appear before him every perfon whofe name is contained in it; the latter make their appearance on the day appointed, and ftrip themfelves naked from head to foot. The mandarin orders his officers to examine them. Thofe who have not the leaft bodily defects, and are robuft, well made, and fitteft for work,

pay

pay a larger tax than thofe whofe infirmities enables them lefs to earn a livelihood. This tax, the profit or revenue of the king, is paid according to the fortune and ftrength of each man, either in gold, *caches* or rice, &c. Every year, in the feventh moon, the tribute of all the provinces is fent to the court. The king, attended by all his coutiers, comes forth to receive it. This reception takes place with a great deal of pomp and magnificence. The court fpends a whole month in rejoicings, and the time paffes away in feafts, plays, fire-works, and all kinds of diverfions.

MANNERS.

The *Cochinchinefe*, compared with the Indians, are brave, active and laborious. They love the truth, and become partial to her dictates, as foon as they know her ; they are poor, ignorant, civil among themfelves, and above all to ftrangers. They have a great efteem for the *Chinefe*, on account of their fine doctrine ;

doctrine; they call China the Kingdom of Light (*Moedaimingh*). Since the French miffionaries came among them, they have more efteem for the Europeans. The king is fond of the latter, and wifhes them to vifit his fea-ports for the purpofe of commerce. The *Cochinchinefe* are much given to women; polygamy is eftablifhed among them; they, in general, keep as many wives as they can maintain, and the law gives them great authority over them, as well as over their children. Thofe who are convicted of infidelity, are condemned to die by the teeth of the elephants. The women cannot boaft of great pudicity. During the hot feafon, they are always naked to the waift, nor do they make any ceremony of ftripping and bathing before every body. The figure of the people of Cochinchina is very analogous to that of the Chinefe, they are only a little more tawney. Their drefs correfponds with that of the Chinefe, worn previous to the irruption of the Tartars. The drefs of their lettered men is the Japanefe habit, they wear their hair,

U

and

and take great care of it, efpecially the women, who let it even drag down to the
ground.

RELIGION.

The Religion is the fame as in China;
the people go to the pagodas, or temples of
Foe and Tfchoua; the literati repair to the
temple of *Confucius*, who is their mafter, as
well as of the Chinefe. At prefent, the
Chriftian religion is not only tolerated, but
free, and makes a deal of progrefs; there are
princes and mandarins of the firft clafs, who
are Chriftians. The kingdom contains about
fixty thoufand perfons, who became converts
to the church of Rome.

LITERATURE.

All the knowledge and fcience of the
Cochinchinefe confifts in reading Chinefe
books, and in being inftructed in the moral
precepts which thofe books contain. It is
their

their improvement in this science which raises them to the dignity of Mandarins.

W O O D S.

Cochinchina is but a ridge of mountains, whose valleys and plains are well cultivated ; the heights are the repair of tygers, elephants, and all sorts of wild beasts. The mountains, however uncultivated, are covered with woods and forests extremely productive. The Cochinchinese draw from them rose-wood, ebony, *sapan*, cinnamon, *calembac*, sandal, and all kinds of fine woods which come from India, either to build their houses, barges, to make furniture, or to extract from them gums, perfumes and balsams. Some of the mountains bear even clove-trees.

G O L D   M I N E S.

The natives of Cochinchina draw likewise a great deal of fruit from those mountains, such as honey, wax, &c. They even find

U 2

there large quantities of ivory and gold. There is a great number of gold-mines, and the moſt celebrated are thoſe of the province of *Cham*, near a place called *Phunrae*, where the French miſſionaries have a church and a great number of proſelytes. This place lies at the diſtance of eight leagues from *Faiſo*. There are likewiſe very famous mines in the province of *Nanlang*. Every body, even foreigners, may work theſe mines. They would be extremely productive, if the natives would apply themſelves to dig them; but as there are but few people fond of that kind of labour, thoſe who are, do not know how to go about it. They never dig deeper than the uſual height of a man. On the ſpot where I have ſeen them work, they ſome-time found whole lumps of very pure gold, which is quite unmixed, and weighed fre-quently two ounces. The gold amaſſed in duſt or bits, is afterwards converted into cakes, and carried to market, where it is ſold like all other commodities; its uſual

price

price is about one hundred and thirty Chinefe *quans.** But it has lately been fold at one hundred and feventeen *quans*. The mountains have a great many iron-mines, and iron is a very important article of commerce in Cochinchina.

PRODUCTIONS of the EARTH.

The cultivated lands of Cochichina are very fertile indeed. They gather every year a double crop of rice, which is almoft given away for nothing. The people of Cochinchina have plenty of all the fruits which India bring forth. Cotton is very abundant, but the natives do not manufacture it well; they have nurferies of mulberry-trees, and rear filk-worms. Of their filk they make very indifferent ftuffs, and they are only clever in manufacturing certain fatins. Raw filk fells very dear; they ufually fell it at *two hundred quans a quan*, Cochinchinefe

U 3   meafure

* We fhall explain the value of *quans, caches,* &c.

meafure, according to the feafon, for more or lefs. Their fugar is doubtlefs the fineft in India. This article fetches them vaft fums of money from China, whence the merchants come to buy cargoes at *Faifo*, which are fhipped for CANTON or Japan, where they get at leaft four hundred per cent. The fineft fugar is fold at four *quans*, *Cochinchinefe* meafure; it is moftly made in the province of *Cham*, near *Faifo*. They do not wait three years before they cut off the canes; their crop takes place every year towards the clofe of autum. The country produces no other European grain, but Indian wheat; they have neither corn, wheat, rye, nor barley. The leguminous vegetation is alfo very backward among them, becaufe they are bad gardeners. Their foil is, literally fpeaking, divefted of all that conftitutes the richnefs of our kitchen gardens.

AGRICULTURE.

AGRICULTURE.

The people of Cochinchina till their field with buffaloes. This animal is ftronger than the ox, and can bear better the mud of the rice-fields. They have a great number of oxen, which are lean, fmall, and almoft good for nothing; they have no fheep, and their markets are very ill fupplied with meat. To compenfate this deficiency, they have a great deal of poultry; chickens, ducks and pigeons are very abundant and cheap; and game fells almoft for nothing. The natives moftly live on fifh, which are plentiful and very palatable. The rivers and feas are both very fifhy.

COMMERCE.

With regard to the commerce of the country, it may well be affirmed, that the Cochinchinefe are neither rich nor able mer-

U 4   chants.

chants. They never had any commerce
abroad, but with the Chinese and Japanese.
The latter have cut off all intercourse by
order of their prince, who has forbidden
them to leave the country. The same orders
have been given in *Cochinchina*, for which
reason the people here are glad to take such
goods as the Chinese choose to bring them.
The Cochinchinese are far from being as
sharp and cunning as the Chinese, who find
it a very easy matter to impose on them.

The goods which they receive from China
consist of red, yellow, and white copper; tea,
china, silk-stuffs, and all kinds of drugs,
spices, &c. for which the Chinese find an
excellent market. They likewise bring a
great deal of paper, which serves to bury
the dead; gilt and coloured paper to orna-
ment the pagodas and sacrifices, and little lots
of nankeen; likewise all sorts of pictures,
vermilion, azure, or pimento, and linens of
hemp and cotton. Ships from *Hognam* bring
variety of pottery, which is speedily dispos-
ed

ed of. The ſhips which come to the eaſtern coaſt of China, either from *Emoy* or *Nienpo,* bring ſometimes goods from Japan : theſe are all well ſold, eſpecially red copper and ſword blades.

The ſhips which come from *Camboge* and *Siam,* bring kali, wrought copper, drugs, furs, &c.

The articles which the Chineſe export from Cochinchina, are gold, ivory, eagle-wood, ſugar-candy, woods for dying, pepper, muſk, certain kinds of ſalt-fiſh, birds-neſts and drugs, which the natives draw from the mountains. The ſhips from *Siam* take in return gold, ſugar, and horſes, which are very cheap in Cochinchina.

The commerce of the Chineſe to Cochin-china is conducted in the following manner : as ſoon as the ſhips come in ſight of harbour, they find Cochinchineſe pilots, who ſteer them ; theſe pilots belong to th mandarin,

or

or governor of the province. They have orders to hold themfelves in conftant readinefs, to facilitate the foreign fhips the entrance of the harbour. Having caft anchor, the captain goes on fhore, attended by fome officers, and carries to court a general lift of all the goods he has brought, and at the fame time the prefents he means to make to the king. It ought to be obferved, that in this country all kinds of contracts and affairs of concern commence and are terminated with prefents; it is very neceffary to have fuch ones as may pleafe the king, becaufe, if he likes them, he exempts the fhip from the fees of anchorage, which is very confiderable, but always proportionate to the quantity and quality of the goods brought by a fhip. The Chinefe pay ten per cent. for all cargoes, according to an ancient tarif, which determines the price of all merchandize.

The captain, being returned from court, has his cargo brought afhore to his factory.
Here

Here the mandarins, as appointed commiffioners of the cuftoms, come to examine
them, only to fee if there is any thing curious, or that might pleafe the king, or the
firft mandarins of the kingdom; thefe cuftom-houfe officers give a lift of the articles
they fhould like to purchafe. All thofe articles that are upon their lift, are feparated
from the reft, and they afterwards ftrike a
bargain with the captain, to whom they give
a note, which is not paid for two or three
months after the delivery of the goods.—
Before this vifit on the part of the mandarins,
the merchant can fell nothing. He muft be
careful not to omit a fingle article in the lift
he prefents to the king at his arrival; becaufe, if the mandarins at their vifit fhould
difcover any thing in his cargo not inferted
in the lift of the king, they would fine him.
He muft likewife make fome prefents to the
minifter and chief cuftom-houfe officer, who
is a very powerful mandarin in *Cochinchina*;
his title is *On-lai-bo-ta-o*. If the Chinefe
apply for the fale of their merchandize to the
mandarins,

mandarins, who are fond of being merchants wherever they can gain much, the latter buy all the deareſt and moſt important articles. For all goods of little value there are truſty women, well verſed in commerce, who, for the ſake of a ſmall premium, will diſpoſe of one or two lots. European captains who come to this country will find rich Chriſtian merchants, very ready to help them to ſell their cargoes.

M O N E Y,

A N D

Value of Gold and Silver.

Goods ſold are paid for in gold or ſilver, but more frequently in *caches*. The *caches* are the only currency of the kingdom. They are filed after the manner of the Chineſe; each file or ſtring contains ſix hundred *caches*, which make a *quan ;* the quan is divided in ten *tiens* or *maſſes*, counting ſixty *caches* to each

each *tien.* The tien is the lowest specie, all
under a *quan* is counted by caches; they
count likewise by the *choo,* which makes ten
quans, or six thousand *caches*; thus the *quan*
or *tael* of Cochinchina makes but six *masses*
of China; a mass is the tenth part of the
tael; of course the *tael* of China makes one
quan, six *tiens* and forty *caches* of Cochinchina.
Gold and silver are articles of trade among
them, they have no fixed price for either,
and heighten or lower it in proportion to the
quantity exported every year by the Chinese.
They know nothing of the value of our piasters; they melt these pieces into cakes,
and a cake, which contains fifteen piasters,
was sold for a long while at the rate of
twenty-two or twenty-three *quans.* Now
they go off at the rate of seventeen or twenty
quans, and the *Chinese* still import vast quantities of them. They get more profit by
this branch of commerce than they would in
China, where a piaster fetches only seven
hundred *caches,* whilst they get at least eight
hundred for it in *Cochinchina.* It is for this

reason

reafon the Chinefe prefer bringing piafters to other goods, which they would not find fo eafy to fell, and by which they would gain nothing, fince they get more profit by the commodities they export from Cochinchina, than by thofe they import in that kingdom. The price of gold rifes or falls according to the number of purchafers.— When the Chinefe fhips arrive, it is hardly to be got for lefs than one hundred and thirty *quans* ; and about the time when they fail again, it rifes to one hundred and fifty *quans* ; but if it were purchafed from the firft moon to the end of the year of Cochinchina, which anfwers to our months of October, November, and December, till the month of March of the next year, it might then be had at one hundred quans ; and people that know the country might get it ftill cheaper.

WEIGHTS and MEASURES.

The meafure ufed by the people of Cochinchina in buying and felling, contains
about

A VOYAGE TO MADAGASCAR. 319

about two French feet; they call it *thiae*;
it is therefore one half lefs, half an inch
fhorter than the French yard, and larger
than the *cove* of the *Chinefe*, for about fix
ponts and four *condorins*. There is no other
meafure, but for rice, which the poor buy by
the meafure; it contains about fix pounds of
Cochinchina. This pound is fourteen ounces
heavier than the French, and ten heavier
than the Chinefe pound, which latter has
about twenty French ounces. The pound
of Cochinchina contains therefore thirty
French ounces. There are certain articles
of trade in Cochinchina, which none but the
king has the privilege to fell; fuch as ivory,
and the wood of *Calembac*. Thefe articles
can only be bought of the king, and to purchafe them of any other perfon would expofe
the purchafer to great difficulties.

All articles of merchandize, whether
bought of the king, or of any other private
individual, pay no duty; they may be fhipped as foon, and in any manner one pleafes.

SEA-

SEA-PORTS.

There are feveral ports in Cochinchina, and the moft confiderable is that which the Portuguefe call *Taifo*, and the natives *Hoyan*; it lies in the province of *Cham*, in the fixteenth degree, lefs a few minutes, and at a few days march from the court. The harbour is deep, and the fhips are fafe in it; it is very convenient for the merchants, whofe fhips caft anchor before the door of the factories. The entrance is very eafy; it confifts of a large river, which flows acrofs the province of *Cham*, and comes from the mountains of *Laos*. *Taifo*, is the moft commercial place in Cochinchina, where there are always near fix thoufand very eminent Chinefe merchants; they are married in the country, and pay tribute to the king. Here are likewife two Roman churches, one belonging to fome Portuguefe jefuits, the other to Spanifh monks of the order of St. Francis. The governor of the province lives at the

distance

diftance of one league. farther, in a place called *Reta*, on the banks of the fame river; it is here the French miffionaries have like-wife a church. Merchants arriving at *Faifo* always find factories to be let; the largeft and moft fpacious go at one hundred piafters the feafon.

There is another port in the province of *Quinhin*, called *Nuoeman*, which. means, the harbour of falt-water It is an excellent, fafe, and well frequented port. What makes it inconvenient is, its remotenefs from the court, where captains are obliged to go feveral times, and from which it lies as far as fix days journey. There are feveral other little harbours, efpecially in the diftrict of *Nanlang*, but they are neither deep nor fafe enough for great. fhips. The Chinefe never vifit them, becaufe they are too far from court.

X   EUROPEAN

EUROPEAN COMMERCE

IN

COCHINCHINA.

WITH regard to the commerce which the Europeans might carry on in Cochinchina, it may eafily be feen by what has already been faid, what commodities they can draw from that kingdom, either to tranfport them to the coaft of India, China, or even to Europe. The moft difficult point is, what merchandize they fhould bring thither, upon which I fhall make the following remarks:

The people of Cochinchina fet great value on all that comes from Europe. Many articles of very fmall confequence in our part of the world, are precious in that country. All kinds

of

of hardwares, glaſſes, light ſtuffs of a fine colour, ſuch as red ones, would find a good
market. All ſorts of arms, manufactured in
Europe, would ſell extremely well, eſpecially
ſword blades, made after a model of thoſe
uſed in that country; all kind of ſtones,
from the diamond to common chryſtal, are
ſold very dear to the king and the mandarins.
The latter demand likewiſe gold and ſilver
wire, and all theſe articles would at leaſt
fetch cent. per cent. provided they are not
exported in too great quantities. Braſs ſells
at leaſt at eight *quans* a Chineſe foot. Great
profits would therefore ariſe from the ſale of
all theſe goods. It would alſo be well to
ſupply them with brimſtone, which ſells very
high; drugs and medicines, ſuch as quin-
quina, and other articles of that deſcription.
There are other European goods, which are
too dear for the people of Cochinchina; being
however, brought in ſmall quanties, they
would go off well; ſome pieces of ſtuff embroidered with gold and ſilver flowers, for in-

X 2   ſtance,

ftance, would foon be bought, fince the people of this kingdom make bags of them to keep their tobacco and *betel*; nay, they ufed to difplay their magnificence in having feveral bags or purfes well gilt. Pieces of fcarlet, carpets, upon the Perfian model, and white linen, would likewife be well received. Among the toys, bracelets, ear-rings, pinchbeck, &c. fhould not be forgotten. I doubt not but a vaft number of other European articles would fell well, but this can only be known by experimental knowledge. If the Europeans would export feveral cargoes, confifting of a great variety of objects, they would foon fee what takes moft the fancy and tafte of the people of Cochinchina.

If any European nation would try the experiment of freighting a fhip to this kingdom, they ought, as I have obferved already, to take care to fend prefents for the king, elfe they would rifk meeting with a bad reception. The prefents which the king would

probably

probably like, would be pier-glaffes, clocks, jewels, brocade, curious cryftals, fome optical inftruments, fuch as the magic-lanthorn, the cylinder, the telefcope; as likewife mechanic contrivances, fuch as hand-organs, &c. woolen carpets and hangings. Thefe would be objects highly calculated to attract the king's notice, for he is curious, his tafte is good, he likes all that comes from Europe, and prefers what is moft ufeful to what is moft pleafing.

The prefents for the mandarins ought to be of a fimilar defcription, but lefs valuable. They ought to be diftributed according to the dignity of each of them. A perfon might create himfelf enemies, were he in the diftribution of his prefents, to deal upon an equal footing with two mandarins of different rank.

I have not attempted in this fketch to give Europe an exact knowledge of the kingdom

X 3   of

of *Cochinchina*, but my only intention was, to point out in a curfory manner, what might, and what might not be ufeful and interefting to a nation defirous of eftablifh-ing hereafter a commercial intercourfe with thofe diftant regions.

SUPPLE-

SUPPLEMENT

TO THE

INDIAN PLANTS.

———————

OMBAVE.—A tree which yields a gum fimilar to gum arabic.

Bontoo.—A tree whofe roots yield a yellow dye ; it grows on the banks of the rivers ; its leaves are thick and ranged by pairs.

Voai-marang —A tree whofe rind ftops the loofenefs of the belly.

Sondi-fa-fat.—A plant growing on the fea-fhore. The natives of Madagafcar rub ther bodies with the leaves of this plant,

X 4   whenever

whenever they are tired : thefe kind of frictions refrefh them and cheer their animal fpirits. They pretend that the leaves of *Sondi-fa-fat* are incorruptible; and apply them very fuccefsfully to wounds.

Vognin-dofong.—A plant of the parafotic kind, whofe leaf is like that of the lily. It brings forth bloffom in July, and announces the whale fifhery. The prow of the canoes are then decorated with large bunches of this bloffom.

Vua-azignc.—Is the ftraighteft and loftieft tree at Madagafcar. Its height greatly furpaffes the reft of the trees; its hard, heavy and yellow wood is ufed for the purpofe of building, and commonly makes the keel of large canoes. The rofin which flows from this tree is as yellow as amber, but vifcous and inodorus.

The Malegafhes extraƈt a very valuable oil from this tree, which being frefh and mixed

mixed with rice, renders that food extremely palatable and delicate.

Tougmonnam.—A tree which grows on the fummit of mountains, its wood of a red or brown yellow, ferves for inlaid work, and to make lances. It is very heavy.

Vohan-filan.—A tree twelve feet high, its trunk, which is full of thorns, is quite ftraight; its leaves of a beautiful green, are four inches and an half long, and two inches and an half broad. The trunk of this tree is leaflefs, but its top bears a very denfe foliage, perfectly round. The wood-pigeons are very fond of its fruit, which has a very fingular form.

Toulooc.—A bufh, fix or feven feet high; its fruit is called the ftrawberry of Madagafcar, which is very delicate and palatable. Both Europeans and natives think it a great dainty.

Finguiera

Finguiera.—A kind of wild fig-tree, which issues a yellow sap by incision. In coagulation, this sap yields a genuine elastic rosin, analogous to that which flows from the *Cavutchouc.* The natives make torches of it, which burn without wicks, and give a good light if they go a fishing by night. Spirit of wine has no effect upon this rosin, but it may be dissolved in æther and linseed oil. The other fat and oily substances operate likewise a great deal on this gum.

The *Finguiera* rises to the height of twenty feet; its leaf is eight inches long, and four inches broad. The fruit resembles a round fig, and is full of little granulary seeds. The Malegashes devour this fig with great eagerness : as for my own part, I found it acetous and caustic.

If we examine with a little attention the bottles and other vases, which the Peruvians make of gum-elastic, we must be sensible

fible how eafy it is to give this fubftance a
form infinitely ferviceable for the purpofe
of chirurgical operations ; probes and bandages fabricated with gum elaftic are very
convenient and advantageous. But this fubftance diffolved in linfeed-oil or æther, lofes
a great part of its elafticity : in this ftate it
is very proper for thread or filk ftuffs, in
order to render them impenetrable to air and
water.

The Chinefe have known, for this long
time, how to diffolve the elaftic rofin, and
to give it different colours.

Bagnets.—A plant from which the Malegafhes extract the real indigo, by a very
fimple mode of procefs. They fteep the
leaves and ftems of this plant in water, as
foon as it brings forth its bloffom ; after pu-
trefaction the water turns in a violet colour.
When it affumes a deep dye, the leaves and
ftems are taken out, and a certain quantity of

oil

oil is poured in the water, which is let off as foon as the fediment is formed. This fediment, dried in the fhade, furnifhes a beautiful indigo.

DESCRIP-

DESCRIPTION

Of a Palm-Tree,

*Which bears a very singular fruit, much cele-
brated in India, and known by the name of
COCOA of the Maldives, or SEA-COCOA.*

T HE *Palm-tree,* which bears the curious
fruit known by the appellation of *cocoa of
the Maldives,* or *fea-cocoa,* rifes to an elevation of fifty or fixty feet. Its top is crowned
with ten or twelve palms, about twenty feet
long. This noble tree has the form of an
enormous fan. Each of its great palms is
fupported by a pedicle fix feet long, whofe
whole circumference is indented.—From
the pit or cavity of the leaves iffues a
ramified panicula, terminated by female
flowers. The piftil of the flowers or bloffom yields, when growing ripe, a fpherical
fruit, having eight or ten inches in diameter.

The

The shell of the fruit is thick and fibrous like that of the common cocoa. Its form is very peculiar and whimsical : the inside of the nut is replete with a lacteous substance, very bitter and unpleasant to the taste : the trunk of this singular tree does not differ much in its form from the common cocoa-tree. It is harder and bigger. *Palm-island* is covered with this species of palm-tree, without there being any in the islands adjacent, nor in any other known place. From this observation it is probable, that the nuts of that species of palm-tree, whose growth is fortuitous in the Maldives come originally from Palm-island, though the distance between these islands be near three hundred leagues. This observation is useful to point out the direction of the currents in this part of latitude.

The Indians appropriate great medicinal virtues to this nut, known to botanists by the denomination of *Nux Medica*. The Asiatic physicians ascribe to it the virtue of an anti-scorbutic, fcorbutic, and pretend that it cures radically all venereal diforders. They alfo confider the fhell as a powerful antidote. The Indian princes have cups made of it, which are richly fet in gold and precious ftones. Thefe cocoa-nuts were fo rare in the year 1759, the epoch of their difcovery, that fome were fold in the Eaft at ten thoufand livres a piece.

A MEMOIR,

A

MEMOIR,

Defcriptive of the Chinefe Trade.

By MONSIEUR BRUNEL

I N an age when commerce evidently determines the preponderance of ftates, an object of fuch magnitude ought to be duly ap-
preciated.   It is the beft means of contribut-
ing to the glory and profperity of an empire;
and, for this reafon, it ought to attract the
notice of every good citizen.   Whether we
confider commerce as domeftic or as foreign,
it is equally fubject to laws; but in both
inftances it depends on neceffity, or temporary abundance.   It depends likewife on the
productions of different countries, and the
induftry of the nations that inhabit them;
for commerce, in fact, is but an exchange

of

of thofe productions, the quality and price of which is fixed by divers circumftances.

France, by the fertility of its foil, and the temperature of its climate, brings forth all that is neceffary or pleafant, in fuch pro-fufion, as renders it independent of all other countries. It has, therefore, been long de-liberating on the important queftion, whe-ther it ought to concentrate its commerce within itfelf, or to extend it abroad? This however ceafes to be a problem. Reafon and calculation, aided by experience (that diurnal leffon the leaft equivocal of any) feem to have refolved it entirely. There is even reafon to hope, that the opinions of mankind will be no longer wavering in fo momentous a concern. The advantage of not confining the productions of a particular climate to one fingle diftrict, and of com-municating the fruition thereof to remote regions, has been fully felt. It has been remarked, that the defires of the Europeans have been roufed by frefh objects, ever fince

Y the

the period they experienced frefh wants; an eagernefs of poffeffing the arts and commodities of other kingdoms has been diffufed among them. Hence it would be a ftroke of bad policy to impede that relative communication which fubfifts between nations. Such a conduct, on our part, would fhamefully devote ourfelves as tributary to our neighbours, and fuffer the balance to be ftruck altogether in their favour.

Our commerce with India has doubtlefs created more new wants among us than real wealth; it would however occafion a great lofs, were we to abandon that branch of foreign trade to other nations, who would not fail to profit by it. The whole of this obfervation was fo congenial to our wife legiflators, that they have endeavoured to remove thofe reftrictions which checked its progrefs and fuccefs. They have fuppreffed that privilege of monopoly which vifibly obftructed it, and rid it from an odious oppreffion; which, inftead of being a national

concern,

concern, interefted but a few individuals, more folicitous of increafing their own private fortunes, than procuring their country's weal.

Love of gain is the only *ftimulus* of European induftry, in the commerce of the Europeans with the Chinefe, fince they might do very well without their productions.— Habits, however, foon degenerate into wants, or at leaft into unpleafant privations, which are nearly a tantamount. We crave after fuperfluities, and China, of all the Eaftern regions, is that which furnifhes them in greateft plenty. A wide-fpread and lucrative commerce, which keeps pace with the wants of the natives, may of courfe be carried on with that empire, as foon as we have acquired precife notions of the principal commodities which conftitute its produce.

CHINESE

CHINESE MONEY.

Though there be rich gold and silver mines in China, yet it is not permitted to open them, without doubt, from an apprehendfion of caufing too great a circulation of money. It is in this light of political and commercial intereft, that we fhould confider a prohibitory law, which proceeds indeed from the fpirit of the government; but this reafon, too artful for popular perception, is exhibited in a more pleafant view, and as a plaufible motive of humanity : it is, they fay, to prevent the lives of the fubjects of the empire being facrificed. Thefe valuable metals being thus procured from other nations, the Chinefe have admitted no other currency than *caches* and halfpence. There are two forts of the latter, the one of brafs, and the other copper. They are both mixed with toutenag; but the allay being confiderably lefs in the halfpence, they are of higher value.

We

We fee on thefe pieces feveral Chinefe characters. At the top and bottom is the name of the Emperor in whofe reign they were coined; and on the fides is engraved *valuable current things,* i. e. currency.

They make an object of traffic with feveral bankers; but the Europeans will by no means meddle with them. There is no other currency in China than thefe *caches* and halfpence. They make their payments by weight, and are frequently obliged to clip gold and filver, to fettle their accounts, both in paying and receiving. The inftrument ufed for this latter purpofe, is called *kias tien.*

In paying large fums, they weigh the gold and filver in fcales; but for thofe of fifteen to twenty *taels,* they ufe a fmall fteel machine.

The Chinefe count by the *leang, tfien, tu-en-ly,* and *hao;* to which the Portuguefe
Y 3   have

have fubftituted the words *tael, mas, condorin, cache,* and *haus.*

1 *Tael*	*has the value of*	10	*Maffes,*
1 *Mas*	————	10	*Condorins,*
1 *Condorin*	————	10	*Caches,*
1 *Cache*	————	10	*Haufes.*

A tael is equal to about an ounce of filver.

An hundred taels are 750 livres, or near thirty-four pounds fterling.

Money being received in China by weight only, all kind of fpecie is taken, but its intrinfic value is moft fcrupuloufly examined. This they call *ky ynfe* and *noufs-took:* the former reprefents the French deniers for filver, and the latter the karat of gold.

The current finenefs of the filver is ninety-four, to which ftandard all money, whether more or lefs in value, is reduced. The fineft filver paffes at ninety-eight, and in trade

trade at one hundred. Thus it happens, that a piece of gilt filver, which is acknowledged to be of the finefs of an hundred, will pafs for an hundred and two.

The French piafters of the colonies were formerly taken at the rate of ninety five, while thofe of Mexico were only paffed at that of ninety; but the Chinefe, who are the fhrewdeft people on earth, with regard to a knowledge of money and metals, obferved the alteration in the former, efpecially in thofe coined fince 1729, now refufe taking them in exchange for gold, or in payment for merchandize.

The French crown, value fix livres, ufed formerly to be taken at the rate of ninety-five, but at prefent it only goes for eight *mazoirs*, its natural weight.

The duties of the Emperor, or of the cuftoms are gathered in fpecie only, at the ftandard of one hundred—for thefe there is a certain fixed tariff.

Y 4 The

The Europeans, who tranfact their commercial bufinefs in their *haufes* or factories, generally rate

		Livres.	Sols.
The French Louis d'or,	at	24	0
The French Crown	—	3	0
The Tael —	—	7	10
The Silver Rupee	—	2	8
The Piafter —	—	5	6
The Gold Pagoda	—	8	0
The Dutch Florin	—	2	4
The Cruzado	—	2	10
The Pound Sterling	—	22	10

Gold Zechins and Ducats according to weight.

G O L D.

The Chinefe have different weights of gold (*toks*) but they will never fell it to ftrangers under the ftandard of ninety-three. The beft comes from Cochinchina. It is wrought in fmall bars, and is far more firm and finer than the common gold. The

various

various figures ſtamped on it render it very diſcernable, but it is not always free from baſe ingredients. It happens ſometimes, that the mark denotes the *tok* to be ninety-three, when in the inſide it is only ninety-one. This fraud is practiced by putting the bar into the fire, with brick-duſt and ſalt. The gold then leaves the fire purified from without; and the Chineſe, after having ſtamped it with a falſe mark, ſell it for gold of a ſuperior ſtandard. Great precaution is therefore required to prevent one's being cheated in purchaſing this commodity.

The Chineſe have the following method to aſcertain the fineneſs of gold, and to guard againſt fraud; they put a bit of gold into a crucible, and purify it thoroughly, by making the allay evaporate. This is effected by means of ſome powder, which they throw in the crucible. That inſtant a thick ſmoke ariſes, and the ſame proceſs is repeated till the ceſſation of the ſmoke ſhows that the gold is perfectly pure. They then pour a
ſmall

small portion of the liquid metal into a hole, contrived on purpose, between two pieces of polished marble, which gives it the form of a small plate one inch long, three lines broad, and as thick as a French twelve-sous piece; on this plate they write the words *Pure Gold.*

Among the residue of the metal in the melting-pot, they throw a Silver penny, and of this gold, whose value, in point of fineness is lowered one penny, they make a second plate. on which they put the superscription of *Gold of ninety-nine.*

The self-same process reiterated a third time, produces a third plate, which they mark with the words *Gold of ninety-eight.*

Proceeding in this manner, they cast as many pieces as they like, of a piece of gold, whose fineness diminishes always in proportion to the quantity of silver thrown in the crucible.

They

They have in general, twenty or thirty of thefe plates, each with a fuperfcription, precifely fhowing its intrinfic finenefs or quality. They form then a kind of chaplet of them, and the merchant who buys gold, either in cakes or ingots, firft puts it to the teft by comparing it with his plates. He then bruifes, on a piece of polifhed black marble, a fpecies of bean, which leaves behind an oily, vifcous matter, on which he rubs the gold; on comparing the colour left on the marble with the plates on his chaplet, its refemblance to fome of them appear, which muft of courfe determine the real value of the gold. In this manner the Chinefe merchants ward off all impofitions.

At Canton, gold is actually valued at the ftandard of one hundred taels; that is to fay, ten taels of gold of the finenefs of ninety-three, is commonly equal to an hundred taels of filver, for in China, gold is fold, or rather bartered, for filver.

WEIGHTS.

WEIGHTS.

The Chinese weights are the *pic*, *caty* and *tael*, which are likewise used by the Europeans. The *pic* answers the French quintal; the *caty* the pound ; and the *tael* the ounce.

The *tael* of weight, as well as the *tael* of money, is divided into *mass*, *condorin* and *cache*. The *pic* goes at one hundred and three French pounds, of eight ounces each ; and one hundred *pics*, are equal to six hundred and fifty *taels*, four *masses*, six *condorins* $\frac{6\frac{2}{3}}{}$ Chinese weight. All raw goods, such as tea, toutenag, &c. are weighed in balances with scales like ours, which are called *tienping*. For smaller articles, a steelyard, called *ten-gorge*, is employed, and for those which are still less, another sort called *ty-teng*.

MEASURES.

MEASURES.

The Portuguefe, and in imitation of them, the other European nations, call the Chinefe meafure *cob*. It contains one foot, eight inches, three lines; whence three *cobs* and one fixth make a French ell. The Chinefe foot goes by the name of *tochi*, and is divided in ten inches.

ACCOMPTS.

The Chinefe do not make their calculation with the pen, but a board, having fmall wooden balls ftrung upon it, at certain diftances; two of them are at the top, and five at the bottom. Each of the top balls is equal to five, and each of the bottom ones goes for one. When they have caft up a fum, they mark it on a board; when the fecond is caft up, they immediately add it to the

firft,

firſt, and generally without making any blunder. This operation is performed with the utmoſt eaſe. The board uſed for this purpoſe is called *ſouon-pan,* or the *counting-board.* The following are the names and ſigns by which the Chineſe expreſs their cyphers :

1	*y*	—
2	*Cule*	=
3	*San*	☰
4	*Sec*	⊐
5	*Oo*	±

MERCHANDIZE.

MERCHANDIZE.

T E A.

The tea grows on a fmall fhrub, from which the leaves are gathered twice or three times a year. Thofe who gather them thrice a year, begin in the new moon which precedes the equinox of fpring, whether it falls in the end of February, or in the beginning of March. At this epoch the leaves are perfectly green, and fcarcely quite expanded; but thefe fmall and tender leaves aie reckoned the beft, they are rare, and extremely dear.

The fecond crop, or the firft for thofe who gether the leaves but twice a year, takes place towards the latter end of March, or in the beginning of April. At this period a part of the leaves are perfectly ripe, and
though

though the reſt have only reached half their growth, yet they are both gathered without diſtinction.

The third and laſt crop, which is the ſecond for ſome, is the moſt abundant, and takes place towards the cloſe of April, or in the beginning of May, when the leaves are full grown, both in point of ſize and abundance. There are people who neglect the two firſt crops, and confine themſelves ſolely to this; the leaves of which are picked out with great care, and ranged into claſſes in proportion to their ſize and goodneſs.

Tea ought to be rejected as bad, whenever old and apparently withered leaves are found amongſt it; which may eaſily be known, by infuſing a ſmall quantity of it in water; for in that caſe the leaves dilate, and return to their natural ſtate.

The leaves of the tree-ſhrub are oblong, ſharp pointed, indented on the edges, and of of a very beautiful green colour. The flowers confift of five white petals arranged in the form of a rofe, and are followed by a pod of the bignefs of a filbert, containing two or three fmall grains of feed, which are wrinkled, and very unpleafant to the palate. Its root is fibrous, and fpreads itfelf clofe to the furface of the foil.

This fhrub grows as well in a rich as in a poor ground. It is to be met with throughout China, but in fome places, the tea is of a better quality than in others. There are people who deem the Japan tea the beft, but we have reafon to be dubious whether there is any real difference.

The manner of preparing tea is very fimple; when the leaves are gathered, they are expofed to the fteam of boiling water, to render them foft; they are afterwards fpread on metal plates, placed over a moderate fire, which gives them that fhrivelled

Z   appearance

appearance which they have when brought
to Europe.

China produces only two kinds of the
tea-fhrub ; but the natives, by their induftry,
have confiderably multiplied each of them.
Thus, if there are large quantities of tea fold
at an exceffive price, there is alfo fome
very common, which goes off cheap. The
Chinefe, however, are extremely fond of
good tea, and take as much pains in procuring it of a prime quality, as the Europeans do in procuring excellent wine.

BOHEA TEA.

The Chinefe call this tea *vou-y-tfcha*,
which means, tea of the kind called *vou-y*.
It derives its name from a mountain in the
province of *Fokien*.

There are three different forts of this tea ;
the firft of which, called common bohea,
grows

grows at the bottom of the mountain; the second, called *cong-foo* or *camphoo congo*, grows at the top; and the third, denominated *faot-chaon* (fouchong) grows in the middle.

Cong-foo tfcha means bohea of a better preparation, and *faot-chaon* fignifies quinteffence. The latter bears this name, either becaufe it grows on the middle of the mountain, and being fheltered from the inclemency of the weather, attains to a greater degree of finenefs than the reft; or becaufe none of the leaves are plucked unlefs they are full and juicy.

The *faot-chaon* fold to the Europeans, is nothing but *cong-foo* of a fuperior quality. The three fhrubs diftinguifhed by the names above mentioned, are in every refpect the fame; and the only difference confifts in the mode of its preparation.

Bohea

Bohea teas ought, in general, to be dry and heavy to the feeling; this is a sure sign that the leaves have been full and juicy. When infused, they ought to give the water a yellow tint, inclining somewhat to green, which shows their freshnefs, for old tea yields a red colour. Above all things, care should be taken to keep out red leaves, and to choose such as are large and entire. This is likewise a sure token of freshnefs, for the longer tea is kept the more it is shaken, which breaks the leaves, pulverizes and mixes them with the dust. The tea-dust is sometimes owing to the manner in which it is put into the box, as the Chinese tread upon it with their feet, to make it hold a larger quantity. The leaves of *cong-foo* and *faot-chaon* ought to have a fine black glofs, to be large and heavy, and to tinge the water with a very bright colour, and to give it a sweet mild taste.

The *pekao* is a singular kind of tea-shrub, the leaves of which are quite black on one side, fide, and quite white on the other. As the real *pekao* is very fcarce and dear, even in thofe places were it grows; the Chinefe, who ftudy the art of adulterating their teas in general, take care, when this valuable fort is collected, to put in a much greater quantity of black than white leaves. They alfo adulterate it by a mixture with little half-grown leaves as yet white, which grow on the top of the common bohea fhrub. This alters the quality of the *pekao*; for thofe leaves being hardly formed, can have but little juice or flavour.

GREEN TEA.

The green teas do not grow on the fame fpot as the bohea. They are brought from the province of Nankin, and diftinguifhed by three forts. The firft goes by the name of *fonglo tea*, but more frequently by that of green *tookay*; the fecond is called *bin*, and the third *hyffon*. There are befides thefe

Z 3   feveral

several other kinds, most of them unknown, or such as do not engage the attention of foreigners. The *songlo* and *hysson* teas come both from one shrub. Their only difference is in their mode of preparation.

The *bin* grows on a different shrub, the leaves of which are thicker and broader than the other sorts; the older it is the yellower are the leaves, which is a very great defect. They also ought to have a burnt smell, not too strong but pleasant; for if they have been kept too long, they have a fishy smell, much like that of pilchards. The French always like in green teas, especially in *songlo* and *imperial* tea, an odour like that of soap.

In the different sorts of tea here enumerated, a particular distinction is to be made, as they are generally ranged into one, two, or three classes, according to the period of their respective crops.

BALL-

BALL-TEA.

There is a kind of tea in China, called *poncul-tfcha*, which the Europeans have denominated *ball-tea*. It is brought from the province of *Fle-tfchien*, or *Yunnan*, and confifts of a compofition of different teas fhaped into balls. When it is to be ufed, a fmall quantity of it is cut off the ball, and the water being poured on it, it is fuffered to draw much longer than common tea. It is not at all pleafant to the tafte, but endowed with the peculiar virtue of curing afthmatic complaints, and facilitating the digeftion of food. Some of this tea comes from *Si-ang-yang*, a town in the province of *Hoo-quang*, but it is inferior in quality to the former. The latter may foon be known, by applying it to the mouth, and breathing ftrongly upon it. If the breath do penetrate it, they hold it to be genuine. The older the *poncul-tfcha* is, the greater is the demand for it; it is

Z 4

even

even afferted, that it has been preferved in fome families, with aftonifhing care, for upwards of a century; but this is a kind of caprice which commerce has nothing to do with.

CHINA INK.

China Ink is a compofition of fifh-glue, ox-gall, and lamp-black. It is poured into fmall wooden moulds when liquid, and in thefe they let it harden.

The people of China confider it as a moft efficacious remedy againft fpitting of blood. Hence they will frequently keep fome of it in their mouths in the fame manner we do lozenges. The very beft is manufactured at *Tcienien*, a city in the province of *Nankin*, fituate on the *Ki-ang*, or *Blue River*. That of the fineft quality is dry, hard, black, and fhining.

GALEGA

GALEGA.

There are two fpecies of galega. The firft and largeft is a thick, heavy plant, covered with a hard reddifh bark, whitifh from within, and of a fharp bitter tafte. Its bloom is like that of the pea, inodorous, fometimes of a blue, and fometimes of a white colour. It gives vinegar a very agreeable tafte, and is reckoned a fpecific in diforders of the breaft.

The fecond fpecies is a hard root, of the fize of a little finger, reddifh within and without, and of a ftronger and more aromatic tafte than the former. The plant arifing from it, has the form of a little tree, with leaves fimilar to thofe of the myrtle. It fhould be felected frefh, juicy, of a high colour, compact, odoriferous, and with a ftrong aromatic tafte. The Chinefe cut it into pieces of the fize of a filbert, in order that

it

it may be dried and carried about with more ease. They confider it as an excellent antidote. Thefe two fpecies of galega are cultivated in the province of *Xanxy*, and the merchants of the city of *Tayven* moftly deal in them.

GAMBOGE.

The Gamboge is a refinous gummy juice, of a yellow colour, extracted drop by drop on incifion, from a thorny fhrub, which rifes very high, and twines round other trees like the ivy. The beft fort is brittle, hard, high coloured, of an infipid tafte at firft, afterwards fharpifh, inflammable, and for the moft part fit for being diffolved in fpirit of wine. This gum, ufed for medical purpofes, comes from *Sigan*, a village in the province of *Kiangfi*. Some prefer the gamboge of *Siam* to that which grows in *China*.

GUM

GUM LAC.

This gum, which is ufed in the compofition of fealing-wax, ought to be chofen in
bright tranfparent leaves. It is brought
from *Quan au-ton*, in the province of *Quei-chu*,
but is greatly inferior to that of *Bengal*.

CURCUMA.

The root of this plant is hard, yellowifh
within and without, and very fimilar to that
of ginger. It bears a purple bloffom; its
fruit is covered with prickles, like the Indian
chefnut; and its feeds, which are as found
as peas, are eatable. They are boiled with
meat mixed with rice, and put in various
ragouts. The plant is likewife ufed in
phyfic, and yields a fine dye imitating faffron. It ought to be felected frefh, fucculent,

lent, compact, heavy, and of a fine yellow.
The beſt comes from *Car-fung*, in the province of *Honan*.

QUICKSILVER.

This ponderous, fluid mineral, which pe-
netrates gold and ſilver, is a natural production of many parts of China and the Eaſt-
Indies. It is uſually found in mountains,
under layers of ſoft ſtones as white as chalk.
It has been remarked, that the plants growing on theſe mountains, are greener and
taller than any where elſe; but the trees
ſeldom bear fruit. When a denſe fog or
vapour which does not aſcend high in the
atmoſphere, is ſeen to ariſe from a mountain,
it is a certain indication that there is a mine
of quickſilver below. The richeſt mines are
ſituate to the North; they are always ſurrounded with water, which muſt be eva-
cuated previous to their being worked.

It

It is a very rare thing to obtain quickfilver pure from the mine; for it is found mixed with earth, or reduced to natural cinnabar; that is to fay, mercury mingled with ful-phur. If mercury is mixed only with a fmall quantity of earth, it is ftrained through a fhamoy fkin, on which the earth remains fequeftered; but when it remains in the form of natural cinnabar, it muft be extract-ed with iron and fire. The iron ferves to de-tach the fulphureous acid which confines the mercury; and the fire gives the mercury an opportunity of pouring itfelf into a receiver full of water, which is required for the pur-pofe of making it condenfate by the coolnefs it meets on its paffage from the fire.

This mineral fubftance, confifting of fmall globular bodies, always detached, is the more difficult to be fixed and retained when it is preffed. If it be fuffered to fettle in one particular place, it remains motionlefs. The late French Eaft-India Company of late years would not receive it on board their

fhips,

fhips, for fear of accidents. It was brought home by the mafters of private merchant veffels, who difcarded thofe apprehenfions, and by taking proper care, they never experienced the fmalleft inconvenience or lofs. The advantage which they gained by this article, ought to incite us to imitate them, fo we do not neglect the neceffary prefervatives.

CINNABAR.

There are two forts of Cinnabar; the one native, which is found in perfection in the bowels of the earth, as we mentioned under the preceeding head; and the other artificial, which confifts of three fourths of crude mercury, and one fourth of fulphur, fublimated and mixed together. The latter having been pounded for a confiderable time on a piece of porphyry, may be reduced to a very fine power, called vermilion, one of the moft beautiful red colours extant. It is

ufed

ufed to make fealing-wax red. Fine cinnabar ought to be of a bright red colour.

BORAX.

Is a falt which has the virtue of accelerat-
ing the fufion of metals. It ought to be
chofen as white and as chryftalline as poffible. It is generally as broad as the palm of
the hand, and between one and two inches
thick when entire. One ought not however
to perfift too much in procuring it always in
large maffes; pieces of the fize of an egg,
will be full as well, fo they are white and
pure. The borax brought from Surata is
greatly inferior to the Chinefe.

RHUBARB.

This is a large root, which thrives in low,
cold, moift fpots, in the provinces of *Hou-
quang* and *Le-ao-tong*. The leaves are broad of
X a dark

a dark green, and have an acid and agreeable tafte, when the root is pulled out from the ground, its external bark is fcraped off, as likewife the thin yellow membrane from below ; it is afterward perforated, and filed on a ftring, for the purpofe of hanging it in the open air, or drying it in the fhade. The largeft pieces are not the beft becaufe, the fuperfices only becomes dry. Rhubarb ought to be felected in pieces of a middling fize, to the utmoft two inches thick : flat, hard, and leafy ; frefh and even on the outfide, and of a faffron or nutmeg colour, veiny in the centre, of a bitter tafte, and an aromatic fcent. The excellency of this plant in medicine, is univerfally known ; it produces likewife a yellow die, which renders it continually an article of vaft confumption.

SMILAX

SMILAX CHINA,

OR

CHINA ROOT.

This plant has a root as large as a child's hand. It is thick, knotty, hard, infipid to the palate, inodorous, reddifh from without, and of a flefh colour in the heart. It emits ftalks full of prickles, rampant, and entwining the trees where it grows. It fhould be chofen full, heavy and compact; of a reddifh colour, and free from rottennefs; for it is much fubject to be worm-eaten. It is fuccefsfully adminiftered as a medicine, in the province of *Onanfi*, where it grows in great abundance. The Chinefe eat it inftead of rice, which contributes much to make them lufty.

A a   MUSK.

M U S K.

Is a kind of bilious, fermented, curdled, and almoſt corrupted blood, taken from the teſticles of a ſpecies of roe-buck, the hair of which is dry, brown, and brittle. When the animal is killed, the *ſcrotum* is cut off, and the curdled blood being taken out, is ſuſpended to dry in the ſun. In this ſituation, it is eaſily converted into a light ſubſtance, almoſt pulverized, and of a brown colour, which is again put into the *ſcrotum* for the ſake of convenience in carrying it about. Theſe animals are taken in the beginning of ſummer, becauſe having been half-ſtarved during Winter, on account of the ſnow, which lies in great depth on the ground, their blood is heated, and in a ſtate of fermentation.

Muſk

Mufk ought to be chofen very dry, and in bags of the fize of an egg, thin, of a ftrong fcent, and much covered with hair, which muft be of a brown colour. Care fhould be taken to examine if the bags have not been opened, and fewed up again, or if any fmall pebbles or bits of lead have been put in them; a cheat very common among the Chinefe. If there be a neceffity of keeping the mufk feparate from the bag, it fhould be put in a leaden cheft, that the coolnefs of the metal may prevent its getting dry and acquiring a bad fmell.

TOUTENAG, or ZINK.

Is a white metalline allay, made of tin and bifmuth; hard, compact, and heavy. The beft, which is in cafks, is very fonorous when ftruck, and pure and brilliant when broken. The Emperor of China has arrogated to himfelf the monopoly of gold, quickfilver, and toutenag.

MOTHER

MOTHER OF PEARL.

This commodity confifts of large, thick oyfter-fhells, of a grey colour on the outfide, and fmooth, polifhed, and filvery from within. The infide exhibits the fame beauty and brilliancy as the pearls which are commonly found in them.

The Chinefe do not draw thofe fhells from their own country, but from Cochinchina and Cambogia. They make all forts of toys of them, and ufe them likewife inftead of panes for their windows, as they reflect almoft as much light as fome glafs in Europe.

They alfo ufe them in making lime, not for the purpofe of building, fince it is not fo ftrong a cement as that made of ftone ; but for plafter and ftucco, it being far whiter and

and finer. Mother of pearl fhould be chofen of a beautiful white, thick, even, and above all, free from yellow and grey fpots and veins.

VARNISH.

The varnifh which China produces is a compofition of a vifcous fap, extracted from different fhrubs, and of a juice fqueezed out of the bodies of fmall reddifh worms, nearly of the bignefs of the filk-worm. Thefe worms having been boiled in water, leave its furface covered with a kind of oleofe matter, which is carefully fkimmed, fixes immediatly, but may be rendered liquid by the heat of fire, when it is wanted for ufe. This fecond fort of varnifh is much better than the firft.

There is however a third fort, which is of the very beft quality, and much fought after. It is prepared of a kind of

A a 3   gum

374 MEMOIR ON THE

gum called *cie*, which diſtils in ſummer
from certain trees, ſimilar to the drops trick-
ling from the pine. The yellow is the beſt,
and the black of an indifferent quality.

The *cie*, when freſh and liquid, exhales
a malignant vapour, which occaſions pale-
neſs and prodigious ſwellings in the face of
thoſe who gather it at firſt. This infection
cannot be cured otherwiſe than by rubbing
the affected parts with the aſhes of burnt
feathers. If this remedy is not applied, the
diſorder increaſes, a fever enſues, and the
patient is expoſed to great danger of loſing
his life.

Works to which this varniſh is applied,
do not get dry but in damp and humid
places, and not before a conſiderable lapſe
of time ; but if they are once dry, they always remain in the ſame ſtate, without the
ſmalleſt alteration. Articles that are well
varniſhed, receive ſeven coats of varniſh, and
they never lay on the ſecond before the firſt

is

is thorougly dry, and follow the fame method to the feventh. For this reafon, the varnifh of thofe pieces of furniture which are manufactured at Canton, and made in hafte, according to orders, and have not got fufficiently dry, retain an offenfive fmell, which is not obferved in thofe of Nankin, which are the moft faleable, next to thofe of Japan. The glofs and brightnefs fo peculiar to the varnifh of Nankin, is effected by polifhing and rubbing into the pores of the wood a kind of powder, which embodies itfelf with the work, and produces that brilliancy fo much admired.

The utmoft care ought to be taken that the different coats be laid on even and fmooth, without pocks or blifters, and that the figures be well painted.

A a 4 CINNAMON.

CINNAMON.

This odoriferous bark, the beſt of which is, doubtleſs, that of the iſland *Ceylon*, is found likewiſe in China. The cinnamon of this empire is ſuperior to that of Cochin-china, and may be purchaſed on very reaſonable terms. This bark ought to be choſen thin, of a beautiful brown colour, like that of Spaniſh ſnuff, and of a very pungent taſte. Cinnamon of the prime quality is in great requeſt.

China produces alſo ſtar-aniſeed, which ſhould be choſen freſh and fragrant. It brings forth likewiſe cardamum as good as that which comes from the coaſt of Malabar. The ſhape of the pods ought to be triangular, and the ſeeds brown from within, and of a ſharp, aromatic taſte. The membrane which covers them ſhould be odoriferous,

and

and of a bright yellow colour. The frefheft
is always the beft.

GINSENG.

This celebrated Eaftern plant grows on
the mountains of Tartary, adfcititious to
certain provinces of the Chinefe empire.
Its ftem, which equals in thicknefs that of
wheat, and is about one foot high, bears at
firft red buds, which expand afterwards into
fix white leaves each, fimilar to that of the
violet. It has almoft the form of the man-
dagora, but it is not fo large, tranfparent,
and interfperfed with fmall black veins,
which iffue in two or three branches. It
has a fweet tafte, with a fmall mixture of
bitternefs; its fmell is aromatic, but far
from being unpleafant. This root is dried
for the fake of being preferved, and it then
turns red from without, and yellowifh within. It is fold very dear, efpecially when it
is of a good quality. Thofe roots which

are

are brown and grey are far inferior to the others.

As worms get fometimes into the ginfeng and gnaw it, it would be unfit to be brought to the market, but for the cunning of the Chinefe, who, with a world of patience, fill up the holes with a yellow powder, which bears great refemblance to the root. They embody this powder with the pores of the plant with fo much art, that he muft be extremely knowing who is not taken in. Be as it will, the Chinefe are frequently dupes in their turn, to a fraudulent contrivance of the European merchants, who mix with their oriental ginfeng a certain quantity of that of Canada, which is far inferior in value and quality. It is not only inferior in point of colour, fcent, and tranfparency, but equally deficient in its virtues and properties. However high the notions be which we Europeans entertain of this plant, yet it falls fhort in all the trials made of it in this

part

part of the world, of the miraculous virtues afcribed to it by the Chinefe.

An immoderate ufe of ginfeng would foon prove fatal. The rich confine themfelves to take a fmall dofe of it every morning, not heavier than a grain of corn. If taken in fmall portions, either infufed or pulverifed, it produces the moft falutary effects on old men, and thofe who have ruined their conftitution by excefs, but it is prejudicial to young people, efpecially to thofe whofe temperament is fanguine. So great is the ftrength and efficacy of this plant, that one and the fame dofe, will ferve twice by infufion, without any farther addition.

The beft ginfeng fhould be frefh, heavy, of a ftrong fmell, and free from rottennefs and worm-holes.

Its name in Chinefe fignifies a *refemblance to the thighs of a man.*

NANKIN

NANKIN SILK.

This filk is the moſt eſteemed for its clearneſs and whiteneſs. If it does not poſſeſs theſe two qualities, it ought to be rejected. Care ſhould likewiſe be taken, that there be not hidden any bad filk in large flocks amongſt the ſkeins, which is frequently done to increaſe its weight.— Moreover, it ſhould not be bought without its having been previouſly well dried and expoſed to the air. The Chineſe are very apt to trick the European merchants, by ſelling them filk which they have kept a long time, in damp and humid places.

SILK STUFFS.

Good filk ſtuffs ought to have fine borders, a fine texture, with concomitant ſoftneſs, ſmoothneſs, and brightneſs. It is not

from

from the weight one ought to judge of the good quality of a piece of filk, for the more Canton filk, which is hard and of an inferior quality, has been ufed in the manufacturing of it, the more ponderous will it be. Stuffs woven of that fort of filk, are not fo fufceptible of taking a good dye, efpecially green and blue, and they are always rough and ftiff to feel. Softnefs, evennefs, and fmoothnefs, decides the goodnefs of a piece of fatin and damafk. If it be manufactured of coarfe filk, it will always be hard and uneven.

The Canton ftuffs have a coarfe woof, which makes them inferior to thofe of Nankin, where the materials are finer, and the workmen far more fkilful, fince it is they that weave the tapeftry, coverings and wearing apparel for the Emperor and his palace.

The beft filk ftuffs brought from China are, plain pekins from 11½ to 12 yards, by 5-8.

Luftrings

Luftrings of 12 yards broad, from 5-8 to 2-3, and of 14 yards by the fame.

Plain gourgourans of 13 yards by $\frac{1}{2}$, and of 14 yards by 5-8.

Plain padefoys of 14 yards by 5-8, and nearly 5-6.

Double padefoys of 14 yards.

Pekin handkerchiefs, twenty in a piece.

Plain, embroidered, and brocaded fatins, from $11\frac{1}{2}$ to 12 yards by 5-8.

Plain and painted gauzes, fingle or double.

Lampaffes for dreffes, of 12 yards by 5-8.

Ditto, for coverings, from $21\frac{1}{2}$ to 22 yards by $\frac{1}{2}$.

Painted pekins for dreffes, of $11\frac{1}{2}$ to 22 yards by 3-8.

Yellow

Yellow nankeens; firſt, ſecond, and third quality.

White ditto, firſt and ſecond quality.

White nankeen cloth, on pieces of twenty-ſeven yards.

PORCELAIN,

OR

CHINA WARES.

We do not know who was the inventor of porcelain nor to what hazard or experiments we owe that diſcovery. There is, however, ſome probability according to ſome of the Chineſe annals, that porcelain was uſed in China before the year 424 of the Chriſtian æra. Since that period it has been brought by degrees, to a pitch of perfection, which induces the moſt opulent people in Europe make uſe of it.

The

The manufacturers of porcelain ufed formerly to refide in the cities of *Tfeon-leang*, *Kin-te-ching*, and *Jao-tfhoo*, in the province of *Kiangfi*. The works which were made there, and exported to foreign countries, had no other name than *valuable jewels* of *Jao-tfhoo* and *Kin-te-ching*. Porcelain was afterwards manufactured in other places; but it is very different both in colour and finenefs. Strangers may eafily difcriminate that which comes from the province of *Canton* and *Fokien*. It is of a coarfe white colour, without either glofs or mixture of thofe delicate tints fo peculiarly characteriftical in the porcelain of *Kin-te-ching*. The latter is, without difpute, the fineft ever known ; and is even bought by the Japanefe themfelves.

The Europeans draw almoft all their porcelain from Canton, except that which they give orders for in the country. The China merchants frequently fend models to *Kin-te-ching* to have various articles executed in the same fame manner, but it oftentimes fo happens, that being fure of a ready fale of their own patterns, they neglect hefe works, and do not mind correcting the defects which may be in the materials or the workmanfhip. Orders of that kind ought never to be given but to merchants of known probity and good character, who may feel it their intereft to have them executed immediately. There is befides another inconvenience attending works executed by orders. Being got ready according to the new models, which are fometimes difficult to be well executed, they are rejected by the Europeans, even for the fake of a few faults, becaufe they make it a rule to purchafe nothing but what is well finifhed. Thus they are turned back upon the hands of the manufacturers, who, not being able to difpofe of them to the natives, as they do not take their fancy put upon the articles they fell an additional price, in order to compenfate the lofs they fuftain by thofe which are returned to them.

B b   The

The difficulty of imitating the models sent from Europe is, to be sure, one of the causes which makes the Chinese manufacturers enhance the price of all the porcelain that is ordered; we must not suppose that the workmen can copy indiscriminately every pattern which is sent them from abroad. There are some which the Chinese find really impracticable to imitate exactly; at the same time they can finish various articles with such superior skill, as would baffle all the imitative efforts of an European mechanic.

There are many people who imagine that porcelain derives an eminent degree of perfection, when it has been buried in the ground. This however is a wrong notion, which the Chinese turn into ridicule. The history of *Kin-te-ching*, in a passage relative to the fine porcelain made there in times of yore, states, that there was so great a call for it, that the furnaces were no sooner opened, than the merchants contended who should fhould have it, which does by no means denote that it was buried in the earth. True it certainly is, that fome very beautiful pieces of porcelain, hid in times of war and revolutions, are now and then difcovered by thofe who dig ruins, or clear ancient decayed walls. What accounts for the beauty of thofe pieces is, the practice adopted by thofe ancient Chinefe of hiding thefe pieces only which they fet the moft value on, with a view of finding them when the ftormy times fhould be over. If they are valued high, it is not for having acquired any real excellence from being buried, but becaufe their ancient beauty is preferved. There are likewife fome connoiffeurs in China, who fix a high price on the moft paltry utenfils ufed by their ancient Emperors. All the change which this burial operates on the porcelain, is confined to its tint and colouring. The fame mark of antiquity is obferved too in marble and ivory; but much more in porcelain whofe varnifh and enamel impede the rapid progrefs of humidity.

B b 2 There

There has been a method, recently difcovered, of imitating the antique porcelain,
or that at leaft, which bears marks of remote antiquity.   Pieces of this kind of
workmanfhip, are generally very thick and
heavy. They are firft dipped in a compofition, or lye mixed with yellow oil, which
gives them, after they come out of the firft
furnace, a fea-green colour ; they are baked
a fecond time in a kind of very oleofe liquor,
made of capons and other meat, and then
put in a foul fewer, where they remain
two or three months, and at the expiration
of that time, they look like porcelain
manufactured two or three centuries ago, at
which period pieces of that colour and thicknefs were much valued by the Chinefe.
Thefe factitious antiques refemble the real
ones, they do not re-echo the found when
ftruck, nor do they produce a hum when
held to the ear.

The Chinefe have a kind of predilection
for the glafs and chryftal wares which are
imported

imported into their country from Europe. Porcelain, however, is preferable to the latter, becaufe it has a kind of tranfparency imitating glafs, and is not fo fragile. It alfo ftands the warmth of liquor, and it may be held in the bare hand with boiling tea, whilft a filver cup of the fame fhape and thicknefs, would not produce the fame effect.

The Chinefe are extremely dexterous in fhaping grotefque figures of men and beafts, of porcelain. This kind of ware is called in the Chinefe tongue, *ifcky*.

Thefe are, in general, the chief productions of nature and art, which might be drawn from China, with the hope of certain lucre. I fhall now point out in a curfory manner, certain oriental commodities which might be brought to that vaft empire, and difpofed of there to great advantage.

Stimulative

Stimulative, or aphrodifiac, and reftora-
tive remedies are eagerly purchafed by the
Chinefe. They are, above all, fond of having a kind of neft, conftructed on the rocks
contiguous to the fea-coaft, by a fpecies of
little aquatic fwallow, of the fifh-fry, and
of clammy foam hardened by the rays of
the fun. They are fold in proportion to
their quality. The ifland of *Java* produces
the beft, and the whiter they are, the rarer
they are deemed.

The Chinefe pay likewife a liberal price
for fhark-fins, fea-priapus, crabs, fago, tripam, and a kind of molucca beans, defcribed
by Rumphius.

The fago is the pith of a palm-tree,
which grows at *Timor*.

The tripam is a little fpungy plant without root, and like a mufhroom. The degree
cf its roundnefs and blacknefs determines
its

its perfection. It grows in great profusion in the ifland of *Celebes.*

As the Chinefe have no relifh for the moft palatable food, and heighten all their victuals by feafoning them ; they of courfe confume vaft quantities of aromatic fpices, fuch as cloves, nutmegs, and pepper.

The beft cloves come from the ifland of *Amboyna.* They muft be full, juicy, heavy, ftrongly fragrant, and of a hot fpicy tafte, and leave a thin oily fubftance on the fingers.

The nutmegs and mace of the ifland of *Banda,* are the moft valued. They fhould be procured frefh, round, heavy, ftrong to fmell, to the palate fomewhat bitter, and yielding an oily juice.

Benjamin and opium, fandal wood, am-bergris, camphire of *Sumatra* and aloes of *Socotra,* may likewife be imported into China. The latter article, which comes

B b 4 from

from the ifland of that name, contiguous to the Red Sea, ought to be bright and tranf-parent, of a tawney colour, a bitter aromatic tafte, and is almoft inodorus.

Benjamin may be obtained from *Bantam*. It is an aromatic gum, ufually fold in boxes of one or two cwt each. It fhould have a ftrong fcent, be marbled in different places, and white from within.

The opium of Bengal excels every other in point of goodnefs. Its confifts of the juice of poppies infpiffated and converted into little cakes. It fhould be a little foft, and of a brownifh colour, of a ftrong fœtid odour, and to give way when fqueezed with the finger. That which is dry, triturable, burnt, and mixed with earth, is of a bad quality.

The Sandal-wood ought to be heavy, fweetly fragrant, without pith, and of a beautiful carnation colour from the infide.

Ambergris

Ambergris may be found on the fea-coaft, in many parts of India. This refinous, fpungy, and inflammable fubftance is deemed good when of a grey colour imitating afhes. It has a pleafant fmell. The maffes are in different forms; but moftly flat, and of the fize of a hand, and confift of different leaves, two or three lines thick; confequently ten or twelve of thefe leaves, being laid upon one another, form a mafs, at leaft, two or three inches thick, which is an infallible mark of their intrinfic goodnefs.

I fhall conclude this head with fome obfervations on the commerce which might be eafily carried on at *Timor*, fituate to the South of the Molucca iflands, and to the Eaft of Java. Thofe articles which are the fooneft difpofed of there, are fufees, firecock flints, iron in bars, common trinkets, cloth of different colours, filver bracelets, coarfe handkerchiefs, Indian cottons, a little opium, and Spanifh or Madeira wine of a rough flavour.

The

The articles which might be obtained in return are rice, faltpetre, tortoifefhell, wax, fandal and japan-wood, and fome gold. Great quantity of *Cadiang*, a kind of fmall beans which the Dutch give as food and medicine to their feamen, may alfo be obtained here.

I fhall forbear expatiating here on that odious branch of commerce, a horror to humanity, reafon and philofophy; whofe efforts could never yet obtain a triumph over prejudice, cuftom, and the avarice of a *handful* of individuals. Alas! when fhall the happy period come, that will banifh flavery from our colonial fettlements.

FINIS.

I N D E X.

A.

Ball

Diſcovery

their

North

Production

Silk

Vapour

Y.

Z.

ERRATA.

Page 111, WALT and BOLTON, *read* WATT and BOLTON.

Page 208, Line 3 and 4, Count Benyowſki, Governor of, &c. *read* Benyowſki to the Governor.

CPSIA information can be obtained at www.ICGtesting.com
Printed in the USA
LVOW13s1117140114

369252LV00001B/49/P